MEDITERRANEAN COASTS OF ISRAEL AND SINAI

Holocene Tectonism from Geology, Geophysics, and Archaeology

D. Neev
N. Bakler
Geological Survey of Israel, Jerusalem

K.O. Emery
Woods Hole Oceanographic Institution, MA

Taylor & Francis
New York • Philadelphia • London

USA	Publishing Office:	Taylor & Francis • New York 3 East 44th St., New York, NY 10017
	Sales Office:	Taylor & Francis • Philadelphia 242 Cherry St., Philadelphia, PA 19106
UK		Taylor & Francis Ltd. 4 John St., London WC1N 2ET

Mediterranean Coasts of Israel and Sinai

Copyright © 1987 D. Neev, N. Bakler, and K.O. Emery

All rights reserved. No part of this publication may be reproduced, stored in a retrieval system, or transmitted, in any form or by any means, electronic, electrostatic, magnetic tape, mechanical, photocopying, recording or otherwise, without the prior permission of the copyright owner.

First published 1987
Printed in the United States of America

Library of Congress Cataloging in Publication Data

Neev, David
   Mediterranean coasts of Israel and Sinai.

   Bibliography: p.
   Includes index.
   1. Geology, Stratigraphic—Pleistocene.
2. Geology, Stratigraphic—Recent.
3. Geology—Israel.   4. Geology—Egypt—Sinai.
5. Archaeology—Israel.
6. Archaeology—Egypt—Sinai.   I. Bakler, N.,
1931–   . II. Emery, K.O. (Kenneth Orris),
1914–   . III. Title.
QE697.N44   1987   555.694   86-30143
ISBN 0-8448-1495-4

The sea looked and fled,
  Jordan turned back.
The mountains skipped like rams,
  the hills like lambs.

What ails you, O sea, that you flee?
  O Jordan, that you turn back?
O mountains, that you skip like rams?
  O hills, like lambs?

PSALMS, 114

Contents

Preface ix

Summary xi

I. Introduction 1
    A. Coastline 1
    B. Coastal Plain and Continental Shelf 3

II. Stratigraphy 7
    A. Late Neogene to Late Pleistocene—Generalized 7
    B. Stratigraphy and Environment of Deposition of the Late Pleistocene
        and Holocene Sequence 7
        Unit 1 ——Dune Sand (Kurkar) 10
        Unit 2a——Soil 10
        Unit 2b——Red Hamra 11
        Unit 2c——Brown Hamra 11
        Unit 2d——Chalky Freshwater Limestone 11
        Unit 3 ——Dune Sand (Kurkar) 12
        Unit 4a——Netanya Hamra 12
        Unit 4b——Caesarea Freshwater Chalk 13
        Unit 4c——Lagoonal Clay 14
        Unit 4d——Brownish Sandy Clay 15
        Unit 4e——Loess-like Mudflat and Coarse Detrital Deposits 15
        Unit 5a——Calcarenite Bank 16
        Unit 5b——Beachrock Terrace of Northwestern Sinai 19
        Unit 5c——Fluvial-Lagoonal Sands 19
        Unit 5d——Dark Brownish Gray Clay 21
        Unit 6 ——Nof Yam Clayey Sand 22
        Unit 7a——Hadera Dune Sands 23
        Unit 7b——Marine Clay+Sand 23
        Unit 7c——Tel Haraz Calcarenite 26
        Unit 7d——Shell Beds 29
        Unit 7e——Lagoonal Evaporites 35
        Unit 7f——Bronze-Age Earthern Structures 37
        Unit 7g——Later Man-Made Structures 38

III. Holocene Tectonic Histories of Coastal Segments and of Significant Sites Along Them 39
   A. Northern Segment (Rosh Haniqra to Mount Carmel) 39
      1. Ancient Akhiv Harbor 39
      2. Akko 41
      3. Tel Abu Hawam 43
      4. Tectonic Framework of Northern Segment——Structural and Geomorphic Indicators 43
   B. Hof Hacarmel Segment (Coast West of Mount Carmel) 45
      1. General 45
      2. Haifa Nose to Atlit Area 45
      3. Dor 47
   C. Hof Hasharon Segment (Caesarea to Yafo) 49
      1. North-South Perspective 49
      2. Caesarea 52
      3. Michmoret 53
      4. Netanya 54
      5. Ga'ash 55
      6. Apollonia (or Tel Arshaf) 55
      7. Tel Michal 56
      8. Tel Baruch and Ramat Aviv C 59
      9. The North-South Trending Ayalon Fault 61
     10. Geological Cross Sections Across the Tel Aviv—Yafo Coast 61
     11. Transverse (East-West) Faults Across the Tel Aviv—Yafo Coast 63
   D. Southern Coastal Segment (Yafo to Rafiah) 65
      1. Yavneh Yam 65
      2. Tel Haraz 67
      3. Ashdod—Ashqelon Area 69
      4. Ashqelon 73
      5. Gaza Area 75
      6. Deir el Balah 76
   E. Coastal Segment of Northwestern Sinai 79
      1. Hydrological Pattern Between Nahal Besor (Wadi Gaza) and Wadi el Arish 79
      2. Post-Pleistocene Tectonic Rise of Coastal Segment Between Tel Qatif and El Meidan 82
      3. Inland Extension of the Coastal Fault 84
      4. Ostrakina (or Felusiat) 84
      5. Mount Casius 88
      6. On-Land Segment of the Pelusium Line 89
      7. Sand Supply into Northwestern Sinai During Holocene 91

IV. Synopsis 93
   A. Tectonics 93
      1. Contemporaneous Upwarp of Continental Crust and Subsidence of Oceanic Crust in Easternmost Mediterranean Region since Late Pleistocene 93
      2. Nature and Magnitude of Coastal Fault System 95
      3. Sequence of Oscillatory Tectonic Movements Across the Coastal Fault System during Late Holocene 95
      4. A Working Hypothesis on the Origin and Mechanism of Oscillatory Tectonic Movements 97
      5. History and Rhythm of Tectonic Movements 99
      6. Contradictory Concepts about Holocene Tectonics near Coastline 100
      7. Tectonic Origin of Kurkar Ridges 102
      8. Seacliff Origin and Evolution 105
   B. Comparison of Tectonics along Entire Coast 106
   C. Depositional History Relative to Climate, Sea Level, and Coastline ... 110
      1. Late Pleistocene (50,000 to 10,000 y BP) 110
      2. Early to Middle Holocene (10,000 to 4000 y BP) 111
      3. Late Holocene (4000 y BP to Present) 111
   D. Cultural History 113
      1. Coastline Positions and Their Relation to Settlements 113
      2. Effects of Coastal Dunes 113
      3. Tectonic Instability (Earthquakes) and Climatic Changes 114

References 117

Index 127

Preface

More than 25 years ago, each of the authors became interested in the topography and geological history of the coastal belt of Israel as a result of their studies of the region's beaches and continental shelf. This interest and subsequent observations led to a decision in 1983 to summarize our thoughts in the form of this little book. We believe that the physiography, stratigraphy, and structure of the region indicate that archaeological and historical evidence of changes in relative sea level along the coast indicates not just simple additions and withdrawals of water from the ocean due to global climatic change, but local tectonic movements of the land and sea floor. Such coastal changes of level are widespread in the world ocean, as inferred from tide gauge records of the past century and probably from less precise radiocarbon datings of now submerged or emerged remains of animals and plants that had lived during the past 25,000 years in the intertidal belt. Evidence for changes of relative sea level during the past 4000 or more years is supported by archaeological data, and the Israeli coast has perhaps the most concentrated reasonably well-studied sites of the past several thousand years.

Even preliminary comparison of archaeological evidence at different sites preferentially supported an interpretation of tectonic movements of land and sea floor rather than changes in volume of the oceans during the past few thousand years, just as revealed by tide gauges during the past century. Combination of archaeological data with environmental and stratigraphic characteristics of sediments deposited within the relevant sites before, during, and after significant tectonic events yielded a more integrated and reliable understanding of the geological and cultural histories. Utilization of this information requires a merging of geological and archaeological records and ways of thinking that appears to be difficult to accept on initial exposure to them. Assembly of our information for the Israeli and northwestern Sinai coasts makes it available for present and future investigators as a better level for launching studies than was available to us 25 years ago.

Early drafts of the manuscript were written at the Geological Survey of Israel and were followed by critical readings by Y. Nir and J. K. Hall of the same organization. Final drafts were written by Neev and Emery during a sabbatical leave of Neev to the U. S. Geological Survey at the Denver Federal Center (courtesy of J. D. Friedman) and at Menlo Park (courtesy of D. W. Scholl). Among our many colleagues who have discussed and contributed ideas and comments are M. Avnimelech, O. Bar Yosef, Y. Gila'd, R. Gophna, Z. Herzog, E. Lindner, S. Lowengart, E. D. Oren, L. Picard, and A. Raban. Special thanks are due A. Starinski and Y. Levy for their reviews and discussion of the chapters on the origin of evaporitic sediments at Deir el Balah and Qadesh Barnea, as well as to A. Kaufman, E. Geyh, K. O. Munnich, J. C. Vogel, and E. Wakshal for radiometric age determinations. Preliminary drafting and typing was done at the Geological Survey of Israel by Saadia Levi, Nehama Shragai, Arieh Peer, and Dina Askenazi. Final drafting was by Emery and final typing was by Charlet Shave of North Falmouth, MA. Photography, photocopying, and other completion costs were supported by the Ocean Industry Program of Woods Hole Oceanographic Institution. We express our appreciation to these individuals and organizations for their aid in this long and complex undertaking.

Summary

During the transition from Pleistocene to Holocene, the floor of the Levantine Basin (eastern Mediterranean) subsided, and the continental crust east of it became uplifted. The coastal belt of Israel and northwestern Sinai functioned as a hinge for this differential vertical movement. During that phase the coastal fault was not reactivated, and the coastal cliff did not exist.

Since about 4000 years BP, the style and nature of the tectonic regimen changed. Uplift of the continental side either completely stopped or appreciably diminished. At the same time, oceanic crust of the Levantine Basin continued to subside, but in phases. Consequently, the continental slope off Israel was downwarped and arched basinward, so that the continental shelf and coastal belt were dragged downward with it. Occasionally (during peaks of the tectonic phases), the land side of the coastal belt also was submerged. Tension produced by westward arching of the slope was concentrated mostly across the coastline, later to be released by reactivation of an old coast-parallel normal fault. As a result, the upthrown or land side of this fault rebounded upward. Such an oscillatory type of downward and upward tectonic movements occurred across the coastal fault at least five times during the past 4000 years: the Early to Middle Bronze phase, the Late Bronze phase, the Middle to Late Iron phase, the Byzantine phase, and the Mamlukian phase. At the end of each phase, the coastal cliff rose to about its original (pre-movement) structural elevation. It is not yet known, however, how much of the entire coastal cliff was submerged during each phase, nor for how long (decades or even centuries) the upthrown block remained submerged prior to rebound. Possibly uplift since the Mamlukian phase continues. Along most segments the top of the cliff has not yet reached its pre-movement elevation, but locally (at Apollonia) it exceeds that level.

Conclusions about displacement across the coastline are based mostly upon seismic stratigraphy combined with detailed stratigraphic analyses of numerous drill holes and outcrops as well as of man-made (archaeological) structures both offshore and onshore. Cumulative post-Jurassic vertical displacement across the coastal hingeline is more than 4 km (divided among several coast-parallel faults between the coastline and about 15 km offshore). Maximum post-Miocene displacements across the central segment (Netanya-Ga'ash) are about 300 m since Messinian, 150 m since early Pleistocene, and about 60 m since early to middle Holocene. Conclusions concerning repeated up-and-down tectonic movements of the continental side of the coastal fault are based upon identification of facies and habitats of shallow-marine and continental sediments as well as of man-made structures in the coastal belt. Tectonic inferences are made with respect to sea levels at times of deposition and present sea level. Dating of events was deduced from archaeological and radiocarbon analyses. Types of sediments include low-energy clayey sand, beach sand, lenticular shell accumulations, lagoon evaporites, mudflat and coastal swamp loams, and coastal dunes.

Although numerous earthquakes have occurred along the coastline of Israel during the past 4000 years, much of the oscillatory movement may have had a creeping nature rather than catastrophic faulting. Apparently, it is due to such a process (but also to the relatively long time spans for each phase) that few historical documents were found in which such occurrences were recorded. A prominent example of such lacunae is the absence of documentation describing the economical and agricultural disaster that the northeastern district of the Nile Delta underwent during the Mamlukian Phase only a few hundred years ago. Until then, this area was one of the most flourishing districts of Egypt and included the important city-harbor of Pelusium. Afterward, the area subsided and became a salt marsh.

Three (perhaps even four) of five recognized tectonic phases are associated with an increased supply of sand from the Nile River to the coastline of northwestern Sinai and Israel and also with climatic changes from drier regimens to wetter ones. Apparently, increased sand is related to increased tectonic activity that caused uplift and disturbance of sediments within the Nile Delta province, thereby leading to increased erosion. Contemporaneous occurrences of phases of increased wetness and tectonism may have been related genetically to increased volcanic activity.

Last but not least is a possible correlation between regional cultural events (such as desertions, conquests, and revolutions) and tectonic and climatic phases. Most prominent were those during the transitions between the Early to Middle Bronze, Middle to Late Bronze, Late Bronze to Iron, Iron to Persian-Hellenistic, Byzantine to Early Moslem, and Mamluk to Turkish rules. Theoretically, such a relationship is reasonable, because the higher the cultural level of a civilization, the more vulnerable it is to destructive effects of tectonic and climatic factors. Superimposed on direct tectonic destructions are sand ingressions across the coastline. Such events, as well as the submergence of at least parts of the Via Maris, were associated with three of the five tectonic phases. These factors made overland transportation between Egypt and the Fertile Crescent more cumbersome for armies.

Map drawn in 1651

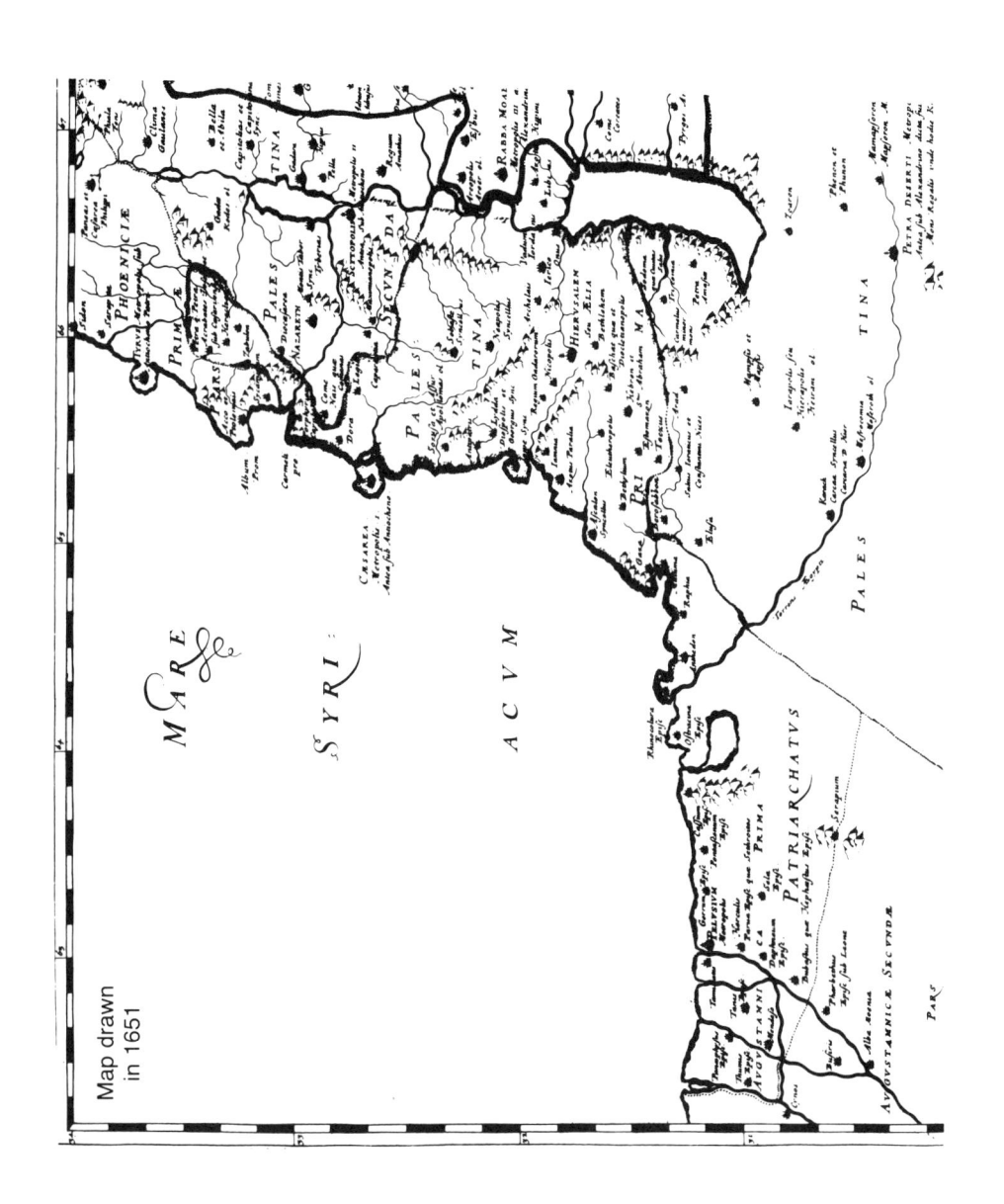

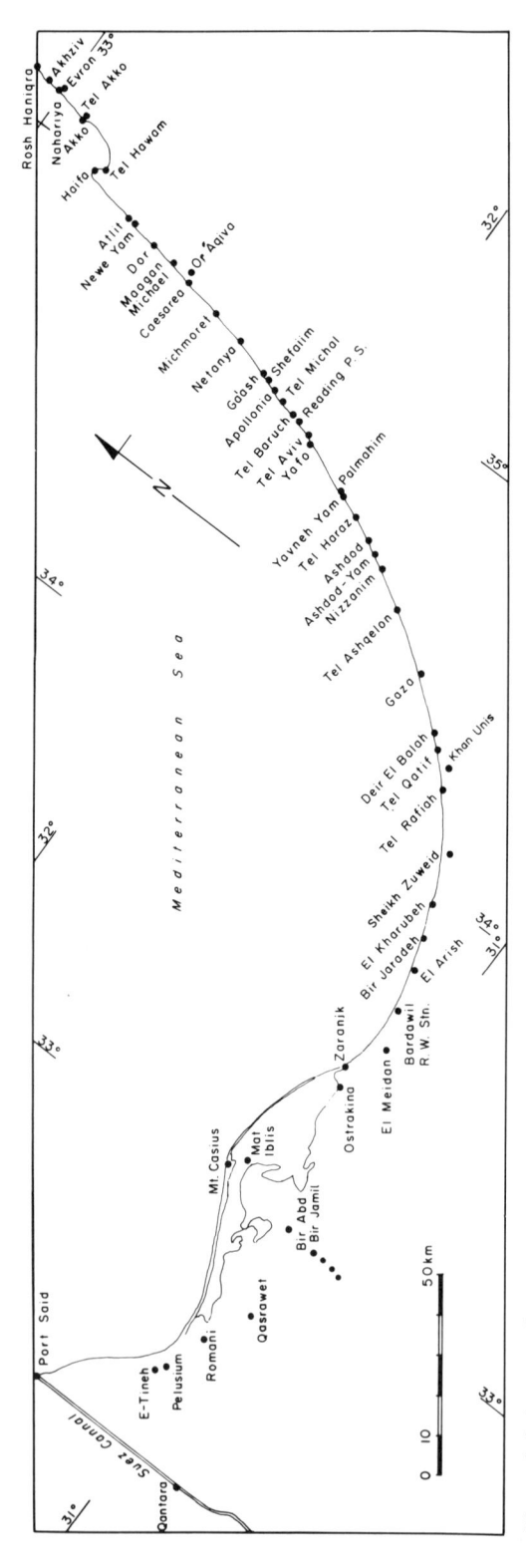

Figure 1. Index map of coastal localities discussed in text. Positions of other features (drill holes, ridges, folds, wadies, etc.) are shown in Figs. 3, 8, 14, 15, 19, 24, 26, 30, 31, 32, and 36.

I. Introduction

A. Coastline

The coast of Israel is broadly concave, generally trending NNE-SSW (Fig. 1). Along northwestern Sinai, the coast gently curves clockwise to trend east-west. The seaward protrusion of the northwesterly-trending Mount Carmel ridge is the only major promontory breaking the smooth linearity of the coastline. Two much smaller promontories, at Yafo—Tel Aviv and at Yavneh Yam (Neev et al. 1976), also are present.

Along almost all of its length, the coastline of Israel lies between two parallel lineaments. The eastern (onshore) lineament is an escarpment that locally is steeper than 45 degrees and rises as high as +50 m above mean sea level. A sequence of late Pleistocene to Holocene age sediments crops out along the cliff. The top of this sequence extends eastward to form the now-elevated alluvial coastal plain of Israel (the Sharon Plain). The western offshore lineament is a low submarine escarpment (Nir 1973) that is identified easily on aerial photographs (Fig. 2), although it partly is masked by an apron of loose sand. It forms the western limit of a patchy abraded terrace that is a few hundred meters wide.

The character and position of the straight coastline could be either an incidental result of marine abrasional activity or a product of tectonic activity. Effectiveness of the abrasional factor is well demonstrated by the physiography of the coastal cliffs; the coastline has transgressed inland rather uniformly from the submerged western lineament to the foot of the subaerial coastal cliff because of marine erosion. The erosional aspect has theoretical support, because the main wave direction is from the west (Emery and Neev 1960; Goldsmith and Sofer 1983). On the other hand, the fact that the coastal cliff is quite linear despite its lithological heterogeneity and varied morphology (the broad and shallow topographic gaps that were entrenched by rivers) indicates an important tectonic influence as well.

In fact, there is ample evidence that the coastal belt is an old geosuture along which tectonism has been active since Jurassic and probably even earlier. Bein and Gvirtzman (1977) suggested that the Levant coast was a Mesozoic paleodepositional hinge belt along the western limit of the Arabian Plate, separating shallow marine to continental facies at the east from deep-water sediments at the west. Neev (1960, 1975), Neev et al. (1976, 1985), and Neev and Greenfield (1984) suggested that this geosuture is a disturbed zone (a combination of warping, folding, and faulting) that extends from a few km inland to 12–14 km offshore. At least two major phases of vertical differential movements have

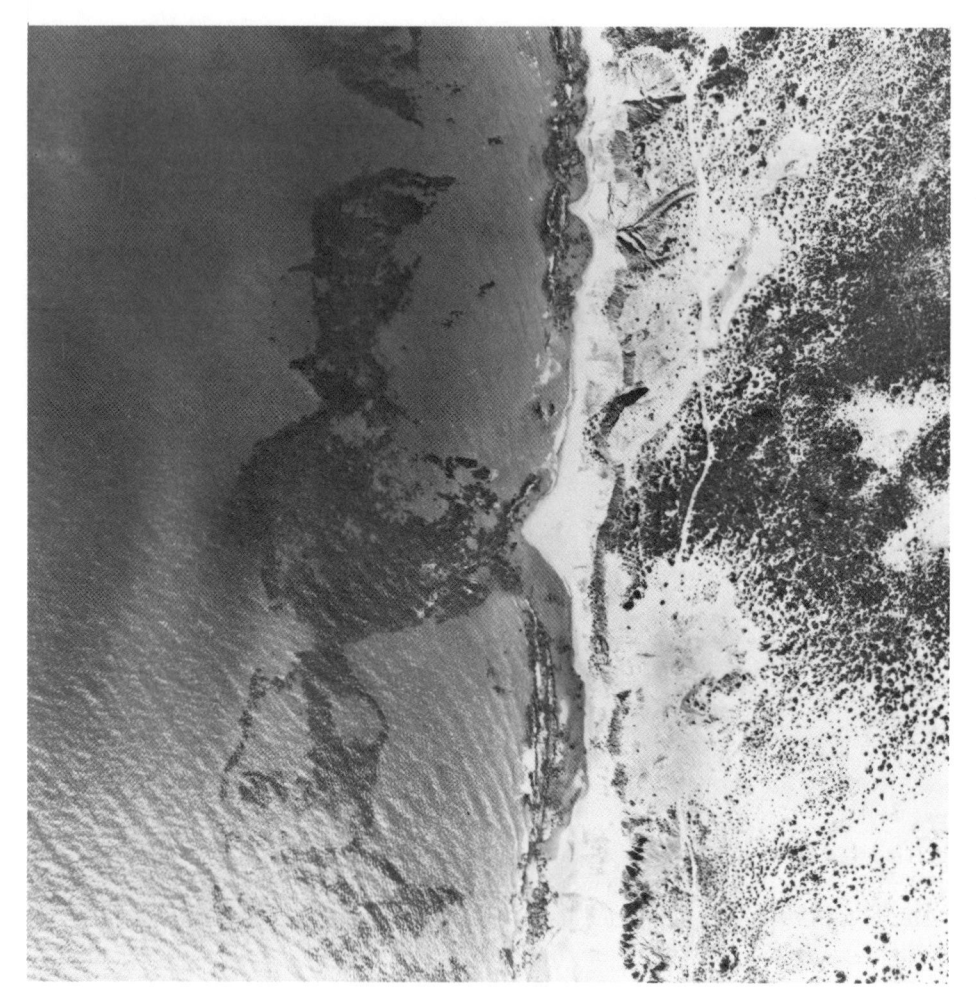

Figure 2. Aerial photographs showing the two cliffs along the coastline: a topographically higher one on land and a much lower one offshore. The latter is identified by the western limits of abraded terraces as far as 200 m west of the coastline (from Neev and Ben-Avraham 1977, fig. 2; and Neev and Bakler 1978, fig. 2; by permission of Plenum Press, New York). Aerial photo courtesy Israel Survey.

occurred along that belt: one near the end of the Jurassic and the other between Middle Oligocene and Early Pliocene times. The cumulative vertical displacement of top Jurassic markers across this wide step-faulted zone ranges between 3 and 5 km. Cumulative displacements of several hundred meters occur across the coastal fault itself. Broad coastal warping also is typical of most other continental shelves of the world (Pitman 1978, and others).

Indications for several phases of tectonic activity during the Holocene along the coastline of Israel and northwestern Sinai were presented by Neev et al. (1973, 1978a,b), Neev and Ben-Avraham (1977), Neev and Bakler (1978), Neev and Friedman (1978), Bakler et al. (1985), and Lewy et al. (1986). The net result of these tectonic activities is a vertical differential movement (uplift of the land and subsidence of the offshore belt). Detailed studies of many sites revealed that some of the late Holocene tectonic events were oscillatory movements, whereby the downthrown block progressively subsided and the upthrown block first subsided and submerged but then rebounded and emerged to its original elevation or even to a slightly higher one. These conclusions were opposed by Mazor (1974), Garfunkel et al. (1977), Arad et al. (1978), Flemming et al. (1978), Ronen (1980), Ronen and Zemer (1981), and Nir and Eldar (1986a,b,c). It is the purpose of this paper to compile and present relevant data that we have observed and studied since 1958 and to deduce from them the late geological history of the coastal zone of Israel.

B. *Coastal Plain and Continental Shelf*

Adjoining the coastline are the coastal plain on the land and the continental shelf beneath the ocean. Both areas contain broadly curved subparallel sand ridges that are similar to each other. The ridges are interrupted mainly by the transverse Mount Carmel (Fig. 3). Smaller interruptions are provided by river valleys and by a few ridge bifurcations. Because the combined coastal plain and shelf narrows to the north and yet has relatively smooth slopes toward an approximately uniform 130-m shelf break, and because the base of each ridge has about the same elevation along its entire length, the ridges necessarily are farther apart at the southwest and converge toward the north. These characteristics are to be expected of deposition of coastal sand ridges, but they are unusual for purely tectonic features.

Best known because of their accessibility are three ridges that have been mapped on land; these are known as kurkar ridges for their hard sandstone that has been used extensively for construction purposes since earliest times. Similar features occur in southern California and northwestern Mexico as parallel ridges several kilometers apart that rise as much as 30 m above a Pliocene wave-cut terrace surface now 100 to 150 m above sea level (Emery 1950). Nine consolidated sand ridges of low relief parallel the coast west of the Nile Delta (Shukri et al. 1956). Others border the coast of the eastern United States and the Netherlands, and occur on many other gently sloping coastal plains of the world where the supply of sand is or has been large. Where the supply consists more of silt than of sand, chenier ridges parallel the shore, as in Louisiana (Gould and McFarlan 1959), northwestern Mexico (Curray and Moore 1964), and in many other deltaic regions of the world, but these ridges are only 10 or so meters high and a few hundred meters apart. Other small relatives composed of uncemented sand or gravel mark the growth of cuspate forelands punctuated by occasional storms on many coasts of the world (Johnson 1938, 404–456). On coral atolls, features termed gravel or boulder ramparts are built by typhoon waves to heights of 5 m above their surroundings (Wiens 1962, 68–70). Only the kurkar ridges of Israel are known to be high enough or properly positioned to support high seacliffs. Four kurkar ridges also have been mapped on the continental shelf off Israel (Fig. 3; Emery and Bentor 1960; Neev et al. 1976, fig. 10; Almagor 1979). This

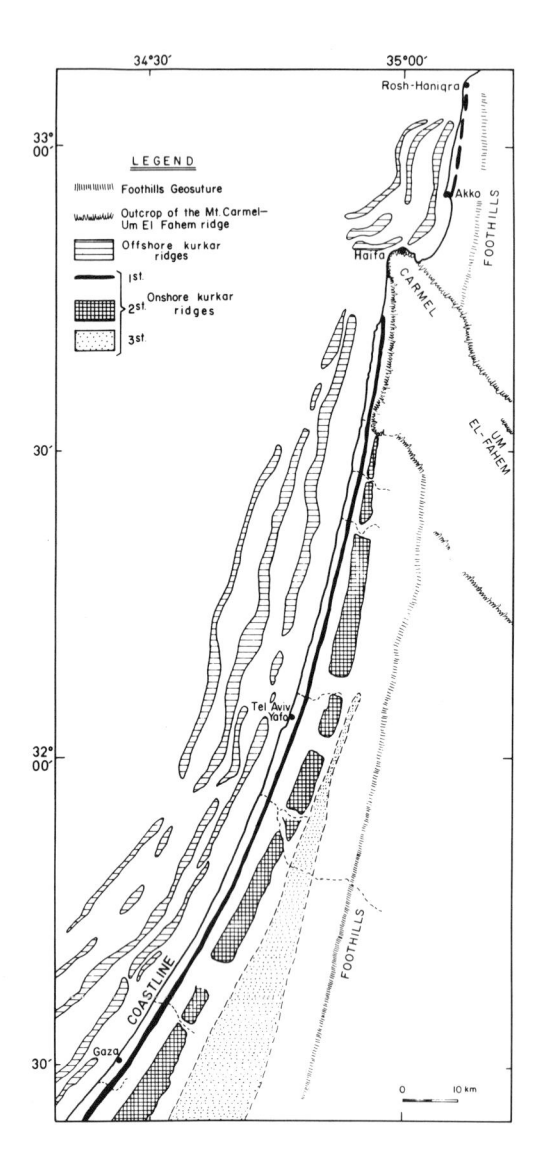

Figure 3. Onshore and offshore pattern of kurkar ridges. Note the (i) general counterclockwise convergence pattern between the foothills geosuture and the westernmost kurkar ridges, and (ii) breaks in continuity and eastward branching features exhibited by the ridges near the transverse faults of Palmahim (south of Tel Aviv), Caesarea—Or 'Akiva (south plunge of Mt. Carmel), Haifa Nose, and Akhziv (south of Rosh Haniqra).

system extends from the littoral zone in the east to the upper continental slope in the west and converges at the north in a pattern similar to the onshore one.

The general pattern of the emerged and submerged kurkar ridges off Israel strongly suggests a depositional origin, essentially the only origin that has been considered in the past. However, the best known ridges (those near the coastline that have been the sites of construction by past cultures and have many exposures caused by considerable ancient and present marine erosion) are believed to have been much influenced by fault activity and associated earthquakes. Several lineaments recently were recognized on LANDSAT images along and parallel to the kurkar ridges in the southern coastal plain off Israel (Bartov et al. 1977). Some lineaments appear to be tectonic in origin. We suspect that the positions and trends of ridges in Egypt also may be tectonically controlled (see Synopsis IV A 7). These facts suggest that tectonism may have been equally important along the emerged and the submerged kurkar ridges where outcrops and other data are more difficult to obtain.

Paucity of outcrops and drill holes from which structural relations can be determined requires that other kinds of information must be considered. Prominent here are stratigraphy and fossil content, details of which reveal changes between marine, brackish, freshwater, and terrestrial environments of sediment deposition at given sites. Thicknesses of sediments and species of fossils yield information about water depths and durations of sediment deposition and erosion. Geophysical surveys, mainly acoustic profiling, yield depths and thicknesses of strata, especially beneath the continental shelf where drill holes are expensive and scarce. Archaeology and radiometric dating serve to establish dates and environments of deposition and erosion; both yield valuable data via published literature, examination of selected new samples, and professional discussion. By these various means we have reexamined the origin of the Late Quaternary sedimentary sequence along the coasts of Israel and Sinai and tried to decipher the story that it tells about changing environments of the region especially during the past 10,000 years of the Holocene. We have provided a synthesis of previously poorly related information to help interpret the geological and human history in this region of complex geology and many cultures. We hope that our work will induce others to use tools and information beyond those provided by single fields of scientific specialization.

II. Stratigraphy

A. Late Neogene to Late Pleistocene—Generalized

On land the Pleistocene Kurkar Group (Picard 1943; Issar 1968; Gvirtzman 1969; and Shachnai 1974) includes a sequence of four sedimentary cycles that are dominated by carbonate-cemented quartz sandstone (locally named kurkar) interbedded with red loams (locally named hamra). Within the red loams are lateral transitions into dark brown swamp deposits. The Kurkar Group, which is about 150 m thick along the coastline, completely wedges out eastward. It changes downward into dark gray clays of the Plio-Pleistocene upper Yafo Formation, which is recognized in drill holes from the coastal zone as well as from the inner shelf. On the continental shelf and slope, the number of depositional cycles within the Kurkar Group increases to six or seven as shown on some single-channel seismic profiles, and lateral transitions into the Yafo Formation also occur. The thickness of the Kurkar Group there increases to about 300 m (Neev et al. 1976; our Fig. 4A).

The precise Pliocene—Pleistocene boundary is difficult to define paleontologically and lithologically. Nevertheless, the total thickness of the Quaternary sequence, which is about 200 m along the coastline (including the upper part of the Yafo Formation; Issar 1968), increases to almost 500 m along the offshore trough that is parallel to the coast, and it locally reaches the unusual thickness of about 1000 meters (in the trough of the Palmahim Disturbance; Neev et al. 1976). In spite of its unconformable nature, the most prominent and reliable marker noted across the coastal plain and continental margin within the Saqiye Group (the Oligocene to early Pleistocene dark gray marly and sandy clay sequence) is the M reflector that marks the base of the Yafo Formation (Fig. 4D, E).

B. Stratigraphy and Environment of Deposition of the Late Pleistocene and Holocene Sequence.

The late Pleistocene to Holocene stratigraphic sequence that is exposed along the coastline of Israel and northwestern Sinai contains seven main archaeological time-stratigraphic units. Most units are further divided into several facies subunits (i.e., 2a to 2b). Following are the seven units:

Unit 1 = late Pleistocene—Early Paleolithic (100,000 to 50,000 y BP);
Unit 2 = late Pleistocene—Middle Paleolithic (50,000 to 30,000 y BP;
Unit 3 = late Pleistocene—Late Paleolithic (30,000 to 20,000 y BP);
Unit 4 = late Pleistocene—Epipaleolithic, (20,000 to 10,000 y BP);
Unit 5 = early Holocene—Neolithic (10,000 to 6000 y BP);
Unit 6 = middle Holocene—Chalcolithic to Early Bronze (6000 to 4000 y BP);

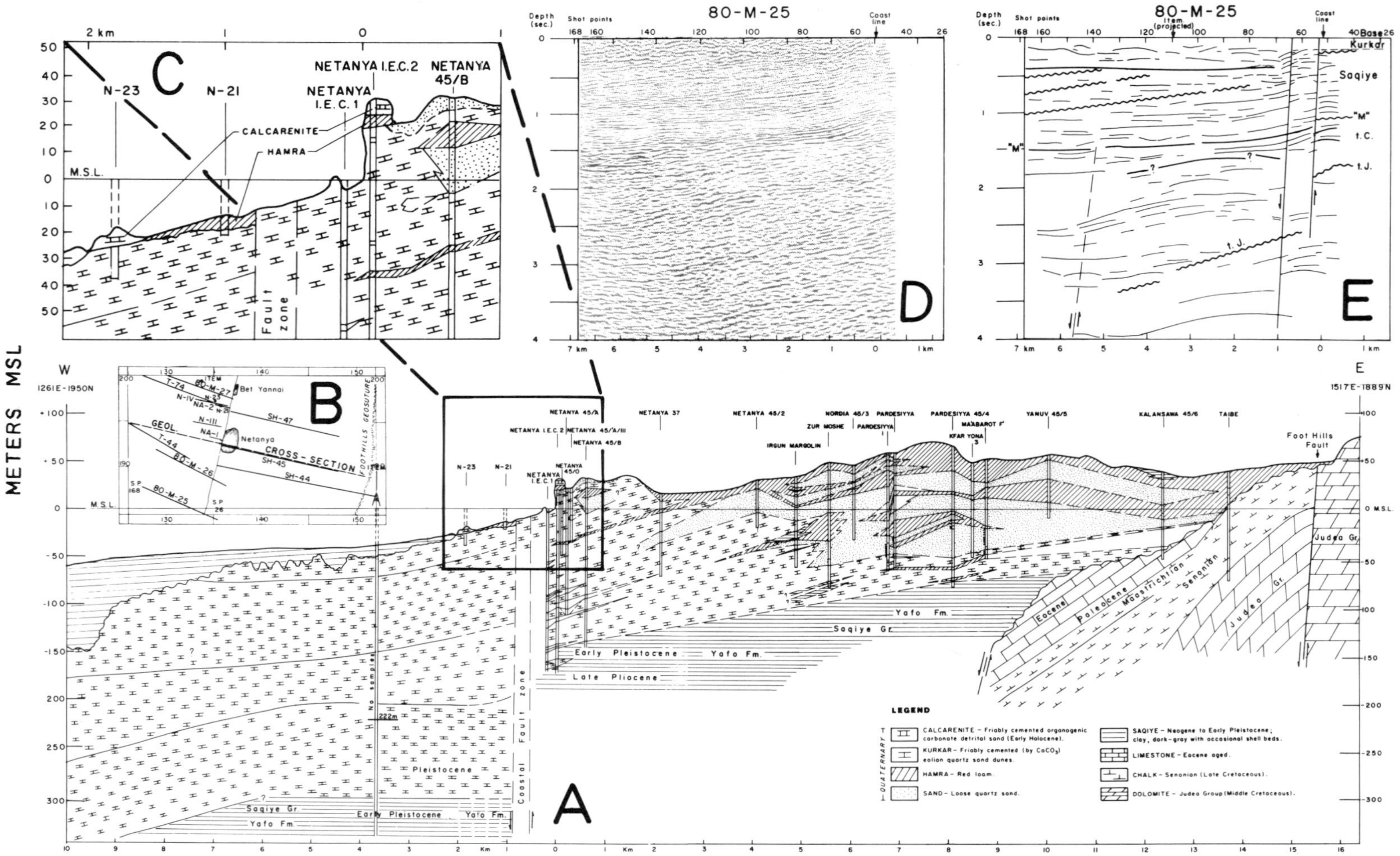
C
N-23
N-21
NETANYA I.E.C.1
NETANYA I.E.C.2
NETANYA 45/B
CALCARENITE
HAMRA
M.S.L.
Fault zone
80-M-25
Depth (sec.)
Shot points
Coast line
D
E
Item (projected)
Base Kurkar
Saqiye
"M"
t.C.
t.J.
B
Bet Yannai
Netanya
CROSS-SECTION
FOOTHILLS GEOSUTURE
GEOL.
80-M-25
80-M-26
80-M-27
SH-44
SH-45
SH-47
METERS MSL
W
1261E-1950N
E
1517E-1889N
NETANYA 45/A
NETANYA I.E.C.2
NETANYA 45/A/III
NETANYA 45/B
NETANYA 37
NETANYA 46/2
IRGUN MARGOLIN
NORDIA 46/3
ZUR MOSHE
PARDESIYYA
PARDESIYYA 45/4
MA'ABAROT F'
KFAR YONA 3
YANUV 45/5
KALANSAWA 45/6
TAIBE
Foot Hills Fault
Judea Gr.
Eocene
Paleocene
Maastrichtian
Senonian
Yafo Fm.
Saqiye Gr.
Early Pleistocene
Late Pliocene
Pleistocene
Coastal Fault zone
No samples
222m
A
Km
LEGEND
QUATERNARY
CALCARENITE – Friably cemented organogenic carbonate detrital sand (Early Holocene).
KURKAR – Friably cemented (by $CaCO_3$) eolian quartz sand dunes.
HAMRA – Red loam.
SAND – Loose quartz sand.
SAQIYE – Neogene to Early Pleistocene; clay, dark-gray with occasional shell beds.
LIMESTONE – Eocene aged.
CHALK – Senonian (Late Cretaceous).
DOLOMITE – Judea Group (Middle Cretaceous).

Figure 4. Geology at Netanya. *A.* Composite transverse geological cross-section from the Foothills Fault in the east, through the coastline at Netanya (modified from Shachnai 1974, SH-45), to 10 km offshore (based on data from seismic profiles and drill holes mentioned in the text). Vertical double lines mark the total depth of drill holes. *B.* Reference map of relevant geological and seismic profiles and drill holes. *C.* Detailed geological cross section of a segment of A. *D.* Offshore CDP Telseis profile No. 80-M-25 that crosses the coastline about 7 km south of Netanya. Horizontal scale along the lower frame of figure. Shot-point numbers along the upper frame of figure. Vertical scale = depth in seconds. *E.* Hand-drawn profile of *D* showing schematic stratigraphic boundaries (tJ = top Jurassic, tC = top Cretaceous, "M" = M Reflector or the Messinian unconformity at top Miocene) and faults.

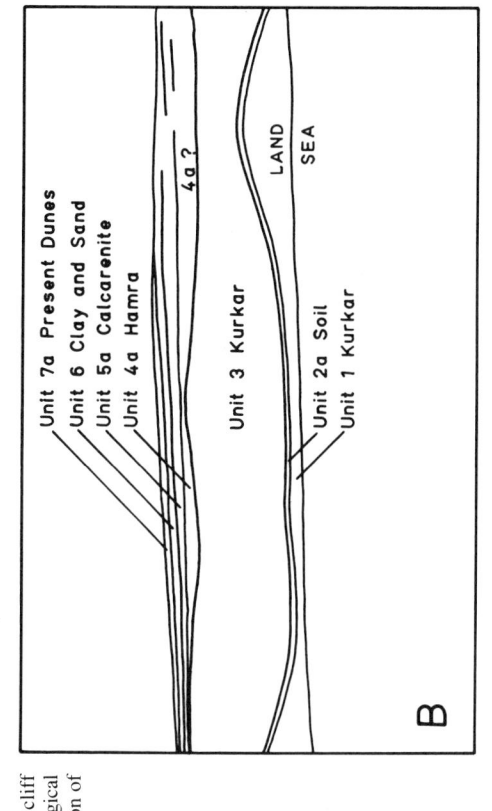

Figure 5. *A* Horizontal frontal view (from the sea landward) of the coastal cliff of the Hof Hasharon segment (III C). *A* = photograph; *B* = Hand-drawn geological cross-section (modified from Neev and Bakler 1978, fig. 4B; for identification of stratigraphic units—see text II).

Unit 7 = late Holocene—Middle Bronze and younger (4000 y BP present).

The seventh unit contains many subunits that are referred to throughout the text. Their dates vary with region, but the following dates are reasonable for Israel:

Middle Bronze—4000 to 3500 y BP
Late Bronze—3500 to 3200 y BP
Iron (Phoenician)—3200 to 2500 y BP
Persian—2500 to 2300 y BP
Hellenistic—2300 to 2100 y BP
Roman—2100 to 1650 y BP
Byzantine—1650 to 1370 y BP
Early Moslem—1370 to 900 y BP
Crusader—900 to 700 y BP
Mameluk—700 to 450 y BP
Turkish—450 to 70 y BP

Unit 1——Dune Sand (Kurkar). A kurkar rock unit consists of barchan dunes that are asymmetric to the northeast: the Ramat Gan Kurkar Member (Horowitz 1979) or the Giv'at Olga Kurkar (Gavish and Bakler in press). The amplitudes and wavelengths of these friable sand dunes are about 20 m and 100 m, respectively (Fig. 5), and their internal structures are dominated by complex crossbedding. A system of northeasterly trending barchan dunes noted on sparkarray Profile 26.6 off Gaza (Neev et al., 1976, fig. 11) also may belong to this unit. Fifty to 60 per cent of the original mineral content is calcium carbonate, mostly bioclasts concentrated within individual laminae. The friable cement is derived from the carbonate grains. The rest of the sand is fine-grained very well rounded detrital quartz with minor (1%) heavy minerals. Its eolian origin is not doubted.

Unit 2a——Soil. The top of the Kurkar (Unit 1) is extensively covered by a rather uniform dark brown to gray soil layer containing calcified roots and shells of land snails. This silty-sand layer was vividly named by Avnimelech (1952) as "Cafe au Lait." Later, it was renamed by Gavish and Bakler (in press) as the Ga'ash Hamra, although at its type locality (the central segment of the coastal cliff) the unit is not reddish. The soil was formed by weathering and dust accumulation after the eolian sands became stabilized at the end of Unit 1 time. Such processes could have accompanied a change from a drier to a wetter climate as well as being related to a reduction in rate of sand supply from the Nile River to the Mediterranean Sea.

A regmatic drainage pattern is formed by two sets of rivers, one that trends transversely across the coastline and another that parallels both the coastline and the kurkar ridges. This drainage system became entrenched into the kurkar of Unit 1 during the following wetter period. We correlate this erosional surface with a prominent uppermost erosional surface (UES) extensively observed beneath the sea floor on high-resolution seismic profiles across the shelf off Israel (Neev et al. 1966, 1976). No artifacts have been found yet within this soil layer. Neither was it possible to radiocarbon date the abundant terrestrial gastropods (*Helix sp.*) in it, as their age is beyond the range of this general technique. Nevertheless, knowing the ages of the overlying units, we assume that the sand dunes of Unit 1 accumulated during a dry phase within the latest glaciation (Würm, or Wisconsinan) and that the overlying soil layer (Unit 1a) formed during a wet phase (Mousterian) that followed.

Unit 2b——Red Hamra. Properly dated (by flint implements) reddish silty-clayey sand beds (genuine hamra) of the same age range as Unit 2a (Middle Paleolithic—Mousterian) were described both from Hof Hacarmel (Ronen 1977, or the Nahsholim Hamra of Horowitz 1979) and from the northern coastal plain between Akko and Nahariya (Avnimelech 1943). They were deposited in an oxidizing environment.

Unit 2c——Brown Hamra. The Pleistocene sequence along the northern Sinai coastline (between Tel Rafiah and El Arish) is rather similar although appreciably thinner than that along Israel (Fink 1969; Zelinger et al. 1971; Zelinger and Bar Yosef 1971). Several hamra-like units are interbedded; however, they are dark to light brown, rather than the red that characterizes the Hamra beds of Israel, and they are much more plastic (less sandy and more clayey).

A 1- to 2-m thick beachrock layer (composed of carbonate-cemented well rounded coarse quartz grains with oolitic spherules and small shell fragments alternating with cross-bedded fine sands) is interbedded between two hamra-like units along the coastline just west of Sheikh Zuweid (N31°13'40" E34°03'30"; Fig. 1). Middle Paleolithic (40,000 y BP) to Late Paleolithic (25,000 y BP) flint implements occur within the overlying hamra-like clay unit (Y. Gila'd, Ben Gurion Univ., Dept. of Archaeology, personal communication). The dark brown well-compacted clay unit that crops out at El Kharubeh—Musaida (Unit 4d; see below) could be an upper member or a lateral facies change of Unit 2c. If the age of the El Kharubeh clays is really Epipaleolithic (Unit 4), the dune sands of Unit 3 (see below) must be absent in this segment. Such a relationship is analogous to that described for the equivalent units at the Akko—Evron area (see Unit 4c below). The El Kharubeh clays are rather similar to the dark brown clay unit that is extensively exposed along the central segment of the Suez Canal (north of Bitter Lake) and may be the same age. The thickness of the hamra-like clayey unit found in drill holes at Sheikh Zuweid is about 25 m (Fink 1969), and it overlies a 15-meter Kurkar Unit that probably is equivalent to Unit 1.

Unit 2d——Chalky Freshwater Limestone. A several-meter thick freshwater porous (heavily burrowed) algal chalky limestone layer is exposed just above the regional watertable at Bir Jamil in northwestern Sinai (approximately +5 m to +15 m msl at N30°56'00" E33°01'40", about 8 km south of the junction of the Gafgafa—Bir Abd and the coastal roads). A freshwater Nilotic faunal assemblage of micro-mollusks, ostracods, and diatoms occurs as detrital pockets within this limestone layer (E. Tchernov, Hebrew Univ., Dept. of Zoology, personal communication). The radiocarbon age of organic carbon disseminated within a thin lenticular clay-horizon interbedded in this unit is 34,770 ± 1,020 y BP. A radiocarbon age of the algal limestone from the same unit is 24,160 ± 520 y BP (K. O. Munich, personal communication). This freshwater unit is underlain by a friable greensih limonitic fine-grained quartz-sand layer. Based on regional data, this unit is underlain by a relatively thick dune (?) sand sequence that we believe correlates with Unit 1 in Israel. The overlying freshwater algal unit was deposited probably during the wet phase that followed (when the soil and the drainage pattern were formed). The same algal limestone layer crops out 700 m and 1800 m south-southwest of Bir Jamil at elevations of about +20 m and +30 to +40 m msl, respectively (N30°56'30" E33°02'07" and N30°55'59" E33°01'22"). In both outcrops, the limestone layers are about 1 m thick and, similarly to the Bir Jamil outcrop, are underlain by limonitic greenish fine quartz sands. The second outcrop of the algal limestone layer (at +30 to +40 m) forms a platform of about 300 sq. m that is tilted 3 to 5 degrees northeastward.

A small erg of active sand dunes farther south is underlain by a dark gray hamada-like plain that crops out in several sites, mostly along the leeward sides of the more than 50 m high linear seif dunes. Two outcrops are 7 and 8 km south of Bir Jamil at elevations of +50 to +60 m msl (N30°53'04" E33°02'06" and N30°52'30" E33°02'06"). A several-meter thick well-bedded sequence of reddish brown (hamra) to greenish limonitic silty sand layers, including some mudballs interbedded with finely layered cream-colored concretionary carbonate-cemented quartz sandstones, has been exposed by wind erosion at these outcrops. Large angular erratic blocks of dense limestone that resemble the Bir Jamil algal limestone layer are atop some of these hamada-like outcrops. An in situ finding of probably the same freshwater limestone layer and also associated with hamra deposits is 35 km east-northeast of Bir Jamil, at Hod al Kufri (N31°00'15" E33°24'00") about +25 m msl. Most likely the Bir Jamil paleofreshwater body was rather extensive; however, it was shallow (not deeper than a few meters) as no physiographic barrier is known to have existed between it and the Mediterranean Sea to the north.

Unit 3——Dune Sand (Kurkar). A younger unit of carbonate-cemented quartz-sand dunes that is lithologically similar to the underlying Unit 1 was deposited atop the Uppermost Erosional Surface (Unit 2a). Its sediments fill the interdune troughs of Unit I along the coastal cliff of Israel (Fig. 5), where it was named the Wingate Kurkar Member (Gavish and Bakler in press). Calcium carbonate content is 40 to 50 per cent, forming most of the cement (the rest being fine-grained quartz). Only small- and medium-scale cross-bedded structures occur in this unit, and no dune structures of appreciable size are associated. Several thin hamra layers are interbedded along the central segment of the coastal plain of Israel. Solution basins were identified within the elevated abraded terrace that is the top of this eolian sand unit at an elevation about +40 m msl in Netanya (Mazor 1960). The lower part of the alluvial fill sequence within the transverse river channels (see above) probably is a time equivalent of Unit 3. This lower part of the fill includes more sand layers than the overlying part.

Unit 4a——Netanya Hamra. The next younger unit consists of the dark red loams (maroon colored Hamra, Gavish and Bakler, in press) that dominate and characterize the coastal plain of Israel. It conformably overlies the kurkar of Unit 3 in the interdunes, but locally it onlaps the peaks of the dunes of Unit 1. It was found also in shallow offshore drillings to about 2 km west of the coastline between Tel Aviv and Givat Olga (Figs. 4D and 5). This red loam is a mixture of sand, silt, and clay in various proportions. A lateral transition to dark gray to black sandy clay is common where plant remains and freshwater fauna are present, thereby indicating its aquatic (swamp) origin. The swamp facies is more abundant where this unit fills part of pre-existing erosional channels and also near the top of the unit. Although most of the Hamra Unit is a uniform and massive bed, some finer bedding also is recognized. This bedding ranges from 0.2 mm to 30 cm thick. Cyclic graded bedding is locally present where the sediments are finely laminated, and fine-grained quartz sand alternates with laminae of clean dark brown montmorillonitic clay. Crossbedding or flaser structures are not evident. Such an arrangement suggests that the fine grains of quartz sand were transported inland by strong westerly winds from nearby beaches toward extensive flood plains that existed then. These sand grains were trapped in the muddy water and settled to the bottom. At the same time, the load of brown montmorillonitic clay particles was continuously settling from the water but at a slower rate.

The source of most of the clay fraction within the Hamra Unit probably is the Quaternary terra-rossa (red soils) that are the typical circum-Mediterranean weathering products of various kinds of outcropping rocks, mostly dense carbonates. Even during present winter floods the residual montmorillonitic (in Israel) and kaolinitic (in Lebanon) red clays are being washed westward from the mountains into the lowlands of the coastal plain as well as eastward into the Jordan Valley (Picard 1943). These processes were more intensive during pluvial (glacial) phases of the Pleistocene, when the clays were deposited within the floodplains and lowlands. In this respect, we disagree with Rim (1950, 1951), Yaalon and Dan (1967), Dan et al. (1968–69), and others, who consider the Hamra to have two components: a minor one due to in situ weathering of the heavy mineral fraction within the eolian sand of the underlying kurkar, and a major one consisting of eolian clay imported from the nearby deserts of Sahara and Arabia. The age of this Hamra Unit 4a ranges from 20,000 to 12,000 y BP, as determined by Epipaleolithic flint implements found within it (Ronen 1977).

Unit 4b————Caesarea Freshwater Chalk. A radiocarbon age of 14,700 ± 250 y BP was determined for a 30-cm thick laminated pure chalk layer reported by Neev et al. (1987a,b, 51) to unconformably overlie Kurkar Unit 1 (or 3?) in the present Caesarea harbor at a water depth of 4.5 m. A uranium age analysis on another sample from this same chalk layer yielded similar results between 20,000 and 10,000 y BP [E. Wakshal, Hebrew Univ., Faculty of Agriculture, Rehovoth, personal communication]. Oxygen and carbon isotopic ratios within this chalk indicate that it was deposited within a freshwater lake environment (Y. Kolodny—Hebrew Univ., Dept. of Geology, personal communication in Neev et al. 1978a). Therefore, a freshwater body is inferred to have existed during this time along the coast just south of Mount Carmel. Absence of quartz-sand grains in this chalk deposit, which today is within the coastal cliff, may indicate that it was deposited during a phase of low rate of sand supply by the Nile River. The absence of reddish-brown clay may suggest isolation of this site from the mountainous provenances at the east and north (the source of the terra-rossa clay).

Unit 4c——Lagoonal Clay. This lagoonal clay is a time equivalent of both 4a (the Netanya Hamra) and Unit 5a (the Calcarenite Bank)—deposited almost uninterruptedly since about 20,000 years ago, ending sometime during middle Holocene. (i) A dark gray clay unit as thick as 12 m and containing brackish water and marine foraminiferans was reported by Sivan (1981, 1982) and Inbar and Sivan (1984) in shallow boreholes along the coast-parallel trough between the coastline of Akko (from its promontory and northward) in the west and the Evron Kurkar Ridge about 2 km east of it (Figs 1 and 14). This clay sequence is interbedded by a 0.5- to 2.0-m thick bed composed mostly of the shells of marine- to brackish-water bivalve species *Cerastoderma glaucum* (Brugiere) that are so weathered that they are unsuitable for radiocarbon age analyses. The dark gray sequence is underlain by a hamra unit a few meters thick, within which Paleolithic (about 50,000 y BP) flint implements were found at nearby outcrops (Avnimelech 1943, 44). The hamra gradually changes facies downward into loose sand, which in turn is underlain by a well-cemented unit of kurkar rock. Three radiocarbon analyses were made of disseminated organic carbon within the marine to brackish dark clay sequence. They yielded the following ages (from the upper one downward): (a) 6240 y BP at the middle of the upper marine clay layer, (b) 14,780 ± 295 y BP just above the shell bed, and (c) 19,110 ± 535 y BP in the upper part of the lower marine clay layer. Pottery sherds, mostly of Hellenistic age (2300 y BP), are interbedded within the uppermost part of the marine clay sequence. Accordingly, Sivan (1981, 84) suggested that shallow marine to lagoonal environments uninterruptedly prevailed within the trough east of Akko since 30,000 or even 50,000 y BP and until late Holocene (Hellenistic) time, about 2400 y BP. A similar sequence of dark gray clays that also contains a shell layer of *Cerastoderma glaucum* at an average depth of -5 m msl occurs in boreholes along the northward extension of the same trough between Akko and Nahariya.

(ii) A 6-m dark gray clay unit was shown by Sneh and Klein (1982, 66 and their fig. 4) to crop out at sea level and to overlie the Kurkar (Unit 1 or 3). It was penetrated by several shallow boreholes drilled along the coastline of Dor (Figs. 1 and 15). Brackish-water foraminiferans within the upper part of this unit suggest a marine to lagoonal origin for the entire unit. Two radiocarbon analyses made on the disseminated organic fraction within clays at the middle part of this sequence (the lower one from a depth of -4.4 m and the upper one from -3.8 m msl) yielded ages of 11,400 ± 420 and 9415 ± 480 y BP, respectively. This same clay unit crops out nearby at a water depth of 3 m about 80 m west of the coastline (Galili and Inbar 1986). It probably is identical with the Hof Hacarmel clays described by Prausnitz (1977), Wreschner (1977), Raban (1983b), Adler (1985), Galili (1985), Galili and Evron (1985), and Galili and Inbar (1986). That unit forms a continuous 1-km wide and 11-km long strip between the Carmel (Haifa) Nose and Atlit. It was deposited within a coast-parallel trough bounded east and west by the flanks of the coastal and first offshore kurkar ridges (Figs. 1, 3, and 15). The highest elevation of the clay outcrops is +1 m msl, and the lowest elevation is -13 m msl (about 900 m west of the coastline). Thus its uppermost surface slopes westward about one degree (locally 1.5 degree). Its lagoonal-brackish water fauna indicates it to have been in hydraulic equilibrium with the nearby Mediterranean Sea. Early Neolithic to Early Bronze settlements were found and excavated in the upper layer, both along the coastline and offshore. The oldest one (8140 ± 120 y BP) was found about 400 m off the coastline at water depths between 12 and 7 m, whereas younger ones are shallower and nearer the coastline as well as onshore at about +1 m msl. The time of initial deposition of this unit, about 11,400 years ago as postulated by Galili and Inbar (1986), seems to us to be too recent, because the dated sample was not from the bottom of the core but from about the top of the lower third of it. Moreover, the age of the lowermost Akko lagoonal clay unit, is older than 19,110 years. On the other hand, we agree with Galili and Inbar (1986) that deposition of this unit ended along the Haifa-Atlit segment about 8200 years ago. This was not the same history as for the southern extension of this trough (the Dor segment), as indicated by the 9415-year age of the sample from 3.8 m beneath the top of the core. Apparently, deposition of the clay unit continued along the Dor segment of the trough until middle Holocene time or even until 4000 years ago. Possibly during deposition of the last phase of this unit the northern segment of the trough was at a somewhat higher structural and topographic level than was the southern segment; subsequently, this relationship became reversed.

(iii) A sequence of alternating brackish-water clay sediments and beach sands was reported by Gifford and Rapp (in press) within the lower half of a 2.5-m deep bore hole just east of the coastline at about +1 m msl. This was drilled into the paleoestuarine fill of the Poleg River (about midway between Netanya and Tel Michal—Fig. 1). The radiocarbon age of articulated *Cerastoderma edule* (identical with *C. glaucum*) shells at -1.1 to -1.2 m msl within one of these layers is 6520 ± 140 y BP. As the brackish-water facies probably continues below the bottom of the hole, this sequence is considered to belong to Unit 4a. Apparently, the brackish-water facies of Unit 4c interfingers with the mud-flat facies of the hamra sediments (Unit 4a) and also with the overlying beach calcarenite sediments (Unit 5a).

Unit 4d——Brownish Sandy Clay. A well-compacted brown sandy clay unit is exposed at elevations up to 12 m above msl along the coastline at El Kharube, the bay of Musaida, and farther northeastward (about 20 km east-northeast of El Arish, central point at N31°11′ E33°58′). Epipaleolithic (13,000–12,000 y BP) implements were found scattered in its upper parts. The unit is overlain by a sequence of hamra-like more sandy layers that are interbedded with yellowish kurkar (friably cemented) and loose sand layers, atop which are sites with Chalcolithic to Middle Bronze I (6500 to 4000 y BP) sherds. This sequence has been affected by tectonic processes, as indicated by its present tilted (mostly to the southeast) and even folded (dome shaped) geometry. Recent dunes (Unit 7) to 15 m high cover part of the Chalocolithic to Middle Bronze more stable surface.

Unit 4e——Loess-like Mudflat and Coarse Detrital Deposits. An extensive terrace of yellowish-gray to tan mudflat sediments is exposed at an elevation of about +15 m msl both east and west of El Arish. Similar sediments occur farther northeastward as far as Gaza. At El Arish, it was correlated by Shatta (1959, 230, 231, and 240) as the Pre-Roman Mediterranean sea-level stage 4, and described as the lower terrace at Wadi El Arish that "occurs at a distance less than 100 m from the present coast." A coarse detrital sequence more than 10 m thick is exposed about 4 km west of Wadi El Arish and about

2 km south of the Mediterranean coastline (N31°06′20″ E33°47′00″) within an artificially excavated interdune trough. Similar depressions are common along the coastal zone between Gaza and El Arish where they are locally named Mawassie. The bottoms of these depressions, which reach the freshwater table at about +1 m msl, are being exploited for intensive agriculture. At the site near El Arish, the coarse detrital sequence becomes gradually finer upward to be topped by a 1-2 m loess-like layer similar to the present floodplain deposits of Wadi El Arish. Pottery sherds of Chalcolithic (about 6000 y BP) and younger ages occur at several sites atop this now-elevated floodplain that presently is covered by scattered dunes. The coarse detrital sequence consists mostly of cross-bedded well-rounded to sub-angular flint and limestone-dolomite sand to boulder-size components. Green-gray and yellowish-brown mudballs, some of which attain very large dimensions (to 1 m diameter), are included. Green-gray marl layers are interbedded at the bottom of this outcrop. Only redeposited Late Cretaceous to Early Tertiary nannoplankton fossils were found within these marls and mudballs as well as in the uppermost layer of the floodplain (S. Moshkowitz, Geol. Surv. Israel, personal communication). The above suggests that: (i) This fining-upward sequence was deposited during the transition period from the latest glaciation (late Pleistocene) to the climatic optimum about 6000 y BP. (ii) The gradient of the El Arish River and thereby also the energy of the river floods may have diminished appreciably because of the more than 100-m eustatic rise of sea level. (iii) The waters that flooded these mudflats were in equilibrium with the nearby sea. (iv) The transgressive coastline stabilized at a location probably near that of today. (v) During the past 6000 years the ancient floodplain terrace must have been tectonically elevated by 15 m or more. Shatta (1960) quoted Moon and Sadeck (1921) in referring to a raised beach near El Arish.

Unit 5a——Calcarenite Bank. A calcarenite unit, or bioclastic sandstone, is known as the Tel Aviv Kurkar Bed of Horowitz (1979) or the Beit Yanai Kurkar Member (Gavish and Bakler, in press). A 4-m layer of cross-stratified calcarenite conformably overlies Unit 4a (the Netanya Hamra) along the central segment of the coastline of Israel, between Giva't Olga and Yavneh Yam (Figs. 1, 4, 5). Outcrops along the coastal cliff indicate the Units 3, 4a, and 5a are lenticular with their thickest sections in the interdune troughs of Unit 1, and they laterally thin and even wedge out toward some of the older dune crests. Both units 4a and 5a also thicken toward the troughs of some of the transversely trending late Pleistocene rivers (such as at Nahal Poleg—Beit Yanai, where initial dips within the calcarenitic unit correspond with the slope of the river's south bank). Although cross stratification on a small scale is abundant, Unit 5a conformably overlies Unit 4a (the Netanya Hamra). The transition is gradual, and alternations of the calcarenitic layer with the upper part of the underlying hamra layers are locally present.

The prominent white of Unit 5a is due to dominance of bioclastic carbonate components (well-rounded algae, foraminiferans, and shell fragments). Total carbonate content increases northward, being 60 per cent off Yafo and 90 per cent at Giva't Olga (Fig. 1), with the rest (10–40%) being well-sorted fine-grained quartz sand. This calcarenitic layer is friable and has high permeability.

In situ molds of burrowers' tubes are sparsely scattered across this unit, their detrital fill having the same composition as that of the matrix. Locally, near the bottom of the unit, the crowded burrows form biostromal lenses to 0.5 m thick and a few meters long. The maximum diameter of individual tubes is 2 cm and their length reaches 20 cm. Some secondary borings through the tubes are hollow cylinders with smooth and perfectly rounded cross-sections; possibly these were made by pelecypods such as *Mytilus* sp. Presence of mollusks within the burrower population is further suggested by successions of concave-upward septa across some of the vertical molds. An alternative interpretation, that the tubes represent calcified roots, appears improbable; internal structures, such as concentric rings as well as external halos of carbonate cement that usually are associated wth calcified roots were not recognized. We conclude that these clusters of tubes are trace-fossils of colonies of burrowers that populated the beach or the upper littoral zone (Fig. 6A,B,C). Convolute load structures locally present within this calcarenitic unit corroborate their aquatic marine origin. Angular truncation and wedge-out features within alternating beds of calcarenite and hamra occur at the top of the Hamra unit at Shefaiim (Fig. 6D). The overlying porous limestone layer (a time equivalent of the burrower lenses) was affected by solution and probably also through vigorous winnowing by waves to form boulder-like tear-apart features (Fig. 6 E).

The Calcarenite Bank should be younger than 12,000 y BP or even 10,000 y BP (the youngest age of the Epipaleolithic culture found within the underlying Hamra Unit; A. Ronen, personal communication) and older than 5500 y BP (the age of Early Bronze settlements within the overlying brownish alluvial loam unit; Gophna 1977; Unit 6). Several radiocarbon dates, ranging between 10,000 and 7000 y BP, were determined for these calcarenites by Gavish and Friedman (1969). Gifford et al. (in press) described a ceramic Neolithic site (about 7000 y BP) 400 m southeast of Tel Michal (Fig. 1). This site is interbedded within a calcarenitic hamra unit that interfingers westward wth the Calcarenite Bank (Unit 5a or the Tel Aviv Kurkar, as defined by Gifford et al.). An age of 10,000 to 6000 y BP is thereby fairly well established for deposition of this unit. We suggest that it was deposited by the transgressive Flandrian Sea.

The presence of cross-stratification and locally abundant shells of terrestrial *Helicidea* gastropods in lenses within this unit cause some authors to question its marine origin as well as its age. The age controversy derives from the results of eight radiometric age analyses made on *Helix* shells sampled from this unit, as reported by Arad et al. (1978). A spectrum of ages between 5500 and 2400 y BP was obtained. The two oldest (5500 and 4600 y BP) are from shells at the top of the unit, whereas the rest of the shells that were sampled in the middle part of the unit or near the base are appreciably younger (ranging from 3300 to 2400 y BP). It is difficult to refer to these results as faithfully representing the true age of this unit, because reliable archaeological dating indicates that the age of the overlying alluvial loam unit cannot be younger than 5000 y BP, corroborating the 10,000 to 6000 y BP radiocarbon age of the Calcarenite Bank. The inverse chronostratigraphic order of the shells' radiocarbon ages may suggest that they were introduced to their final burial positions by some process (such as downward transport through cracks and solution channels after final regression of the Flandrian Sea). The same arguments also question the reliability of these terrestrial shells as indicators for the environment of deposition of the Calcarenite Bank (such as terrestrial dunes, as suggested by Arad et al. 1978).

18 *Stratigraphy*

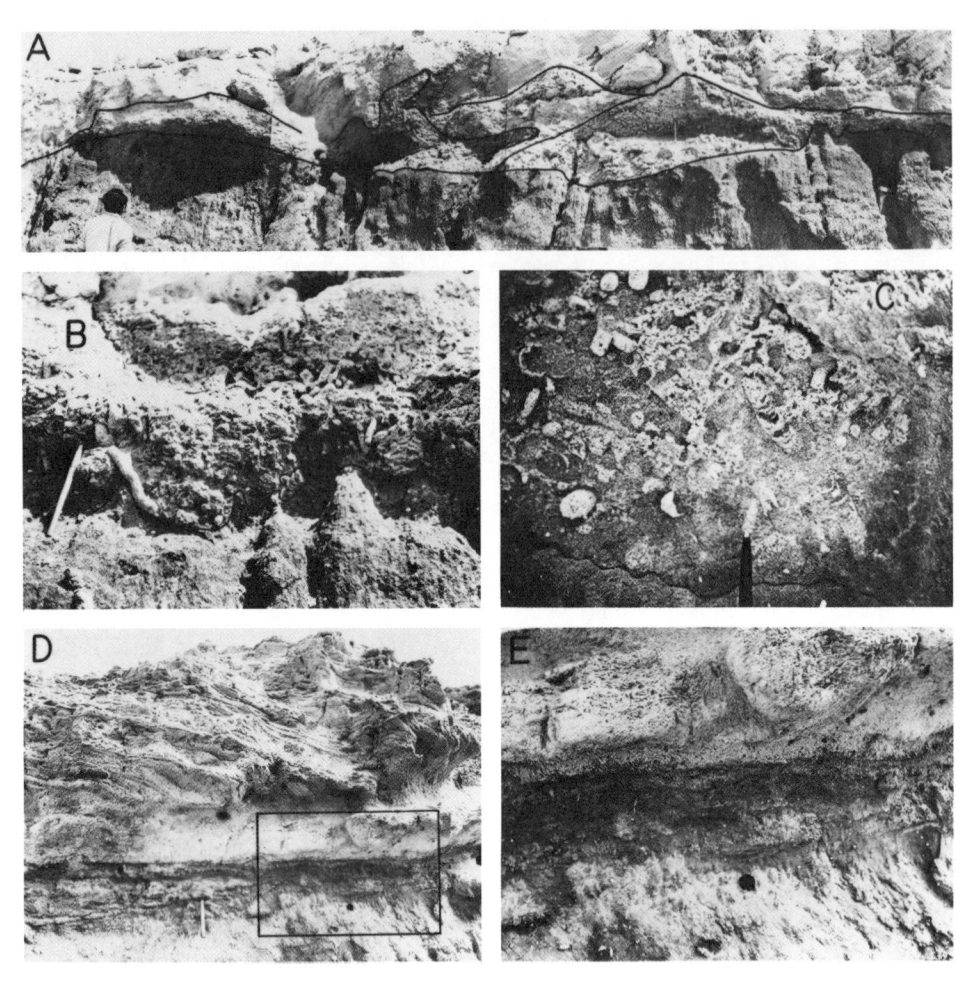

Figure 6. The Calcarenite Bank (Unit 5a) (*A,B,C*—at Netanya; *D,E*—at Shefaiim). *A*. The cross-bedded Calcarenite Bank overlying the Epipaleolithic Hamra (red loam) beds (Unit 4a). An irregularly bedded (lenticular to 0.7 m thick) layer of burrower colonies concentrated at the bottom of the bank. Many colonies have deeply invaded through the top of the Hamra layer to form pockets within it (*C*). Black lines indicate limits of burrower lenses. *B*. A closer view of densely populated colony of burrowers. *C*. A sequence of concave-upward septa within a burrower tube, suggesting the mechanism of bioclastic infilling of the tube by the animal (above pen). Secondary bored cylinder through burrower's tube (above and left of pen). *D*. Angular truncation across a sequence of alternatingly deposited hamra and calcarenite laminae near the contact between the two units. The base of the Calcarenite Bank contains boulder-like tear-apart features (middle right). An Early Bronze site was found atop the Calcarenite Bank. *E*. Boulder-shaped features formed in situ within a 40-cm thick porous limestone layer deposited at the bottom of the Calcarenite Bank (also indicated in panel *D* within the framed quadrangle). Such a tearing-apart mechanism could have been formed by the combined effect of solution and wave winnowing.

A dense bioclastic limestone unit containing the same faunal assemblage as the friable Calcarenite Bank (H. Frenkel, Geol. Survey of Israel, personal communication) was found off Netanya in an offshore borehole drilled with a chisel and bailer at a water depth of 20 m (Figs. 1 and 4C). It overlies a Kurkar sequence belonging to Units 1 or 3. A Hamra layer (probably Unit 4a) found east of it in a nearby offshore borehole has a similar stratigraphic relationship (see above, Fig. 4C). A unit of loosely cemented calcarenitic bioclastic rock more than 20 m thick with the same faunal assemblage was found in another drill hole atop a now-submerged kurkar ridge off Yafo in a water depth of 30 m (see below III C 10 and drill site TA-12 in Fig. 21) We correlate these two offshore occurrences of calcarenitic units with Unit 5a (Bakler 1976).

Chances for miscorrelation between this early Holocene calcarenitic unit and others of similar lithography but greater ages are small. The closest known stratigraphically older bioclastic unit that petrographically resembles the Calcarenite Bank is the Tyrrhenian (middle Pleistocene) *Marginopora* Sandstone Formation (from the second and third ingressions described by Issar 1968). Nevertheless, no *Marginopora* sp. shells have been observed within the calcarenites of Unit 5a in either onshore or offshore areas. The following is a written personal communication from L. Buchbinder (1984) on that subject: "The faunal affinity of the calcarenitic unit of the coastal cliff (Unit 5a) is similar to that of the two calcarenitic zones found within the Kurkar Group at depths of 42–58 m and 92–95 m respectively in the Ashdod Yam 1A borehole (L. Buchbinder and G. Friedman 1980). Other calcarenitic zones found in this borehole above these depths are of different affinities." The late Holocene Tel Haraz calcarenitic beds (see below, Unit 7c) consist almost entirely of fragmented platy particles of pelecypod shells. Correlation between the two submarine outcrops of calcarenite mentioned above and the onshore Calcarenite Bank (Unit 5a) seems assured.

Unit 5b——Beachrock Terrace of Northwestern Sinai. A few-meter thick low and flat beachrock terrace (lumachelle deposits dominated by *Cardium* sp. shells) crops out in several sites south and southeast of Bardawil Lagoon at elevations between +5 m and +15 msl. The most extensive ones are near the abandoned El Meidan (N31°04′40″ E33°34′20″) and Bardawil (N31°05′30″ E33°40′00″) railway stations (see Fig. 1) where they were quarried for road construction. Two radiocarbon analyses made on samples from these two sites yielded ages of 7780 ± 160 y BP and 6550 ± 85 y BP (A. Kaufman, Weizmann Inst. Science, Isotope Dept., personal communication). Therefore, these lumachelle terraces were deposited probably in the Flandrian transgressive sea. A coquina bank associated with a calcareous quartz-sand deposit is reported from the inland sabkhas south of Bardawil Lagoon (Levy 1972); however, the radiocarbon ages of these samples ranged from 35,500 to 2800 y BP. Oxygen isotope analyses of their carbonate fractions suggest precipitation under marine conditions.

Unit 5c——Fluvial-Lagoonal Sands. The lower half of the almost 60-m high coastal cliff of Mount Casius (at the apex of the arcuate bar of Bardawil Lagoon in northwestern Sinai, Fig. 1) is a sequence of loose cyclic fluviatile sands (Neev 1967; Bakler et al. 1972). Another outcrop of this sequence is near the southwestern end of the 3-km long coastal cliff (at N31°12′30″ E33°03′16″), where the strata dip 20 to 30 degrees to the east. The following characteristics suggest deposition within a lagoonal-deltaic environment: (i) graded cyclic layers (each a few cm thick) of very coarse- to very fine-grained quartz sand. The coarse grains (1 to 3 mm diameter) are well-rounded and pitted; (ii)

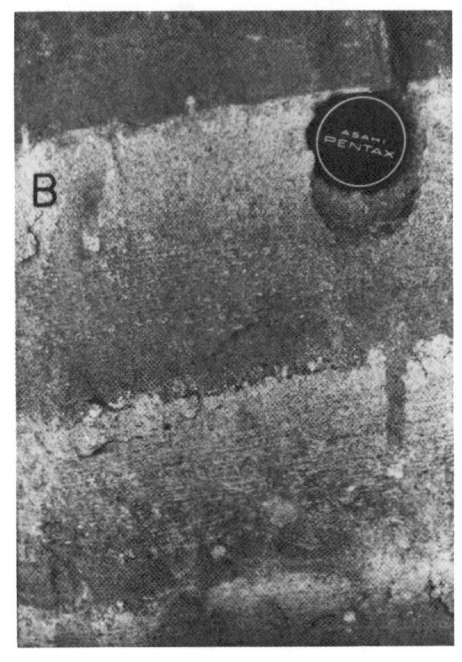

Figure 7. An early Holocene cyclic sequence of bedded and graded sediments at southwesternmost part of Mount Casius (bordering Bardawil Lagoon). Fine striations parallel to bedding consist of coarse- to medium-size quartz sands; white calcium-carbonate precipitates are disseminated through the upper part of each major cycle and are densest at the tops. Some burrowing activity is present. Environment of deposition was a shallow lagoon with minimal influence of currents (no cross stratification) but with cyclic dessication. Layers originally were horizontal, but presently they dip to the east and southeast as much as 30 degrees because of late Holocene tectonic tilting.

friable white calcium-carbonate precipitates cement the laminae at the tops of many of the graded cycles (Fig. 7); and (iii) light-brown clay layers interbedded within the lower part of this sequence. The 20- to 30-degree eastward dips express a tectonic tilt rather than large-scale cross stratification. This conclusion agrees with an earlier observation (Neev 1967) that the entire promontory of Mt. Casius is a tectonically warped dome located along a northeast-southwest-trending tectonic lineament that later was named the Pelusium Line. Domal structure is indicated by the configuration of a hamra-like reddish clayey sand layer that tops the fluviatile sequence. It is assumed that deposition of this hamra layer was associated with the regional water table of that time, because it was originally horizontally layered at an elevation near sea level. This red loam layer is overlain by a sequence of loose eolian sand layers each 0.5 to 1 m thick. At the top of each layer are coarse granules of quartz sand, small fragments of marine shells (lag deposits?), and abundant shells of the terrestrial gastropod *Helix* sp. A radiocarbon age of 4430 ± 190 y BP (A. Kaufman, personal communication) was measured for *Helix* shells from one of these layers about 0.5 km south of the coastal cliff (at N31°12′25″ E33°03′40″). The upper half of the coastal cliff at Mount Casius is an active longitudinal seif dune. Pottery sherds of Persian to Roman ages are at the contact of the red loam layer and the active seif. No relicts of earlier cultures were found on this promontory. These observations suggest that the transition from aquatic (deltaic) to terrestrial (eolian) environments occurred after the Flandrian regression, perhaps during Early Bronze time. The warping process of the Mt. Casius promontory occurred and was rejuvenated since that time.

Results of a study of a 48-m drill hole at Tel el Fadda just east of the Suez Canal and west of E-Tineh (Fig. 1) are reported by Sneh et al. (1986). The lowermost 6 m of the section is well-sorted marine-littoral sand (indicated by a wide spectrum of fauna including an 8480 ± 280 y BP solitary coral at the top of the unit). The rest of the section includes four units, all of which are open marine to lagoonal-deltaic clays and silts in different proportions. A prominent faunistic interval of hypersaline environment occurs about the middle of this sequence. By interpolating the ages of the top (present) and bottom of this section, we infer that this break is near the transition from Early to Middle Bronze ages. Apparently, the very coarse to fine and well-rounded fluviatile-lagoonal sand unit of Mt. Casius is the time-stratigraphic equivalent of the marine sands at the bottom of the Fadda hole (see fig. 2 of Sneh et al. 1986) and perhaps also of the overlying dark clays. The facies of the former characterize the domain east of the Pelusium Line (see III E 6), whereas that of the Fadda hole represents typical deltaic environments.

We concur with Sneh et al. (1986) that the coastline at the Tel Fadda site did not shift significantly landward since the beginning of the Holocene. This conclusion contradicts Said (1981, 80, 105), who wrote that the shoreline of the delta gradually retreated southward about 50 km from the present 100-m bathymetric contour during the Holocene. Moreover, the marine sand unit at the bottom of the Fadda hole may extend downward to the time-depth equivalent of 20,000 or 30,000 y BP. Such a relationship of coastline position and water depth during the most critical stage of the Pleistocene—Holocene eustatic sea level change is analogous to that described for the Akko and Dor sites (see above Unit 4c).

Unit 5d——Dark Brownish Gray Clay. Dark gray sediments that are time-equivalent to the calcarenites of Unit 5a were deposited both south and north of the central segment of the coastline of Israel. At the south, a Neolithic settlement (radiocarbon age of 6740 ± 90 y BP for a bone sample; Yeivin and Olami 1979) was found within swamp deposits onshore near the coastline of Nizzanim (Fig. 1). The radiocarbon age of lignitic sediments sampled in a submarine borehole a few kms off Caesarea at a depth of -35 m msl is 8900 ± 270 y BP (Neev et al. 1978a). Freshwater mollusks and terrestrial plant remains also were found in these sediments. Part of the brackish-water sedimentary sequence drilled at Dor and Akko (see above—Unit 4c), as well as outcrops of swamp deposits at Akhziv (Lewy et al. 1986) and along the littoral zone off Mount Carmel (Raban, 1983a,b) also belong to this unit.

South of Gaza as far as Tel Qatif (Fig. 1), the Uppermost Erosional Surface (the top of Unit 1) is unconformably overlain by a bedded sequence of aquatic-terrestrial sediments. It forms extensive elevated terraces, whose lithologic characteristics change from dark reddish-brown hamra-like loam with lateral transitions into swampy dark gray-brown clays to light yellow-brownish loess-like loam. Their ages extend (according to the ages of the interbedded archaeological sites) from Epipaleolithic to Persian—Iron Age time (12,000 to 2600 y BP; Y. Gilad and E. Oren, Ben-Gurion Univ., Dept. of Archaeology, personal communication).

Unit 6——Nof Yam Clayey Sand. A unit of dark brown to black (locally gray) sandy-clayey sediments a few meters thick was deposited during Early Bronze time (5500 to 4000 y BP' Gophna 1977; Gophna and Ayalon 1980; and Gavish and Bakler in press). The Nof-Yam Clayey Sand now occurs atop the central segment of the coastal cliff, where it overlies the Calcarenite Bank (Unit 5a), as well as atop the first kurkar ridge about 2 km farther east, where it covers Kurkar Units 1 or 3 and in places also the Ta'arukha Hamra beds of Unit 4a (Horowitz 1979). These Early Bronze marsh plains were sparsely inhabited by hunters who occupied small sites that differed appreciably from contemporaneous urban and fortified settlements a few kilometers farther east (R. Gophna, personal communication). One hunter's site is at Ramat Aviv C just north of Tel Aviv and the Yarkon River at about +30 m msl, where it is interbedded within light-brown sandy-clay sediments (Ritter-Kaplan 1979). Chain-forming phytoliths (siliceous platy concretions, constituents of reed tissues) still are linked together in these sediments, thereby suggesting their situ burial. Diatoms and siliceous cysts of Chrysostomaceae (spores of freshwater algae) are present (A. Ehrlich, Geol. Survey of Israel, *in*: Ritter-Kaplan 1979; personal communication). These swamp deposits are conformably overlain by a dark-gray to black cohesive clayey sand layer that is devoid of phytoliths, diatoms, and freshwater algae. Differences between these two layers presumably result from an increase in runoff and/or a few meters rise of water level within the swamps. Such an event agrees with an earlier deduction of a climatic wet phase during the transition from Early to Middle Bronze

Table 1
Swamp Environments

Location*	Material	Age	Elevation	Source
Akhziv	Dark Gray Clay + Archaeology	Late Neolithic to Early Bronze	0 to +4.4 m	Lewy et al., (1986)
Haifa Bay (Carasso Well)	Peat + Clay	5420 ± 540**	?	N. Bakler A. Kaufman
Ma'agan Michael	Peat overlain by freshwater fauna	4843 ± 400**	?	
Caesarea coastline	Peat	3810 ± 180**	−2 to −4 m	E. Shachnai A. Kaufman; Neev et al. (1978a)
Hadera Electric Power Plant	Peat	5160 ± 330**	?	N. Bakler A. Kaufman
Ashdod coastline P=2	Peat	4100 ± 380**	−2 m	N. Bakler A. Kaufman

* See Fig. 1
** Radiocarbon ages in y BP

periods and concurs with data from the Dead Sea—Jordan rift (Neev and Emery 1967; Neev and Hall 1977; Neev 1978).

The prevalance of swamp environments along the entire coast of Israel during the time span of Unit 6 (6000 to 4000 y BP) is corroborated by Table 1. Sediments of similar facies (dark brown to gray and black marsh-clay layers) occur along the coastal zone even in later times, in fact, almost to the present. Some are interbedded with shell beds (Unit 7d), but they were not defined as a separate time-stratigraphic unit.

Unit 7a——Hadera Dune Sands. Two or even three layers of loose quartz dune sand (Horowitz 1979; Gavish and Bakler in press) successively accumulated above the Early Bronze continental aquatic deposits (Unit 6) and in some areas atop older units (1 to 5). They represent a phase of rejuvenated extensive sand supply from the Nile Delta to the coast of Israel. In places, a brownish-gray sandy soil a few tens of centimeters thick separates the lower and upper sand layers (first and second generations). Radiocarbon analyses on both charcoal fragments and shells of the terrestrial gastropod *Helicidea* sampled from the intervening soil layer at the same site (Shefayim, N32°12'30" E34°48'45") yielded ages of 3690 ± 40 and 3320 ± 120 y BP, respectively. The lower layer (or the older generation) of dune sand is appreciably thinner than the upper one. Barchan dunes to 10 m high having slip-faces that dip to the northeast developed within the upper layer and were active until recently (when most of them were either stabilized, quarried, or built upon). The main lobes of these ingressive sand sheets are associated with the wide mouths of late Pleistocene rivers such as the one just north of the Yarkon River (Fig. 8). Smaller lobes also occur atop the +30- to +50-m high coastal cliff, where they form a discontinuous patchy pattern (Figs. 2, 8). Long axes of both types of lobe trend northeast. As no coast-parallel seif dunes were formed atop the coastal cliffs, it is assumed that most of the sand that migrated inland from the nearby beaches drifted northeastward (Fig. 8) with the dominant southwesterly storm winds. However, such a process could not occur today where the coastal cliff is steep (45–75 degrees) and high (+30 to +50 m) and where the beach is narrow (10 to 30 m) (Fig. 9). Under these circumstances, massive transport of beach sand to the top of the cliff, even during the strongest storms, seems highly improbable. The youngest settlements covered by the upper dune layer are a Byzantine site atop the cliff (+40 m) at Ga'ash (N32°13'40" E34°49'05"), and Late Roman to Byzantine warehouses south of Caesarea Harbor (Fig. 1). This coastal sand dune was deposited prior to Early Moslem time, as graves of that age as well as of Crusader age were dug into it. Early Moslem settlements were located on the Hamra (Unit 4a) plains near Ashdod (Fig. 1; Issar 1968). Therefore, the upper layer of sand was deposited probably after Roman times. As the Sharon Plain near the coastal zone in the Apollonia—Arsuf and Ga'ash areas (which is now covered by dunes—Figs. 1,2,8) was rather heavily forested during Crusader times (Lamb 1930, 152), a third generation of sand-dune ingression occurred probably during the past few hundred years.

Unit 7b——Marine Clay+Sand. A loose dark-clay clayey sand or sandy clay unit is now being deposited offshore beyond the high-energy belt at water depths greater than 10 m. This unit unconformably overlies and onlaps several rock units that formerly were

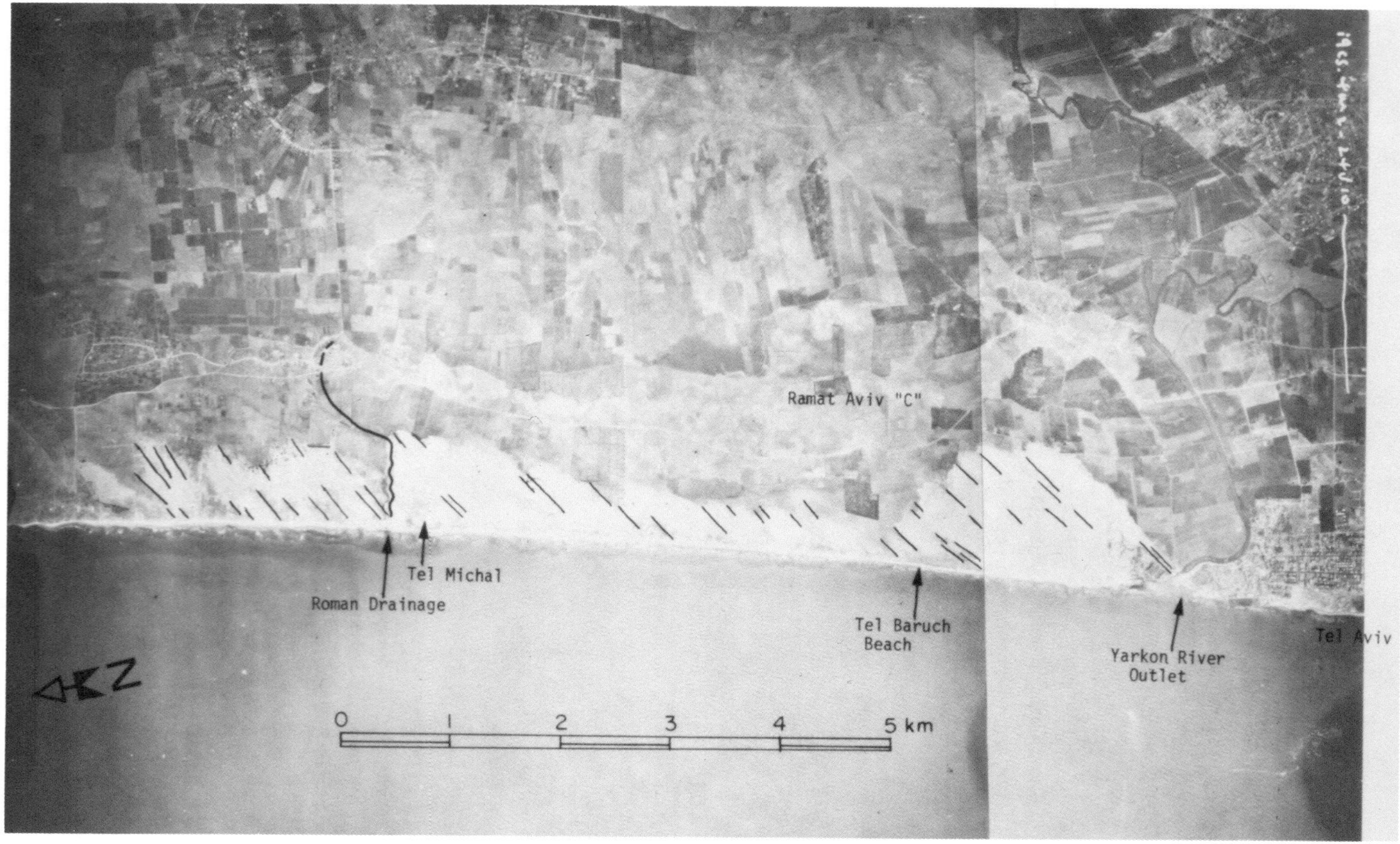
Ramat Aviv "C"
Tel Michal
Roman Drainage
Tel Baruch
Beach
Yarkon River
Outlet
Tel Aviv
0
1
2
3
4
5 km
N

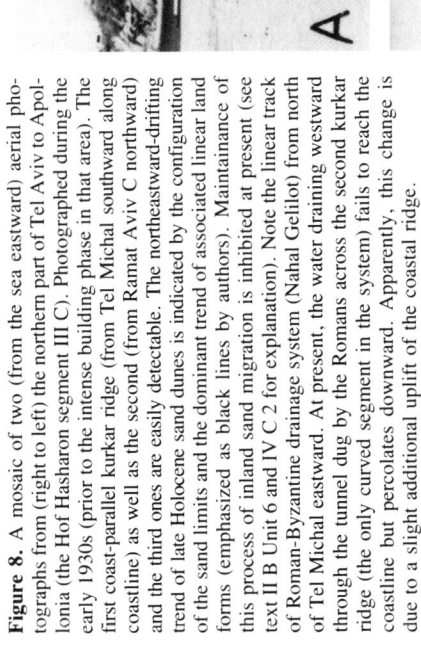

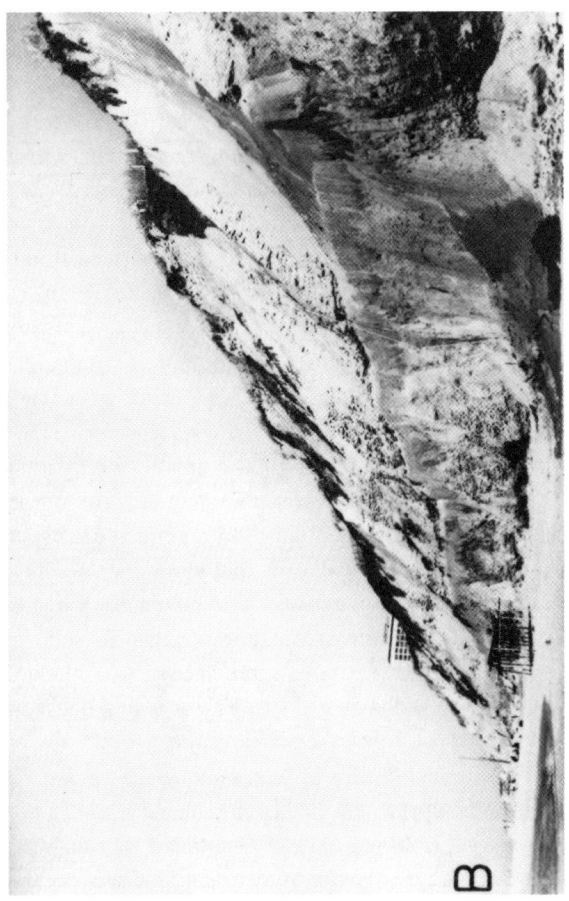

Figure 8. A mosaic of two (from the sea eastward) aerial photographs from (right to left) the northern part of Tel Aviv to Apollonia (the Hof Hasharon segment III C). Photographed during the early 1930s (prior to the intense building phase in that area). The first coast-parallel kurkar ridge (from Tel Michal southward along coastline) as well as the second (from Ramat Aviv C northward) and the third ones are easily detectable. The northeastward-drifting trend of late Holocene sand dunes is indicated by the configuration of the sand limits and the dominant trend of associated linear land forms (emphasized as black lines by authors). Maintainance of this process of inland sand migration is inhibited at present (see text II B Unit 6 and IV C 2 for explanation). Note the linear track of Roman-Byzantine drainage system (Nahal Gelilot) from north of Tel Michal eastward. At present, the water draining westward through the tunnel dug by the Romans across the second kurkar ridge (the only curved segment in the system) fails to reach the coastline but percolates downward. Apparently, this change is due to a slight additional uplift of the coastal ridge.

Figure 9. Views of the coastal cliff at Netanya. Note at the lower part of photographs the undulating dune morphology that is emphasized by the soil layer atop the dunes. (II B Unit 1).

exposed across and beyond the littoral zone. Thickness varies with underlying physiography and may exceed 30 m (Neev et al. 1966). The following age data indicate that this unit accumulated within the littoral zone during only the past four or five thousand years: (i) a radiocarbon date 4595 ± 230 y BP (A. Geyh, personal communication—uncorrected MASCA) of *Glycymeris violacescens* (Lamarck) shells found at the bottom of a 4-m Vibrocore drill hole in a water depth of 37 m off Tel Aviv within beach sand that underlies this unit, and (ii) ages that range between 3900 ± 60 and 3380 ± 80 y BP (A. Kaufman, personal communication) for shells scattered through the lower part of Unit 7b in drill holes 14, 15, and 16 off Tel Aviv (Bakler 1976).

Unit 7c——Tel Haraz Calcarenite. A friable calcarenitic sequence was found at Tel Haraz, which is on the coastal cliff between Yavneh Yam and Ashdod Harbor (Figs. 1, 24; N31°52'35" E34°40'25"). This sequence was named the Tel Haraz Beach Rock Terraces (Neev and Bakler 1977; Bakler et al. 1985), or the Tel Haraz Beds (Garfunkel et al. 1977). It is several meters thick and consists of alternating laminated fragmented platy shell particles and medium-to fine-grained quartz sand (Fig. 10A,B,C). Extrapolated regional information indicates that along the present coast it is underlain by the extensive swamp deposits of Unit 6 (see above, the Early Bronze peat at the Ashdod coastline; Table 1). The grain size of the fragmented shell particles decreases from more than 5 mm at the beach to about 2 mm about 2 km inland. No similar distinct visual differences were noted for the quartz-sand grains within the samples. A nearly horizontal 200-m wide terrace whose top is at an elevation of +2 m msl borders the coastline. Horizons of unbroken shells (mostly *Glycymeris* sp.) having different sizes are interbedded mostly within the upper part of this terrace. An age of 3800 ± 210 y BP (uncorrected MASCA values; A. Kaufman, personal communication) was determined for such a shell sample. A beachrock layer onlaps this calcarentic sequence along the present coastline. It contains gravels and pottery in addition to quartz sand but not the typical Tel Haraz fragmented shell sand, and it dips to the west.

Toward the east, the +2-m terrace of the Tel Haraz beds gradually rises to an elevation of about +4 m at the foot of the coast-parallel kurkar ridge. Farther eastward, this sequence onlaps the ridge to elevations of +20 to +30 m msl to form a sedimentary apron. Unbroken *Glycymeris* shells, typically concave downward, occur within this sequence just to the top of the +4-m msl terrace (Figs. 10C and 24B). Radiocarbon analysis of these shells yielded an uncorrected age of 3450 ± 400 y BP. Load casts and convolute structures are common within certain layers of the +4-m terrace where the cementation is relatively better developed than elsewhere (Fig. 10A). Low-angle cross-layering and burrow molds also are present. Weathered and rounded pumice in sizes ranging from granules to pebbles that are typical of eastern Mediterranean beaches was found in one of the fine quartz-sand layers underlying the +4-m terrace. All of the pumice samples from the Tel Haraz site were derived from a hitherto unknown source somewhere in the eastern Mediterranean Sea. The volcanic eruption that produced it occured "a few tens of years before the great Late Minoan eruption (1500 y BC) of the Santorini volcano" and was much greater than the latter. The destruction on Crete "could be attributed to this mysterious volcano" (Vincenzo Francoviglia, Consiglio Nazionale dela Richerche, Italy, personal communication). Sedimentary structure, mineralogy, and geochemistry of the carbonate cement within the entire Tel Haraz sequence suggest a marine or beach freshwater-seawater mixing zone as its environment of deposition (Bakler et al. 1985). Most of the Tel Haraz beds very much resemble genuine beachrock deposited in the inner littoral belt, although their lithologic characteristics differ appreciably from those of the nearby recent beachrock.

The apron of the Tel Haraz beds extends southwestward along the western coast-parallel kurkar ridge and wraps around it where it plunges toward the coastline. This sequence also onlaps the ridge on its eastern (inland) flank, and its sediments have filled the Central Trough that separates the coastal ridge from the adjacent second ridge at the east (Fig. 24). Steep initial dips were observed across the apron along the ridge; angles of up to 25 degrees to the northwest and southwest were measured. On the other hand, angles up to 30 degrees to the southeast were measured in the Tel Haraz beds within the inland Central Trough. The sequence there is more than 15 m thick, and it forms a large-scale cross-stratified sand body. Steepest dips are at the bottom of the sequence and the topset beds are almost horizontal. Individual better-cemented tabular calcarenitic strata that are interlaminated within the Tel Haraz Sequence can be traced more than 100 m along its strike. The quartz-sand fraction within the Tel Haraz Sequence markedly decreases from both west and east toward the crests of the coastal as well as the second kurkar ridges. Thinly-bedded fragmented shell layers a few centimeters thick from which most quartz grains have been winnowed were traced along stretches of several meters at the crests of these ridges (Fig. 10B).

These characteristics contrast markedly with those noted for the nearby recent loose calcarenitic sand, that is a weathering product of the Tel Haraz Sequence. Sand within this sheet is blown and drifted by the present prevailing winds to form large (1-m wavelength and 20-cm amplitude) asymmetric megaripples (Fig. 10D,E). These megaripples seasonally change their strike in agreement with the prevailing wind direction (northwesterly in winter and northerly in summer). The average granulometric and mineralogic affinities of their sands are the same as those of the sand in the Tel Haraz sequence. During the drifting process of these dune-like megaripples (Fig. 10E), the fragmented shells and quartz sands are segregated. These megaripples are unique along the coastline of Israel. They differ appreciably in detail both from the horizontal long flat and smooth bedforms that characterize the Tel Haraz beds as well as from the bedforms of the nearby pure quartz-sand dunes (Unit 7a). Therefore, we disagree with Garfunkel et al. (1977), who considered that most of the Tel Haraz Sequence (above +4 m msl) was deposited by wind and that the lower part of this sequence (below +4 m; see above) consists of storm deposits (transported and deposited only by waves that can reach such a high level during storms).

Involvement of tsunami waves in the deposition of the Tel Haraz Sequence as well as of the elevated shell beds (see below Unit 7d) also was mentioned by one of the reviewers of Bakler et al. (1985). Most effects of these high waves on the shelf and coastal zone are those of scouring and erosion. Sediments brought into suspension usually should be derived from several different environments of deposition and must include an extreme variety of grain sizes. They should settle rapidly, mostly subaerially, because of decreasing energy of the advancing water mass, especially after breaking on barriers such as the

TEL HARAZ

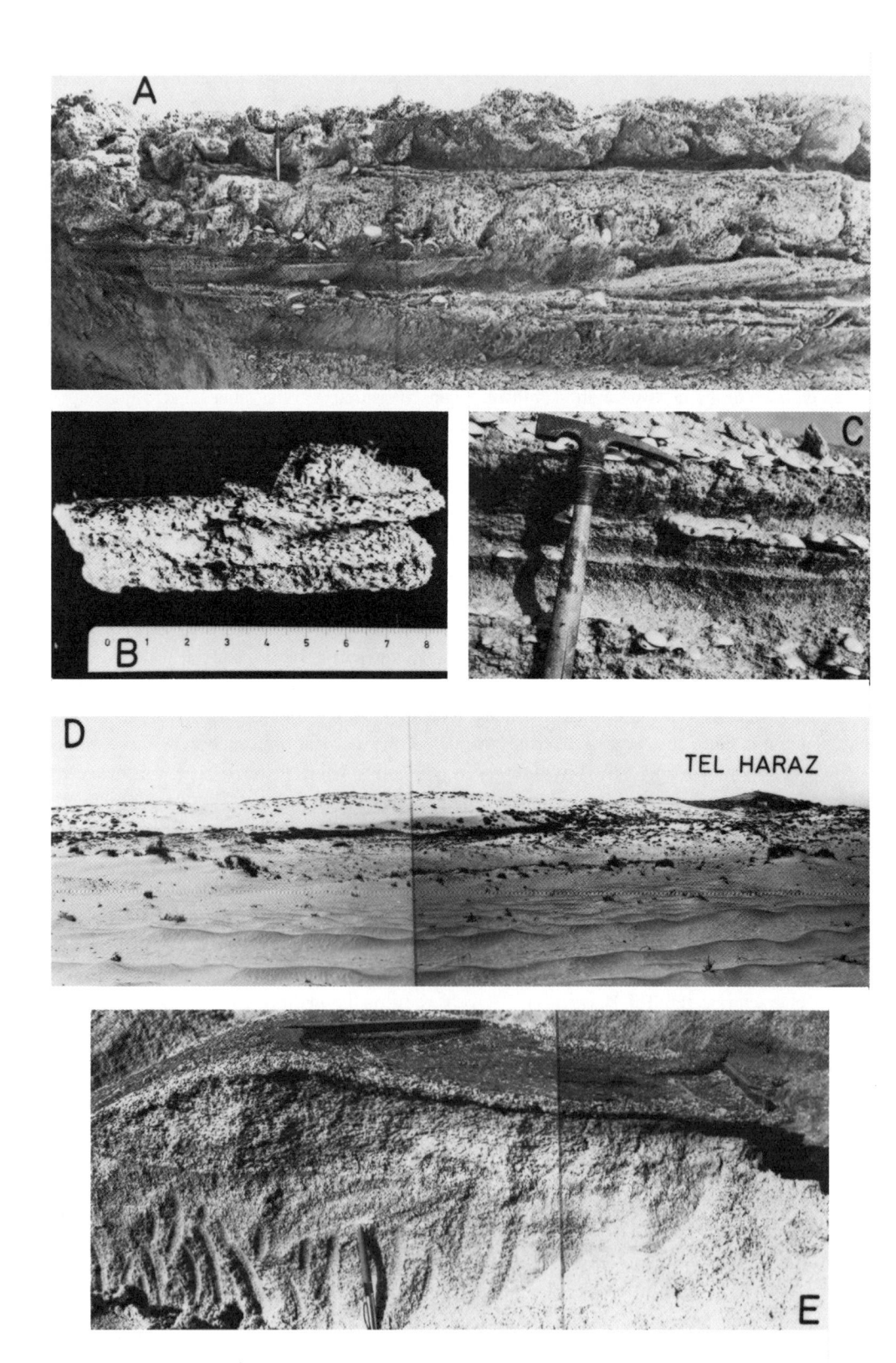

coastal cliff or kurkar ridge. Much of the finer-grained sediment is swept back to the sea by the returning water. Under such circumstances, sediments that are left behind should be poorly oriented and sorted. Processes of aragonite cementation and regular cyclic lamination such as found at Tel Haraz occur during relatively long times of quiet water, and these sediments must differ greatly from those of the catastrophic and very short duration tsunamis. An analogue may be poorly sorted sediments to 326 m on Lanai, Hawaii, believed deposited by a giant wave generated by a local landslide during the late Pleistocene (Moore and Moore 1984).

The Tel Haraz calcarenites have a specific petrographic nature that differs both from its older analogue (Unit 5a) and from the calcarenites now present along the northern beaches of Israel. The sequence is overlain by quartz-sand dunes (Unit 7a), in which fragmented shells (except for those from the terrestrial *Helicidae* gastropods) are not present in significant quantities.

We suggest that the entire Tel Haraz Sequence was deposited in a marine inner-littoral environment a short time prior to the Santorini (Thera) eruption about 3500 y BP.

Unit 7d——Shell Beds. Lenticular layers of loose shells dominated by *Glycymeris violacescens* (Lamarck) and commonly containing imbricated pottery sherds are interbedded in several levels within the late Holocene sedimentary sequence of the coastal cliff. Locally, they occur in terraces at elevations as high as +30 m msl to distances of 1 or even 2 km east of the coastline. Texturally, these lenses are similar to the well-cemented shell lenses incorporated within beachrock along the coastline. Pottery sherds also are present within these beachrocks.

On the basis of the following criteria, the loose shell beds are interpreted to be naturally-deposited beach sediments:

(i) The dominant orientation of the concavity of the *Glycymeris* valves, as well as their pattern of packing: these shells, when transported along the beach by longshore currents and swash, are more stable when they are oriented concave downward, because the friction coefficient is higher than that for the opposite orientation (Fig. 11A). In fact, most shells of the beaches below high-tide level are oriented that way (Emery 1968). On the other hand, most shells that fall freely onto the beach when thrown shoreward by high storm

---

Figure 10. The Tel Haraz Calcarenite (II B Unit 7c, III D 2). *A.* Low-angled cross-bedding within the +4 m msl bank of the Tel Haraz sequence. Note the load structure (convolute bedding) in the upper two layers and the scattered shells of *Glycymeris violacescens* having predominantly concave-downward orientation. Pre-Santorini pumice granules (see text) are within the lower part of this bank (from Bakler et al. 1985, fig. 2A). *B.* Laminated plate-like calcarenite layer from which most of the quartz grains have been winnowed. Found mostly onlapping the tops of the kurkar ridge. *C.* Alternatingly laminated calcarenite with abundant quartz sand, interbedded by concave-downward shell deposits within the +4 m msl bank. *D.* Megaripples across the embayment and Central Trough (see Figure 24B,C). They consist of recent wind-drifted platy coarse-grained calcarenite disintegrated from the Tel Haraz sequence that onlaps the two adjacent kurkar ridges. Tel Haraz and the western kurkar ridge are shown on the horizon. The relief of a patch of southward-dipping layers that onlap the southern plunge of the western kurkar ridge is seen on the left part of panel (from Bakler et al. 1985, fig. 2D). *E.* Cross section perpendicular to the axis of one of the megaripples composed of the loose calcarenite sand impregnated by resin. The upper 10–20 cm layer consists mostly of well segregated plate-like calcarnitic particles that drifted from right to left atop the truncated surface of the much finer grained quartz-sand layer (from Bakler et al. 1985, 2E; by permission of Earth and Planetary Science Letters, Amsterdam).

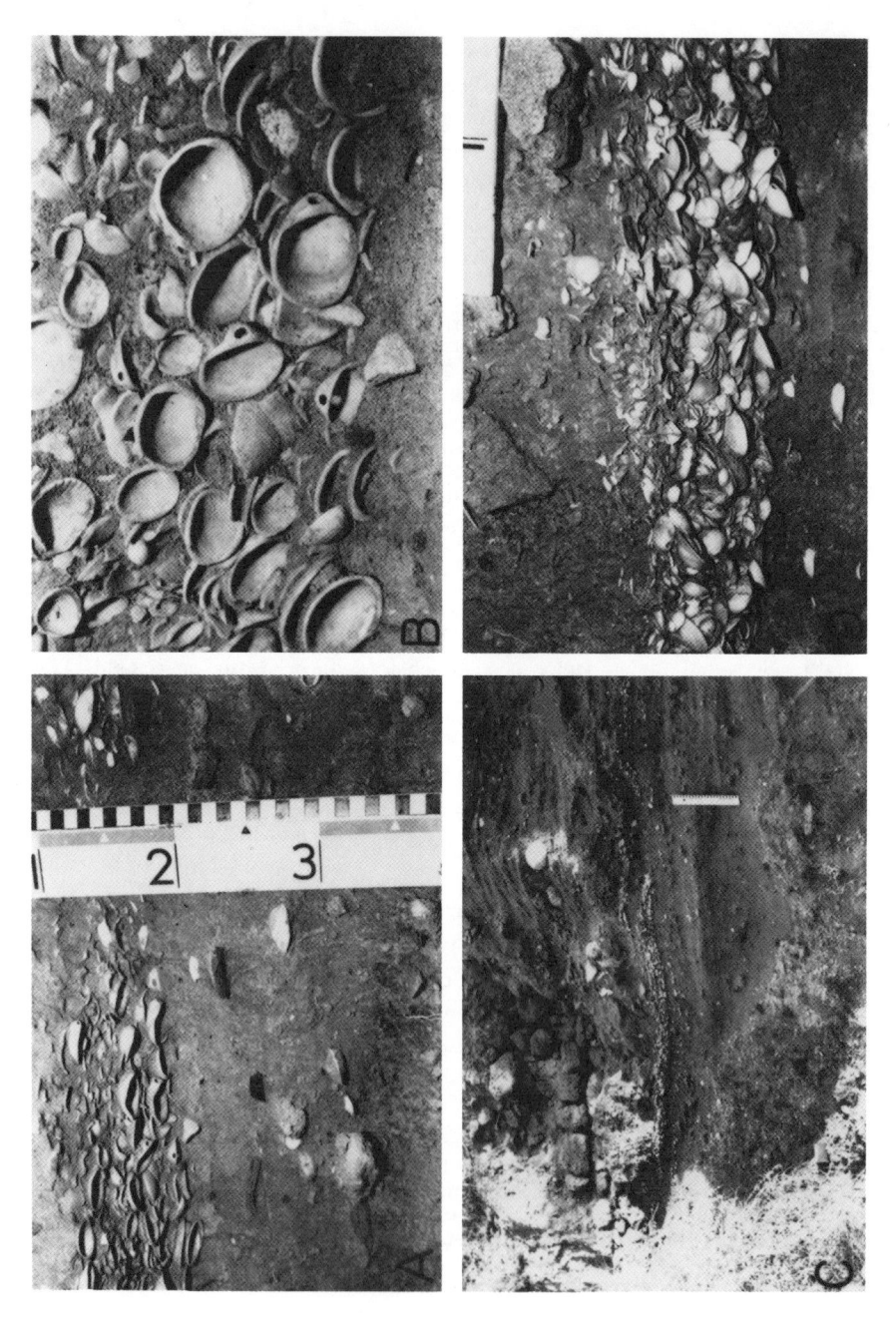

Figure 11. Sedimentary structures across shell lenses deposited by beach processes within and around remains of Crusader buildings at Ashqelon at elevations of +8 to +12 m msl. *A.* Dominantly concave-downward oriented shells at the tail of a lense (from Neev and Bakler 1978, fig 5*A*). *B.* Dominantly concave-upward loose shells after artificially dumping on land. *C.* A long and narrow shell lens interbedded in a layered sequence within Crusader ruins. The sedimentary structures presented in Figure 12 are within this sequence. *D.* Imbricated (nestling) structure within a shell lens, indicating relatively high hydraulic energies of tidal (?) currents when these shells were deposited (from Neev and Bakler 1978, fig. 9*B*, by permission of Hakibbutz Hameuhad Publishing House, Tel Aviv).

waves or by settling freely to the sea bottom through a relatively thick water column or from a turbidity current (Allen 1984) land in a concave-upward position. This is reasonable, as their center of gravity is near their apex of curvature and their convex side is more streamlined (less friction). Similar results were noted in reproducible experiments that we made by artificially dumping shells from buckets held at about a meter height to form a man-made layer; these shells are oriented dominantly concave upward (Fig. 11B; Neev and Bakler 1978, fig. 5B). In both examples the shell accumulations are loosely packed.

A third variant forms when shells are transported and swept along the sea bottom by strong and persistent currents, such as in tidal channels. When impeded by an obstacle these shells tend to stabilize with their convex sides facing upstream. If a large number of similar shells are involved, they tend to stack one behind the other to form chains in which the shells lean forward and their concave sides point downstream. Such a well packed nestling texture forms a systematically imbricated and oriented pattern (Fig. 11D). It would therefore appear that shell accumulations exhibiting the above attributes indicate natural beach environments of deposition. On the other hand, concave upward accumulations may indicate either an artificial (man-made) origin or a storm-wave deposit.

There are two exceptions: (a) Systematic concave downward orientation could also result from artificial arrangement for decorative purposes. In fact, such an example was found at an Iron Age site near Deir al Balah (T. Dothan, personal communication). At that site, shells of exceptionally large size and nice appearance had been selected and inserted in the surface layer with their concave sides downward, whereas those found beneath the ornamental surface layer were broken ones, haphazardly oriented, and much smaller. (b) Strong winds on land may overturn individual shells that are scattered on the surface to form a hamada-like lamina of concave-downward oriented shells. But this cannot happen in massive accumulations of shells thicker than one lamina.

The shell orientation criteria discussed above are opposed by Ronen (1980), who studied our observations and reproduced our experiment (manual dumping of the shells), as well as making additional studies (such as counting the shell orientation and making statistical analyses, which we did not consider necessary because the results were qualitatively obvious without them). His relevant measurements corroborate ours. The agreement is even better when his results (including the three analyses associated with the floor at Yavneh Yam [see III D 1] and two of the four shell analyses associated with the Shiqmona floor) are compared with his two analyses of recent naturally-deposited shell accumulations made at the Yavneh Yam beach. His comparison with analyses from beaches in the United States, where the bivalve assemblage consists of entirely different types (shapes) than those along the Israeli beaches, could conceivably introduce an unnecessary inaccuracy. To our surprise, his conclusions extremely contradict ours. Assuming an artificial (man-made) origin for the shell beds, he explained that the change in the shell orientation from a concave-upward position (following the manual dumping) to a concave-downward one was due to artificial sweeping of the shells by a rake or a hard broom. It is hard to accept such a proposed mode of origin for relatively thick shell beds such as the +13-m msl terrace at Ashqelon, which is more than 1.5 m thick, or for smaller lenses of shells that are interbedded within a sedimentary sequence that was naturally deposited according to other criteria (see below). Nor could we agree with Ronen's statement that his "conclusions only release from the need to explain and to worry about alleged formidable fluctuations of sea/land level during the last few centuries."

(ii) The second criterion is offered by sedimentary structures in fine-grained sand layers interbedded within a sequence of layered detrital sediments that fill partly destroyed medieval structures at Ashqelon (Fig., 11C) or which form the coastal cliff east and northeast of the Yavneh Yam promontory (see below). These structures include flaser and graded bedding as well as load structures (Fig. 12), thereby indicating an environment of aquatic (probably beach) deposition.

(iii) The third criterion is offered by the presence of articulated bivalves found as individual specimens or in lenses within sand or mud layers. Sediments in which they occur are considered to have been deposited naturally in aquatic environments. If a bivalve did not die in a burrowing position or was not buried by sediments shortly after death, its valves eventually and naturally open and become separated from one another because the muscles and ligament of a bivalve usually decay rather soon after the animal dies. A sequence of calcarenitic well-rounded loose sand in which lenticular accumulations of articulated bivalves are interbedded was found along a narrow elevated (about +8 m msl) coast-parallel strandline at the low coastal cliff of the ancient Akhziv harbor site (Lewy et al. 1986; III A 1; Figs. 1, 13). The assemblage of articulated shells within these lenses includes both brackish-water species (*Cercastoderma glaucum* Brugiere) and freshwater ones (*Unio* sp.), thereby suggesting an estuarine environment into which the freshwater specimens were swept and rapidly buried. Purely marine gastropod shells also were present but in much smaller numbers. As most of the articulated shells were concentrated in lenses and not in a genuine burrowing position, it could be argued that they were deposited at their present higher elevation by storm waves and then were rapidly buried. However, in this specific instance, the assemblage contains so few marine shells that such a scenario seems improbable. As Persian to Byzantine pottery sherds are mixed with this calcarenitic sequence, it must have been deposited (if it had been at sea level) during Late Roman times or later (close to 1500 y BP). About 100 m farther eastward, this sequence onlaps a low coast-parallel kurkar ridge beyond which the Nahariya Plain extends. A black soil layer containing freshwater *Unio* sp. shells and mixed with Roman pottery sherds crops out at the Nahariya Plain (Avnimelech 1943, 42) at elevations near +10 m msl. It is highly probable that this Late Roman (or younger) freshwater swamp (Unit 6, last paragraph) was in hydraulic equilibrium with the nearby beach, estuary, and lagoon of the Akhziv Harbor site at the time of its existence.

(iv) The fourth criterion upon which we base our interpretation regarding the natural or artificial origin of these sediments is the following argument: if the sediments in which the shell lenses are interbedded were deposited in marine, lagoonal, or swamp environments, the lenses themselves must be of identical environmental origin. Two of many relevant examples are demonstrated in elevated terraces (+3 to +4 m msl) along the coastline at Dor (north of the tel, N32°37'25" E34°55'15"; see III B 3) and of Michmoret (N33°24'08" E34°51'54"; see III C 3). These terraces consist of dark brown and dark gray clay layers containing shell lenses that were deposited in swamp environments. The time of deposition should be somewhat later than the Roman and Persian sites that they

Figure 12. Flaser structures and graded bedding within a Crusader ruin at Ashqelon. *A*. Layered sequence of fine quartz-sand and silt in which much coarser detritus (including shells and abundant pottery shards) is imbricated (see also Figure 11*D*). *B*. Same—showing wedging out of a clean sand layer containing a bivalve shell.

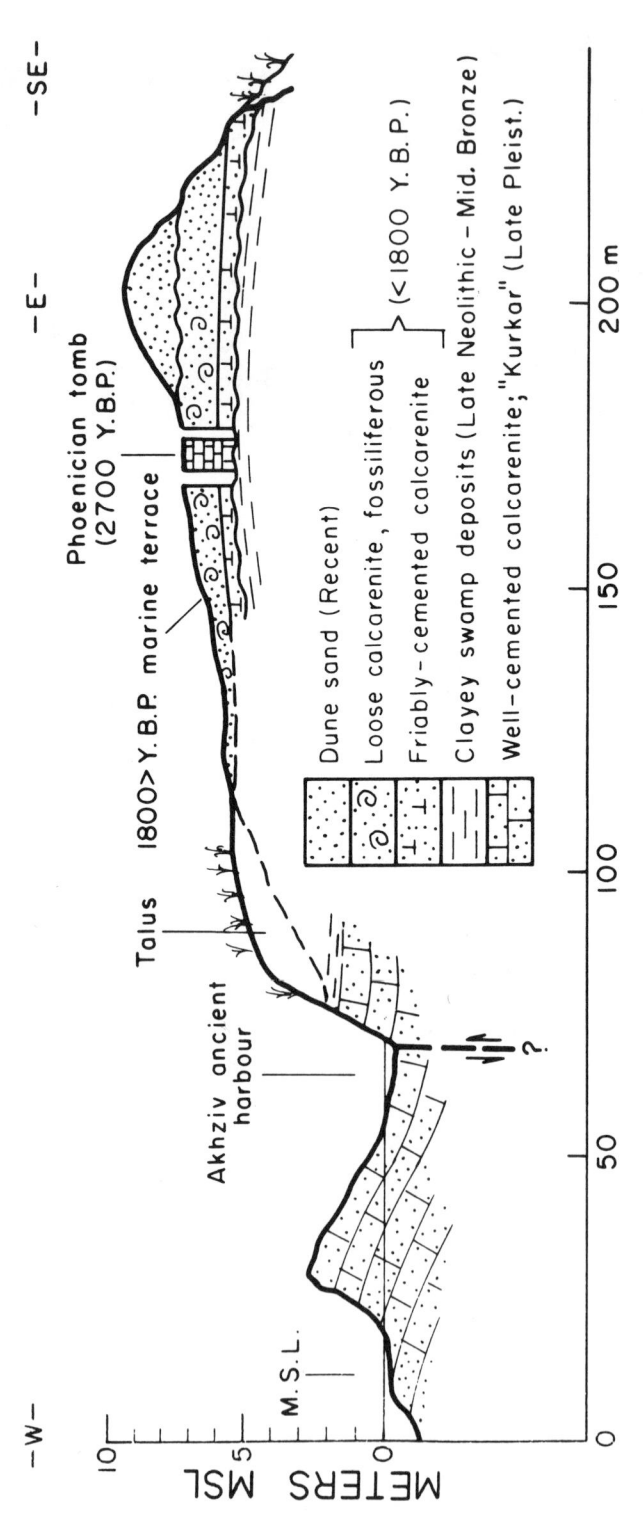

Figure 13. A schematic east-west geological cross section at the Akhziv Harbor site (from Lewy et al. 1986, fig. 2). Abundant articulated brackish and freshwater bivalves in lenses within a post-Roman calcarenite layer that onlaps a 2700-year-old tomb suggest that this site underwent an oscillatory tectonic movement sometime after Roman time (see II B Unit 7d, and III A 1). By permission of Quaternary Research.

overlie. Considering the nearness of these sites to the coastline and the mean sea level of that time (near that at present) as well as the absence of impermeable barriers between them and the sea, we deduce that these freshwater bodies were in hydraulic equilibrium with sea level at that time.

Unit 7e——Lagoonal Evaporites. A sequence of lagoonal-evaporitic sediments a few meters thick lies atop the coastal cliff south of Deir el Balah beach (Fig. 1) at an elevation of about +20 m (N31°24'43" E34°19'17"; III D 6). This sequence onlaps and overlies Iron Age structures (E. Oren, personal communication), some of whose earth-brick walls to 5 m height have been preserved. The overlying sequence is finely laminated green-gray to dark-brown sandy marls. Lenses of marine pelecypod shells (dominated by *Glycymeris* sp.) oriented concave downward are locally interbedded in this sequence. Lateral transitions into rather uniform horizontally layered tan fine sands are present. In some layers, a darker hue of the green-gray marl indicates higher moisture content than in most marls, thereby suggesting the presence of hygroscopic salts. Seven samples were taken at a site where one of these layers crops out for several tens of meters. Chemical analyses for the main ions of the water soluble salts were made by the Geochemical Laboratory of the Geological Survey of Israel. Results are given in Table 2, with concentrations of the different ions expressed as percentage of dry sediment weight. The ionic ratios of the Na/Cl, Ca/Mg, Ca/HCO$_3$ plus Ca/SO$_4$ (expressed in equivalents) are shown in Table 3. Values of the same ratios in five different water bodies are included for comparison in the same table. These water bodies are (i) normal sea water, (ii) artificially evaporated Mediterranean seawater, (iii) typical marine sabkha brines, (iv) calcium-chloride sabkha brines from sabkhas named Hawash and Hayareah near Bardawil Lagoon in northwestern Sinai, and (v) drinkable water from wells near Bardawil Lagoon. All are based on data from Levy (1977).

The following conclusions concerning original characteristics of the Deir el Balah brines can be drawn from these results: (i) The high content of water soluble salts in these marl samples (ranging between 0.5 and 4.7%) from the middle part of the marl sequence

Table 2
Chemical Composition of Water Soluble Salt from Sandy Marls atop Coastal Cliff South of Deir el Balah Beach. Concentrations Expressed in % of Dry Weight.

Sample No.	Na	K	Ca	Mg	Cl	SO$_4$	HCO$_3$	Total
20/12/79	1.08	0.036	0.49	0.08	2.87	0.07	0.12	4.75
2a/80	0.52	0.046	0.16	0.015	1.12	0.05	0.176	20.9
2b/80	0.336	0.026	0.134	0.011	0.724	0.033	0.19	1.45
3/80	0.236	0.02	0.096	0.010	0.497	0.058	0.16	1.09
4a/80	0.276	0.048	0.174	0.019	0.738	—	0.185	1.48
4b/80	0.074	0.014	0.046	0.004	0.142	0.034	0.178	0.492
5/80	0.212	0.021	0.218	0.018	0.696	0.067	0.141	1.37
Average	0.391	0.303	0.182	0.022	0.970	0.060	0.164	1.82

Table 3
Ionic Ratios (Equivalents) Based on Results of Table 2 and on
Data Presented by Levy (1977; see text above).

Sample No.	Na/Cl	Ca/Mg	Ca/(HCO$_3$+SO$_4$)	Ca/HCO$_3$	Ca/SO$_4$
20/12/79	0.58	3.7	7.1	12.3	17.0
2a/80	0.70	6.3	2.1	3.0	8.2
2b/80	0.72	6.7	1.8	2.1	9.6
3/80	0.74	6.0	1.2	1.8	4.0
4a/80	0.58	5.4	—	3.0	—
4b/80	0.82	6.9	0.64	0.7	3.3
5/80	0.47	7.5	2.9	4.8	8.0
Average	0.66	6.1	2.6	4.0	8.3
Normal seawater	0.86	0.2	0.34	8.3	0.4
Evaporated seawater	0.76-0.50	0.01-0.06	0.03-0.02	4-50	0.01-0.05
Bardawil 1. Normal Sabkha Brines	0.79-0.86	0.01-0.14	0.04-0.15	1.8-26	0.04-0.05
2. Ca-chloridic Sabkha Brines (CaCl$_2$)	0.33-0.08	0.3-1.0	12-160	107-2756	12.6-193
3. Drinkable Well Water	0.63-0.87	0.95-1.8	1.6-2.7	8-30	1.7-30

suggests that they are the dried residue of interstitial pore water of concentrated brines, and they are not just the residue of seawater spray that fell on the emerged land. (ii) The dominance of chlorine in the anions indicates that the original brine was chloridic. (iii) The relatively low Na/Cl ratio (0.47 to 0.82) as compared with normal seawater (0.86) suggests that halite (NaCl) was deposited from the original brine because of excess evaporation. Assuming that the source of these brines was seawater, the latter had to become concentrated at least 10 times to reach saturation for NaCl (Neev and Emery 1967) or to about 30 times (Levy 1977). (iv) The very high Ca/Mg ratios (3.7 to 7.5) as compared with normal seawater (0.2) suggest that these brines went through a process of Ca-Mg exchange during dolomitization of previously precipitated CaCO$_3$ minerals. This process is similar to the one described by Levy (1977) for some recent sabkha sediments and brines in the Bardawil area. (v) The relatively high Ca/(HCO$_3$+SO$_4$) ratio corroborates the calcium-chloride nature of the brine. It should be noted that upon dilution of the calcium-chloride brine with meteoric water, the resultant water preserves its general ionic ratios.

Ion exchange is a well-known process between clay minerals and their interstitial waters. In fact, illites and montmorillonites are rather abundant in the Deir el Balah sediments, although appreciably less so than quartz and calcite. In order to learn whether such a process has affected the behavior of Ca^{++} in the interstitial water of the Deir el Balah sediments, concentrations of exchangable cations were analysed in six of the seven samples (of Tables 2 and 3). The results (Table 4) include the Ca/Mg ratios.

Table 4
Exchangeable Cations (meq/100 gr)

Sample No.	Na	K	Ca	Mg	Ca/Mg
2a	—	0.18	17.3	2.08	8.3
2b	0.39	0.33	13.8	1.69	8.2
3	0.28	0.23	0.10	1.15	5.3
4a	1.26	0.05	16.1	1.50	10.7
4b	0.78	0.23	11.0	0.73	15.0
5	0.46	0.20	12.4	0.45	27.5
Average	0.63	0.20	11.9	1.27	12.5

Comparison of the Ca/Mg ionic ratios in the interstitial water (Table 3) with those of the exchangable cations in the clay minerals (Table 4) indicates that the two are unrelated. Whereas these ratios are rather uniform and consistent for the interstitial water samples (4 to 7), they vary over a wide range (5 to 27) for the clay minerals. It is concluded that the source of calcium and magnesium in the interstitial water is not the cations absorbed by the clay minerals, but it may be the brines of the lagoons or sabkhas from which these sediments were deposited.

These conclusions suggest that the Deir el Balah brines were formed by processes identical with those that formed the calcium-chloride brines of the Bardawil inland sabkhas (Table 3). The latter also are postulated to be of marine origin. It is assumed that, after a marine regression, they were flushed from surrounding topographically higher dune areas and concentrated and re-evaporated at the present sabkhas (Levy 1977). This stage is an unstable one, because, if the flushing process continued, the calcium chloride brines must eventually have drained into the Mediterranean Sea. The youth of the Deir el Balah evaporitic sequence (about 2700 y BP, see above), the relatively low rainfall in that region, the present topographically isolated and high location, as well as the impermeable nature of the host sediments (marls), may explain why these soluble salts have been preserved within the sediments until now.

Badly preserved shallow-water marine fauna and euryhaline gastropods were found in some of the seven samples (L. Grossovitz and S. Moshkovitz, Geol. Survey of Israel, personal communication). This information corroborates our conclusion that, during the Iron Age, the Deir el Balah water body was near the Mediterranean coastline, probably as a lagoon similar to Bardawil Lagoon.

Unit 7f——Bronze Age Earthen Structures. Huge earthern structures were built during the Middle and Late Bronze ages along the coastline of Israel. These structures have rectangular shapes formed by earth walls (Yavneh Yam; Kaplan 1978; N31°55'20" E34°41'35"; III D 1) or by ramps (Tel Michal; Herzog et al. 1978; Herzog 1981; N32°09'38" E34°47'45"; III C 7). At neither site are any of the rectangular walls or ramparts parallel to the coastline—as though the builders were unaware of the effects of seacliff erosion that later truncated the western flanks of these structures.

Unit 7g——Later Man-Made Structures. The last part of this time-stratigraphic unit consists of tectonically tilted, subsided, or uplifted man-made structures of Greek (2400 y BP) to Mamlukian times (600 y BP). The best examples are in Caesarea (the subsided and submerged Herodian harbor, the westward collapsed Late Roman obelisk, and the westward tilted Crusader walls; Raban et al. 1976; Neev et al. 1978a; III C 2). Examples from different environments are known from the Roman to Byzantine settlement at Ostrakia (El Felusiat, N31°07'00" E33°25'45") that unfortunately is yet undescribed (E. Oren, personal communication; III E 4). This settlement at the easternmost end of Bardawil Lagoon was an important caravan station along the Via Maris, the most convenient trade route between Egypt and Israel (Syria). The Via Maris followed the coastline and functioned only between Persian and Mamlukian times (sixth century BC to fifteenth or sixteenth century AD; Neev and Friedman 1978; IV C).

Tectonic subsidence of a few meters with about three degrees of northwestward tilt toward the trough of the Bardawil syncline was noted at El Felusiat, (Oren, Site 152) and at a nearby site (Oren, Site 153, N31°07'22" E33°25'50"). Subsidence is indicated by the present low levels (either constantly or occasionally flooded by seawater) of large segments of the Via Maris and its adjacent structures (both houses and water wells) that originally were a few meters above mean sea level. Any known eustatic rise of sea level since Byzantine (sixth century AD) and even Mamlukian (fifteenth–sixteenth century AD) times is insufficient to explain a change of level mounting to several meters. A continuously sampled drill hole to a depth of more than 4 m at the latter site (Oren, Site 153) showed that the base of a house at that site is 25 cm below present sabkha level. Clean dune sand gradually changing downward into brown-red loam extends downward 1.75 m. It is underlain by a sequence of beach sands with interbedded lenses of marine shells to the bottom of this hole. Two age analyses for these shells (at about 2-m and 4-m depths, respectively) yielded ages of 3800 ± 160 y BP and 3250 ± 160 y BP, respectively [A. Kaufman, personal communication]. These data suggest a high rate of deposition, perhaps associated with tectonic subsidence sometime prior to Roman (or Persian) times (note that the radiocarbon ages of the shells indicate the date that they lived but not necessarily the date that they were deposited, which would have been later).

III. Holocene Tectonic Histories of Coastal Segments and of Significant Sites Along Them

Our knowledge of present elevations, environments of deposition, and exact ages of marine sediments deposited during the Holocene permits us to infer the tectonic history of different locales. Knowledge of the curve of eustatic sea-level changes since late Pleistocene would be helpful, but these changes are subordinate to local land movements. It is generally accepted that, at the beginning of the last glacial stage (70,000 to 100,000 years ago), sea levels dropped drastically. At the end of that stage, about 15,000 years ago, sea levels were as low as 130 m below the present level. A eustatic rise caused by return of meltwater lasted until about 6000 y BP, when sea level had risen to a few meters below the present level. The overall curve still is slowly rising, but with irregular fluctuations of one or two meters (Fairbridge 1961; Curray 1965; Milliman and Emery 1968; Flemming 1968; Bloom 1971; Einsele el at. 1974). Many other fluctuations are due to local tectonism associated with melting of glacial loads on the land and to plate movements (Emery 1980; Aubrey and Emery 1983, 1986; Emery and Aubrey 1985). Following are short descriptions of findings at selected sites along the coast of Israel and northwestern Sinai, plus respective histories of tectonic movements that are implied.

A. *Northern Segment (Rosh Haniqra to Mount Carmel)*

1. Ancient Akhziv Harbor (N33°02′25″ E35°05′55″). This summary is based on the data of Lewy et al. (1986) as well as II Unit 7d iii. Sometime in Post-Roman or Post-Byzantine time (younger than 1500 y BP), the coastal zone at Akhziv tectonically subsided and was submerged and then emerged to an elevation of +8 m. This oscillatory down- and-up movement occurred along a hinge line that corresponds with the Akko—Akhziv coast-parallel fault (Figs. 13, 14). Another fault, trending perpendicular to the coastal fault, appears to limit this site on the north. The ancient Akhziv Harbor site, thus, is at the apex of a tilted fault block that is uplifted on its north and dips moderately to the south. These conclusions are based on the following observations: the uppermost layer of sediments at this site is loose calcareous sand deposited within a brackish environment (estuary or lagoon). At present, the site is on a +10 m msl elevated terrace bordering the coastline. The eastern limit of the paleolagoon was along the coast-parallel kurkar ridge that now is about 100 m east of the coastline at an elevation of about +10 m msl. Freshwater swamp environments prevailed east of the ridge along the Nahariya trough (see II B Units 6 and 7d iii). Highest elevations of sediments within these two paleowater

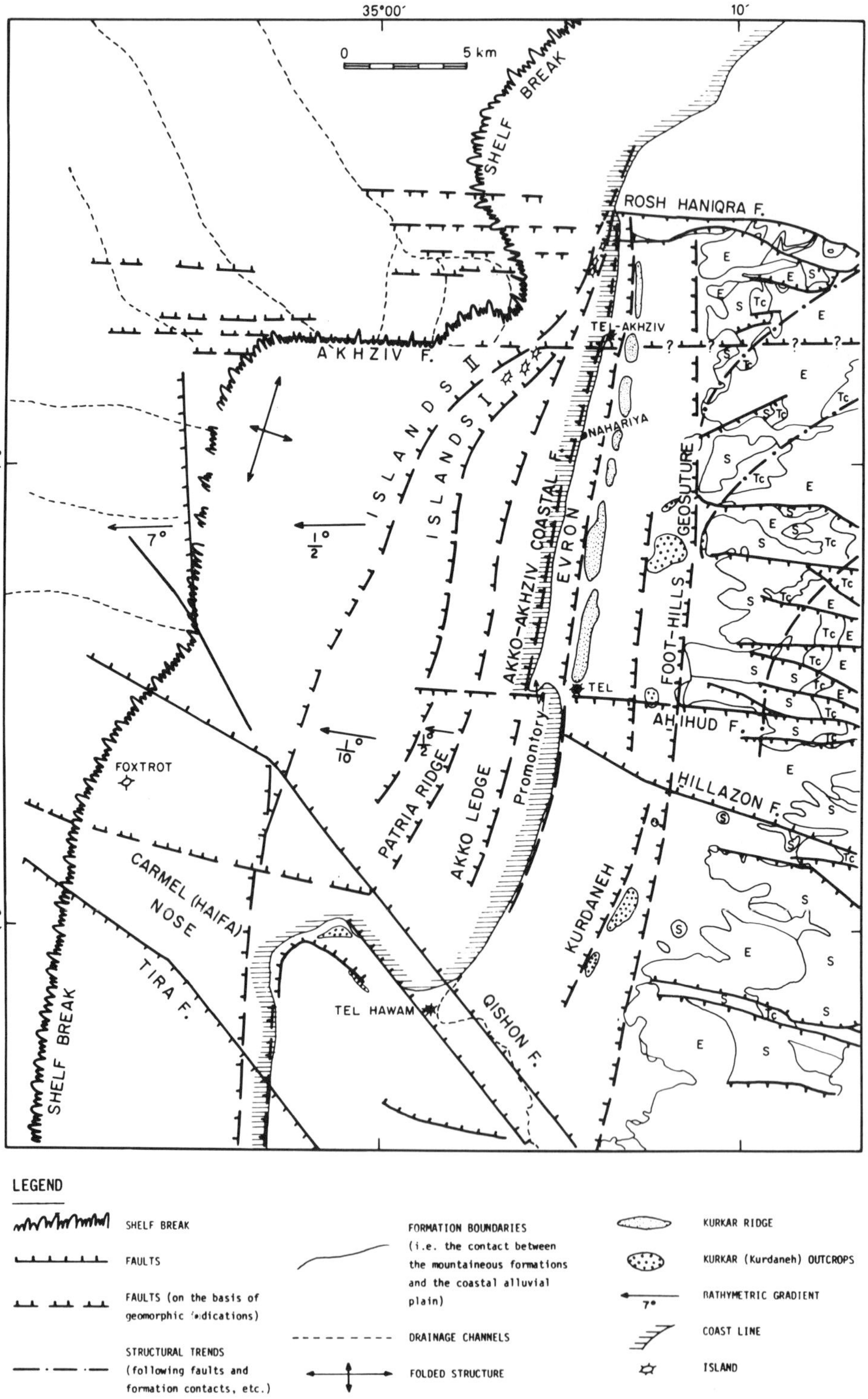
35°00′
10′
0
5 km
33°
00′
32°
50′
SHELF BREAK
ROSH HANIQRA F.
AKHZIV F.
TEL-AKHZIV
NAHARIYA
ISLANDS II
ISLANDS I
AKKO-AKHZIV COASTAL F.
EVRON
GEOSUTURE
FOOT-HILLS
TEL
AHIHUD F.
HILLAZON F.
Promontory
AKKO LEDGE
PATRIA RIDGE
KURDANEH
FOXTROT
CARMEL (HAIFA) NOSE
TIRA F.
TEL HAWAM
QISHON F.
SHELF BREAK
7°
1/2°
1/10°
E
S
Tc
LEGEND
SHELF BREAK
FAULTS
FAULTS (on the basis of geomorphic indications)
STRUCTURAL TRENDS (following faults and formation contacts, etc.)
FORMATION BOUNDARIES (i.e. the contact between the mountaineous formations and the coastal alluvial plain)
DRAINAGE CHANNELS
FOLDED STRUCTURE
KURKAR RIDGE
KURKAR (Kurdaneh) OUTCROPS
BATHYMETRIC GRADIENT
COAST LINE
ISLAND

bodies on opposite sides of the kurkar ridge are about the same, +10 m msl. Ages of both sediments were determined to be Post-Roman, perhaps even Late Byzantine about 1500 y BP, according to the youngest pottery sherds within them. This conclusion is corroborated by the fact that the paleolagoonal sediments onlap and cover a Middle Iron Age (Phoenician, or 2700 y BP) tomb (Fig. 13).

The Phoenician tomb was built on the remains of a Middle Bronze IIb structure that overlies a sequence of swamp deposits, whose age ranges from Late Neolithic to Early Bronze (7000–4000 y BP; see II B Units 4c and 5d), which in turn overlies late Pleistocene Kurkar Sandstones (Unit 1). Assuming that the watertables of these early Holocene swamps were in hydraulic equilibrium with the level of the nearby Mediterranean Sea and considering the eustatic curve of rising sea level during the past 7000 years, it is inferred that this site was tectonically uplifted simultaneously with the rise of sea level. This process continued at least until Middle Bronze time (about 4000 years ago), and perhaps it continues even today.

Flemming et al. (1978, 45) postulated that "there has been no change of relative sea-level" at the coastline of Akhziv since the Middle Bronze. This may be true for the Tel Akhziv site, which is within the structurally low block just north of the east-west trending Akhziv Fault (Fig. 14); however, it obviously disagrees with the data and conclusions presented above that concern the nearby Akhziv Harbor site.

A now-submerged coast-parallel kurkar ridge extends 3 to 4 km beyond the Akko—Rosh Haniqra coastline (Neev et al. 1976). The few small islands that project above sea level off Akhziv and Rosh Haniqra appear to be peaks along the crest of the ridge. These islands were intensively quarried during Phoenician to Roman or even Byzantine times. On the basis of the lowest level of quarrying there, it is concluded that "submergence of the order of 40–50 cm has occurred" (Flemming et al. 1978, 46). Assuming that during the past 4000 years the offshore littoral belt was subject to tectonic subsidence (see below), submergence of these islands could have been appreciably more. Also the remains of additional quarries in deeper water could have been destroyed or camouflaged (Safriel 1975; Tsur and Safriel 1978; Raban 1983a) by the very fast rates of both biogenic and physical processes of abrasion that affect carbonate rocks near the sea surface. The significance of this ridge within the framework of more regional tectonic pattern is discussed later.

2. Akko (N32°55'20" E35°04'25"). During the relatively long period between about 20,000 and 2400 y BP, the Akko promontory and the trough east of it were covered by very shallow seawater. This cover is recorded by an uninterrupted sequence of marine to lagoonal deposits 12 m thick in drill holes within the trough (see II B Unit 4c i and 5d). Considering the more than 100 m of eustatic rise of sea level since the end of the

---

Figure 14. Distribution of tectonic elements across northernmost segment of Israeli coastal belt (III A). Note the northeastward branching and convergence pattern formed by the Islands Faults upon approaching the transverse Akhziv fault. Faults in the mountainous province on the east form a similar pattern.

past glaciation, a corresponding tectonic rise of the Akko site is implied. Most of this tectonic rise must have occurred during the latest Pleistocene or early Holocene.

The Akko promontory (Fig. 14) was first settled in historical time during the Persian period (sixth century BC), after the promontory and the coastal kurkar ridge that is its northern extension had emerged from the sea. We postulate that this coastal ridge became an elongate island or a peninsula by rejuvenation of the coastal fault just prior to Persian time. That fault borders the west side of the present abraded terrace and is a direct extension of the coastal fault off Akhziv (Fig. 14). The Akko promontory has been inhabited ever since, and occasionally it is affected by earthquakes and tsunamis (Shalem 1956).

Submergence of a vault of the Crusader period at the southwestern fringes of the promontory (A. Raban, personal communication; Flemming et al. 1978) indicates that another phase of tectonic activity occurred sometime during Mamlukian or Turkish times. This subsidence was along an east-west trending fault extending westward from the southern periphery of the promontory to about 6 km farther west, as implied by detailed bathymetric and subbottom profiler surveys of that area (Hall 1976, 30–31 and fig. 10). These results suggest that a post-Kurkar Unit (latest Pleistocene to earliest Holocene) vertical differential movement of about 5 m (downthrown to the south) occurred across this fault. The fault probably is a seaward extension of the Ahidud fault, which is the northern boundary of Haifa Bay and the Hillazon Graben (Kafri and Ecker 1964; fig. 22; our Fig. 14). The throw across this fault diminishes westward (Hall 1976, 8) and is not marked on the map west of Tel Akko.

Tel Akko (+36 m msl, N32°55'33" E35°05'30") is named also Tel Al Fukhkhar or Mount Napoleon. It is at the southern plunge of the Evron Kurkar Ridge about 2 km east of the coastline at the Akko promontory. The tel was first inhabited during historical times by the Early Bronze I (about 5300 y BP) people (M. Dothan, Haifa Univ., personal communication). Remains of their city overlie an elevated abraded terrace atop the north-northeast trending Evron Kurkar Ridge. This kurkar platform is now fragmented and slightly tilted in various directions. A cultural break lasting about 800 years followed the Early Bronze occupation unitl the tel was reoccupied by Middle Bronze IIa people. An almost uninterrupted cultural occupation followed, lasting until a few hundred years ago. A similar stratigraphic sequence occurs farther northward along the Evron Ridge, as indicated by analysis of pottery sherds collected around Tel es Summeiriya (N32°58'10" E35°05'30"; 0. Yogev, Ministry of Education, Dept., of Antiquities and Museums, personal communication).

The Evron Ridge extends northward as a linear feature more than 17 km, where it is terminated by the east-west trending Rosh Haniqra Ridge (Figs. 1, 14; Picard 1955; Issar and Kafri 1972). Its western flanks are believed to be a structurally-controlled coast-parallel feature: (i) The narrow (½ to 1 km) and short (1 km) coastal plain just south of Rosh Haniqra is a down-dropped block bordered by a regmatic fault pattern. This pattern is compiled from geological maps of Picard (1955) and Kafri (1972) as well as from coast-parallel cross-sections AA' and BB' of Issar and Kafri (1972, figs. 3 and 4). Within this pattern, the eastern north-south trending fault is the northern extension of the Evron Ridge (Fig. 14). (ii) The western flanks of the Evron Ridge appear to be a hinge line along which monoclinal westward downwarping is recognized (Issar and Kafri 1972, figs. 6, 10). (iii) The NNE–SSW geomorphic alignment of this ridge extends smoothly southward along the eastern shoreline of Haifa Bay (Fig. 14). (iv) During the Early Bronze period, this ridge was dry land occupied by a fortified city (Tel Akko) and other types of settlement, while the Akko Ridge was either submerged under the sea (such as at Akko promontory) or covered by swamps (as at Akhziv Harbor). The final shaping of this ridge could have been caused by renewed vertical differential movement of appreciable magnitude (about 20 m) across the western flank of the Evron Ridge since Pre-Early Bronze times.

3. Tel Abu Hawam (N32°48′20″ E35°01′08″). The top of the Tel Abu Hawam site at +9-m msl is about 1 km southwest of the outlet of the Qishon River (Fig. 14). Remains dating from Middle and Late Bronze to Hellenistic times were found there (Anati 1959, 1975; Flemming et al. 1978, quoting Hamilton 1934). The Late Bronze layer itself was transgressed by the sea, as indicated by a dark gray clay layer on it and that contains abundant mollusks of lagoonal environment, such as *Ceratoderma edule* and *Puranella* sp. in burrowing positions and mostly still articulated (S. Moshkovitz, personal communication). It was then reoccupied by a Persian culture whose relics are found there. A beachrock deposit that overlies a 2800 y BP layer at +1 m msl was artificially cut to build a wall during Persian times (A. Raban, personal communication). This sequence suggests that the site underwent tectonic subsidence of a few meters followed by uplift to its original elevation or more some time during the Iron Age (3000 to 2500 y BP). These movements are quite similar to those of the Late Roman to Byzantine phase farther north at Akhziv (see 1 above).

4. Tectonic Framework of Northern Segment—Structural and Geomorphic Indicators.
A system of six or seven longitudinal geomorphic features exhibiting a northward-convergent pattern was traced both onshore and offshore of northern Israel. The easternmost element within this system, the Foothill Geosuture (Neev et al. 1985), is the contact between the coastal alluvial plain and the mountainous regions (Cretaceous to Eocene). It extends as a rather straight line subparallel to the present coastline and is recognized from Rosh Haniqra to northwestern Sinai and perhaps even to the northern tip of the Gulf of Suez. Its continuity is interrupted at the northwest trending Mount Carmel—Um el Fahm ridge (Neev 1975), although the alignment of its trend is maintained. The next element to the west is expressed by the intermittent north-northeasterly alignment of the Pleistocene (or late Neogene) Kurdaneh Calcarenite. The third element is the Evron Ridge and its southern extension along the coastline of Haifa Bay. Although we hitherto considered this segment of Haifa Bay as non-tectonic, its alignment with the Evron Ridge suggests association with a tectonic lineament. Then comes the coastline from Akko to Rosh Haniqra and its southward submarine extension across Haifa Bay and along the Akko Ledge and Foxhound Reef, respectively (Fig. 14). These latter are mostly of kurkar and calcarenite rocks (Hall and Bakler 1975; Bakler 1976; Hall 1976).

Many segments of the coastline north of Akko are marked by abraded terraces that truncate the coastal kurkar ridge. These terraces are terminated on the west by a precipitous coast-parallel alignment having the form of a submarine cliff a few meters high. Similar topography borders the coastline of Caesarea (Neev et al. 1978a; also below), where the coast-parallel submarine cliff has been shown to be fault-controlled. The tectonic nature of the coastline at Akhziv already has been discussed. The next element to the west is Patria Ridge (Hall 1976) and its extension to the north-northeast off Akko and Nahariya (Almagor and Hall 1980). The "Islands I and II" linear features (Fig. 14) are defined off Haifa Bay as marking ancient coastlines (Levy 1972). They are expressed as buried kurkar ridges covered by a layer of late Holocene clayey sediments a few meters thick. Moreover, bathymetric breaks (changes in gradients) are recognized across the westward very moderately sloping sea floor atop these ridges. The buried ridges stretch roughly along the 30- and 50-m isobaths, respectively. The two groups of islands off Akhziv and Rosh Haniqra are the northern extension of the submerged ridge bounded by the Island I and II elements (Fig. 14).

The shelf break off northern Israel, roughly corresponding with the 100-m bathymetric contour (Almagor and Hall 1980), should be considered another longitudinal element. It has three segments: off Rosh Haniqra, off Akhziv—Akko, and off Haifa Bay—Mount Carmel, respectively. The divide between the first and second segments is near Akhziv, where the trend of the shelf-break lineament sharply curves (almost 90 degrees) from north-northeast to east-west and then again curves due north at the head of Akhziv Canyon. The divide between the second and third segments is marked by a kink in the trend of the shelf break corresponding to interception of the shelf break by the western extension of the Carmel Nose (Fig. 14). Delineation of the fault pattern in this area is based on data of Ginzburg (1971), Golik (1978), Almagor and Hall (1980), and Garfunkel and Almagor (1985, fig. 7). Marked differences are present in the nature of the sub-bottom across the shelf break between the second and third segments. Off Mount Carmel, the shelf break expresses a very young (Holocene) hinge-line, across which the continental slope has been downwarped to the west (Neev and Greenfield 1981). Off Akko—Akhziv, however, the break is bounded both by a fault (along the upper slope) and by the western flanks of a Late Cretaceous folded structure that is asymmetrical (steeper) to the west (Fig. 14). This structure lies along the outer shelf east of the coast-parallel fault.

Neev and Greenfield (1981) considered the east-west trending Akhziv and Rosh Haniqra fault system to be the northernmost transverse fault within a system of five major east-west faults off Israel. The submarine extension of the Akhziv Fault also was detected on deep seismic reflection profiles. Details of the entire fault pattern along this tranverse feature (Fig. 14) were determined on the basis of geomorphology, mostly by plotting the bathymetric breaks and the heads of associated submarine canyons (after data from Almagor and Hall 1980) and by extrapolated extensions of existing faults on land (after Picard 1955).

The longitudinal elements between the Evron Ridge and Islands I and II exhibit a convergence pattern that intensifies and curves strongly from a trend of north-northeast to northeast upon approaching the Akhziv transverse fault (Fig. 14). Similar patterns were noted by Neev and Greenfield (1984) where longitudinal structural elements associated with the north-northeastward trending Pelusium Line branch off to the right (east) upon approaching the east-west traverse faults. Such bends are typical where the Pelusium Line approaches the transverse faults off Gaza, Palmahim, and Or 'Akiva—Caesarea. Another example is on land east of the Akko—Rosh Haniqra coastline where structurally controlled elements (such as faults and middle to Late Cretaceous formation contacts) branch off to the northeast from the north-south trending Foothills Geosuture (Fig. 14). These faults are identified on the basis of data from Picard (1955), Vroman (1958), and Kafri (1972). The information above suggests that the northeastward convergence and curving (branching off) pattern of the kurkar ridges off Akhziv is tectonically controlled and is not purely a depositional feature.

B. Hof Hacarmel Segment (Coast West of Mount Carmel)

1. General. The narrow (2 to 4 km) coastal plain west of Mount Carmel (Fig. 15) is bordered on its east by a prominent linear escarpment that is the western flank of Mount Carmel. This escarpment was considered by Michelson (1970, 56; 1971) to be abrasional rather than tectonic in origin because of: (i) the smooth nature of the now-westwardly tilted and buried unconformable plain that separates the Pleistocene and middle Cretaceous sequences, and (ii) the general lithologic similarity and lack of reliable markers within the outcropping and subcropping Cenomanian carbonates east and west of the escarpment. Nevertheless, the subdivision of this escarpment into straight and linear secondary segments that differ slightly from each other in their trends (NNW and NNE; see Fig. 15) suggests involvement of a tectonic factor (faulting) as well.

Three kurkar ridges are present, both onshore and offshore, along the western periphery of this coastal plain (Fig. 15). The westernmost one defines the coastline between Atlit and Dor, and between Ma'agan Michael and Caesarea, where it is biogenically eroded to patchy terraces. The western fringes of the remnants of this ridge form submerged cliffs that together produce a straight lineament. The submerged northern extension of this ridge was detected and mapped in the offshore area as a coast-parallel feature from the Carmel (Haifa) Nose to off Atlit (Fig. 14, 15). The next ridge to the east could be detected on land between Dor and Atlit (Fig. 15) and offshore as far north as the Haifa Nose (Adler 1985; Galili 1985). The easternmost ridge is recognized as a linear feature along the entire coastal plain of Mount Carmel. It abuts the coastline from Carmel Nose (Haifa) to Atlit Bay. Farther south, it continues smoothly as a coast-parallel ridge about 1 km east of the coastline.

2. Haifa Nose to Atlit Area. Important conclusions about Holocene tectonism of the narrow and long (1 x 11 km) littoral belt between the Haifa Nose and Atlit are drawn by us on the basis of available geological literature and recent archaeological studies by Prausnitz (1977), Wreschner (1977), Raban (1983b), Adler (1985), Galili (1985), Galili and Evron (1985), Galili and Inbar (1986). A 20,000 to 9000 year-old unit of lagoonal

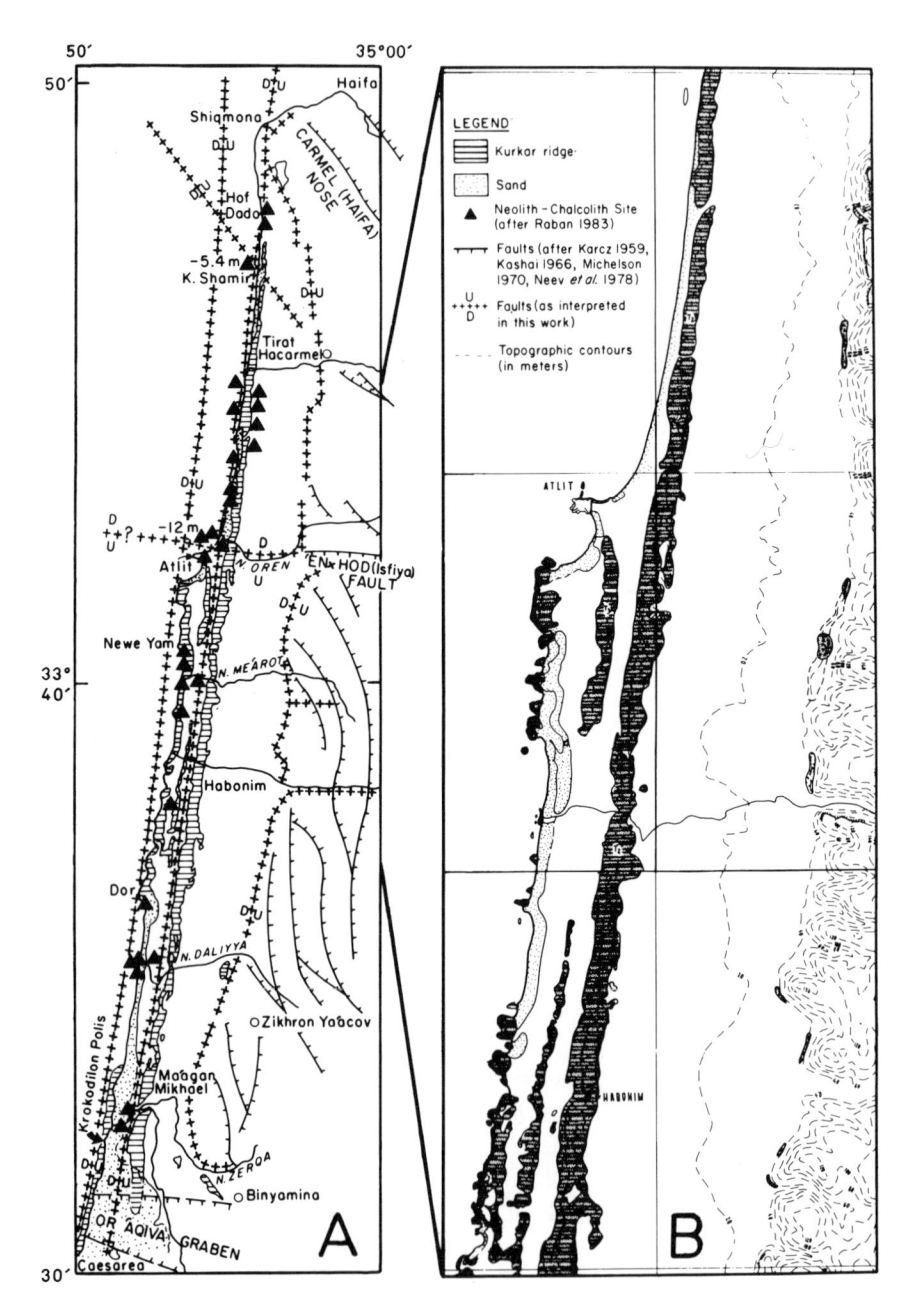

Figure 15. Kurkar ridges of the Hof Hacarmel segment of the Israeli coastal belt (III B). *A*. Map distribution of tectonic elements, kurkar ridges, and Neolithic to Early Bronze sites (both offshore and onshore). *B*. Enlargement of section north and south of Atlit in which kurkar ridges and onshore topography (contour interval = 20 m) are detailed.

to brackish clay deposits a few meters thick occurs offshore along that belt. It pinches out eastward toward the coastal kurkar ridge and westward toward a now submerged kurkar ridge. This clay unit was deposited in the trough of a coast-parallel lagoon, the water of which was in hydraulic equilibrium with Mediterranean Sea water. Apparently, most of its clay particles were derived from the top-soil of the nearby Mt. Carmel and washed into the lagoon during winter floods. The suspension gradually settled downward to form a layer of slurry in a density current that crept along the bottom toward the lowest parts of the lagoon and eventually formed an extremely flat and horizontally bedded clay bed. The clay bed now slopes westward almost 1.5 degree (from +1 m at the coastline to -13 m about 1 km offshore along the eastern flank of the now-submerged kurkar ridge). We infer that this westward slope was caused by tilt that also involved faulting. This tectonic movement occurred probably after Early Bronze time, because now-submerged Early Neolithic to Early Bronze sites at the top of the clay bed are abundant across the trough from the coastline to a water depth of 12 m. Also several beachrock terraces onlap the tilted clay unit from the coastline to a water depth of 5 m. We found a Persian amphora embedded in the highest beachrock terrace just at the coastline (+1 m) in the Bay of Atlit.

These conclusions disagree with those of Raban (1983a, 1986) and of Galili and Inbar (1986) who related most of the 13-m submergence of the Hof Hacarmel lagoonal clay unit to the eustatic rise of ocean level during the past 5000 years. Although the Atlit clay unit is identical with the lagoonal clay unit of Dor (II Unit 4c ii), there is an important difference between them. The former ceased to be deposited about 9000 years ago, but the latter was uninterruptedly deposited until middle or even late Holocene time. This difference could be related to differences in tectonic histories north and south of the transverse Atlit Fault. This east-west trending fault bounds the south end of the Haifa Nose—Atlit rectangle, as well as Atlit Bay and its promontory (the Crusader fortress). It extends farther eastward as a lineament along the lower part of Nahal Oren and joins an east-west trending fault just north of En Hod (Fig. 5; Karcz 1959, geological map). Although the throw of this down-to-the-south fault is rather small, it may be genetically connected with the major east-west Isfiya fault system that separates the Higher Carmel at the north from the Lower Carmel at the south (Kashai 1966). The downthrown side across the En Hod—Isfiya fault zone is to the south. On the other hand, Atlit Bay has subsided tectonically with respect to the strip of land just south of it. Thus, over its entire length, this fault may be termed a scissors fault. Several other east-west (transverse) faults, the downthrown sides of which are systematically to the north (Adler 1985) cross the submerged segment of the coast-parallel ridge north of Atlit.

3. Dor. The following finds at Dor are relevant to the tectonic history of the coastline since the Pleistocene—Holocene transition. An uninterrupted brackish-water sedimentary sequence that accumulated along the present coastline between about 20,000 y BP and about 5000 y BP (see II B Unit 4c) suggests a gradual tectonic rise of appreciable magnitude (more than 100 m) simultaneously with the eustatic rise of sea level. Coexistence of this marine-affiliated sequence and the nearby freshwater swamps (just south of Dor—see below) corroborates the postulate of hydraulic equilibrium between these two water bodies.

Solidly-built Middle Bronze (3900 y BP) structures occur along the western flanks of Tel Dor atop an abraded terrace that afterward was subjected to both faulting and tilting (+4 m and +1.5 m msl at the southwestern and northwestern peripheries, respectively—Raban, 1983a; personal communication) and possibly also +14 m msl at the center of the tel (Sneh and Klein 1982). A layer of dark gray-brown loam (swamp environment) overlies Iron Age structures at the southern fringe of the tel (about +3 m msl). These data suggest differential vertical movements across the coastline since the Early to Middle Bronze transition (4500 to 4000 y BP). They also suggest that an oscillatory movement affected this site sometime during the Iron Age.

Naturally deposited shell accumulations, dominated by *Glycyimeris* sp. and alternatingly interbedded with dark brown clay layers (see II B Unit 7d iv, and Unit 6) occur along the rocky bays north of Tel Dor up to a level of +4 m msl. A fresh outcrop provided by recent quarrying of the shells for use as a supplement in chicken food permitted detailed study of the stratigraphy and sediments. This sequence locally overlies (with a lateral transition) Roman quarries within the kurkar ridge. An up to +10 m msl coast-parallel plain of dark-brown loam extends a few hundred meters eastward. It is inferred that these clays were deposited within swamp environments and that these now-elevated swamps were in hydraulic equilibrium with the swamp along the western flanks of the coastal cliff. A Post-Roman oscillatory tectonic movement (a downwarping and submergence of a few meters followed by a rebounding tectonic rise) is implied.

The model that explains the mechanism of such vertical oscillatory movements (see IV A 4 and Fig. 35) involves two stages: (i) tectonic subsidence and submergence of both the landward and offshore blocks across the coastal fault, which at Dor follows the western rim of the abraded terrace (see Fig. 15A), and (ii) a tectonic rebound of the landward (upthrown) block. The exact date of this tectonic event could not be determined; it could have occurred either in late Byzantine time or at the end of the Mamlukian reign (IV A 3). We consider the younger age as the more plausible one. The following are three additional sets of data suggesting that the upthrown (landward) block across the coastal fault at Dor is still tectonically rising, thereby supporting the second (rebound) stage of the Mamlukian phase. (i) A water well that was dug sometime during Roman or later (even Moslem?) times into the kurkar rocks is today just west of the coastline of Dor, so that its neatly built and well-preserved top is totally submerged under seawater during high tides. Although the water of this well was still utilized during the 1930s (Raban, personal communication, 1986), the precise date of its construction can be determined only by redigging. Its partial flooding by seawater could have been avoided or reduced if the well had been dug just a few meters farther northwest on a mound of kurkar rock a few meters high. Eustatic rise of sea level may be ruled out as an explanation, because the range of sea-level changes during the past 2000 years is small (probably less than about a meter); on the other hand, tectonic subsidence of the continental block could explain the sequence of events. (ii) Large segments of the very linear Via Maris (the Roman coastal road), most of which was cut into kurkar, are now partly submerged under seawater along the coastline just a few kilometers south of Dor. The same arguments that support the tectonic explanation for the submerged water well are applicable here. (iii) An east-west trending road, as well as floors of buildings along both sides of it, was cut during Roman times into an abraded terrace at the coastline off the northwestern end of Tel Dor. Today, these relics, together with the one or two lowest rows of masonry in the building's walls and a few collapsed granite pillars, are flooded by seawater during high tides. At present, the walls are slightly tilted to the west (seaward). Apparently, the tilt has a tectonic origin, as the masons of this well-planned site must have mastered the use of the plumb bob. These data are interpreted differently by Galili (1985) and Raban (1985), who consider that this site was built as a shipyard so that the tilt and partial submergence were purposely planned and that there has been no tectonic change since Roman times.

C. Hof Hasharon Segment (Caesarea to Yafo)

1. North-South Perspective. The coastal segment between Caesarea and Yafo is defined by Gvirtzman (in press) as the Hof Hasharon Escarpment. It is associated with a broad north-south trending structural uplift whose apex is near Ga'ash (Figs. 1 and 16A). The type locality of the seven late Pleistocene to Recent stratigraphic units (Fig. 5; Neev and Bakler 1978) is along this segment near the apex of the dome-shaped uplift just north of Ga'ash. The white Calcarenite Bank (Unit 5a) near the top of the sequence exposed along the Hof Hasharon Escarpment is a prominent guide horizon that emphasizes the structurally high (domal) nature of this nearly 50-km long segment. Considering the origins (environments of deposition) and ages of both the Calcarenite Bank and the underlying Hamra (see Stratigraphy II B 5a and 4a, respectively), we suggest that: (i) The coastal zone along this segment was tectonically uplifted by more than 100 m during Early Holocene contemporaneously with the major eustatic rise of sea level. This phase was accomplished during the peak of the Flandrian transgression (about 6000 y BP). (ii) An additional phase of tectonic rise, amounting to as much as 60 m at the apex of this dome (Netanya to Ga'ash; Fig. 16A) occurred subsequently. Nevertheless, each of these young phases should be considered a rejuvenation of a much older and larger movement; the Ga'ash dome is known to have been uplifted a cumulative amount of about 1200 m (with respect to the depth of the top Talme-Yafo surface at Tel Aviv) since middle Cretaceous (Fig. 16B, after data from Gvirtzman 1981; Klang and Gvirtzman 1983).

The beach origin of the calcarenite bank (Unit 5a) indicates that, during the early Holocene (10,000 to 6000 y BP), this segment could have been structurally lower than the Hof Hacarmel segment (see III B), where a swamp environment habitable by people prevailed. The Hof Hasharon segment is bounded on both its north and south by two transverse fault zones: the Or'Aqiva and the Yafo-Yarkon, respectively. Existence of these two fault zones is supported by shallow- and deep-penetration offshore seismic data as well as by subsurface and field mapping data (see also relevant text sections above and below). However, we did not find support for the systematic sinistral strike-slip shiftings across these two transverse faults reported by Klang and Gvirtzman (1983, 8,

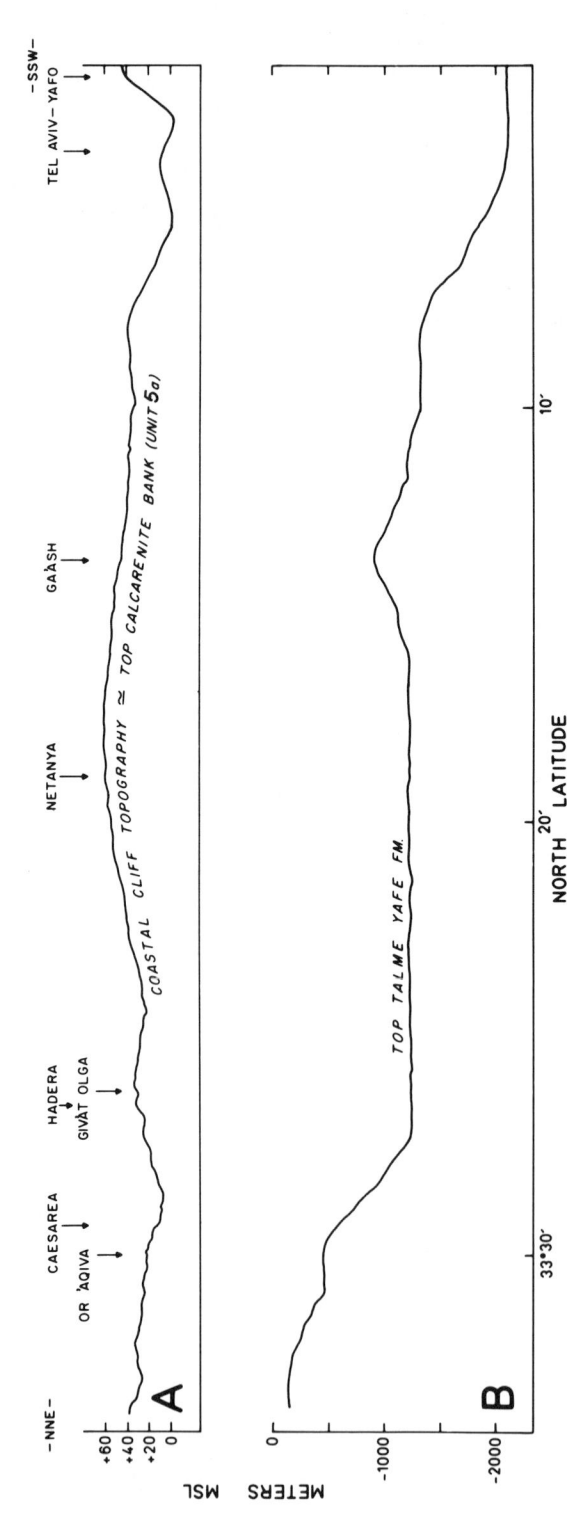

Figure 16. Geology of the coastal Hof Hasharon Segment (III C). *A.* North-south topographic profile along the coastal cliff between Mt. Carmel and Tel Aviv—Yafo. The profile approximates the structural relief of the Calcarenite Bank II (Unit 5a). *B.* A structural profile made on the Talme-Yafe formation (mid-Cretaceous). Despite the difference in vertical scales of profiles A and B, there is an apparent similarity between them, suggesting that intensive tectonic uplift along this coastal segment since middle Holocene (see text and Figure 4) is a rejuvenated phase of a much older process.

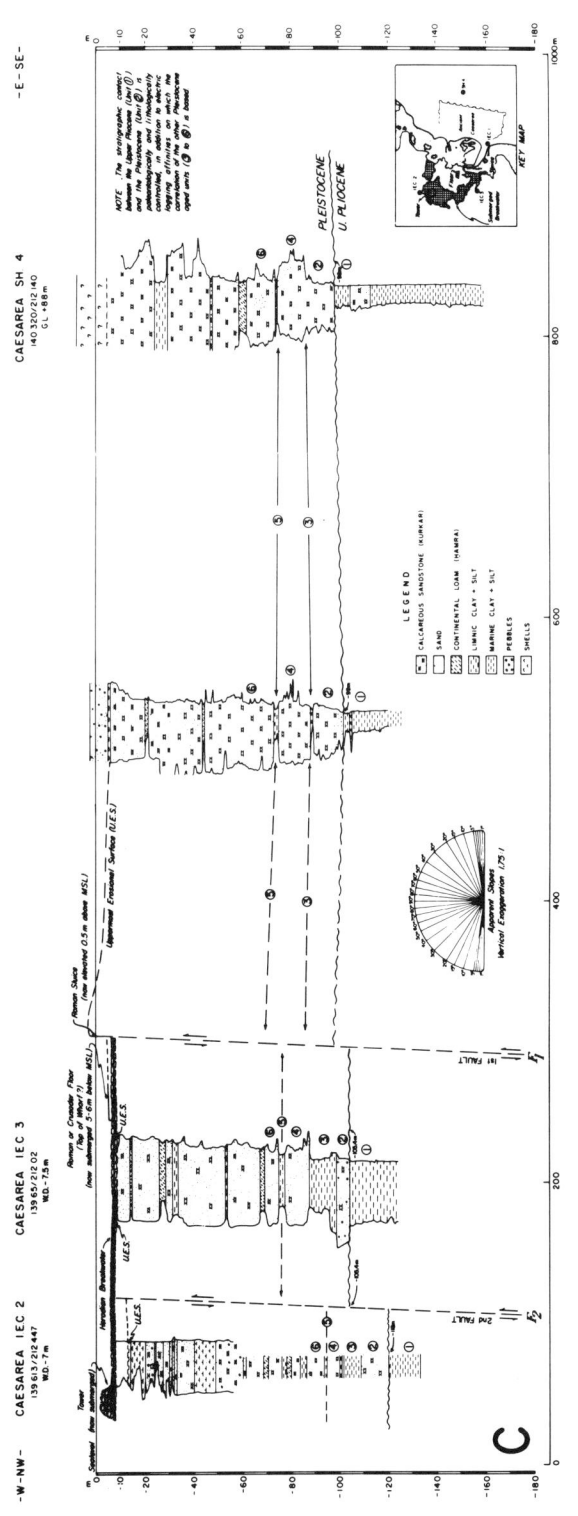

Figure 16. Geology of the coastal Hof Hasharon Segment (III C).C. Transverse east-west geological cross section through the late Pliocene to Recent sedimentary sequence at Caesarea. The section extends from west of the sunken Herodian breakwater to east of the Crusader city wall (from Neev et al. 1978a, fig. 10). The Pre-Roman (F-2) and Post-Roman (F-1) faults were identified (13 m and 5 to 6 m throws, respectively) from precise age analysis of stratigraphic contacts in drilling and present elevations of the now-submerged man-made structures (breakwater, floor, and sluice). By permission of Israel Journal of Earth-Sciences, Jerusalem).

13–16, fig. 5) and by Gvirtzman (in press). According to their model, the "Edge of the Platform" (an onshore and offshore coast-parallel belt) is divided by a pattern of transverse faults into seven or eight blocks extending from the Carmel Nose in the north to Yafo in the south. Moreover, if lateral shifts actually did occur along these transverse faults, they had to be dextral ones (as suggested by the eastward branching patterns along the axes of the coast-parallel folds and faults near the transverse faults—Neev and Greenfield 1984).

2. Caesarea (N32°30'10" E34°53'30"). The structural high of Caesarea (Neev et al. 1978a; Gvirtzman and Klang 1981) is at the junction of three tectonic elements: (i) a northeast-southwest trending folded structure that formed after Early Cretaceous (and perhaps even before) and in which folding activity continued until late Pleistocene; (ii) a north-northeast trending post-Jurassic—pre-Cretaceous normal fault that roughly corresponds with the present coastline as well as with the present coastal fault system; and (iii) the Or 'Akiva east-west (transverse) trending fault zone (or graben) (Gvirtzman and Klang 1981; Neev and Greenfield 1981). Neev and Greenfield (1984) reported that the post-Jurassic coast-parallel structural element branches off from the Pelusium Line eastward at the Or 'Akiva transverse fault.

Freshwater pools occurred atop the Caesarea structure both on land and present offshore from latest Pleistocene (about 15,000 y BP) until Neolithic time (about 9000 y BP; see II B Unit 4b, 5d, and 6). As the freshwater bodies probably were in hydraulic equilibrium with the Mediterranean Sea, we suggest that this joint shelf and coastal belt were low and flat. A regional tectonic rise of both littoral and coastal belts by more than 100 m during late Pleistocene and Holocene is implied. The westward slope of one degree, as measured on the Pliocene—Pleistocene contact (onshore) and on a late Pleistocene reflector (offshore) (Neev et al. 1978a), resulted from a contemporaneous movement (a recent tectonic tilt) that may have been related to the same origin.

Three coast-parallel faults are postulated along the littoral zone off Caesarea (Neev et al. 1978a, fig. 6). Two faults (the ones nearest the coastline, Fig. 16C) were identified on the basis of onshore and offshore studies that included detailed stratigraphic analyses of boreholes (including precise elevations of the Pliocene—Pleistocene boundary) and detailed underwater archaeological excavations (Raban et al. 1976). A third offshore fault (beyond the western limit of Fig. 16C) was identified on the basis of shallow-penetration seismic profiles and geomorphic considerations. Cumulative throws during Holocene across the first two faults total nearly 20 m in a distance of about 400 m. The Herodian harbor subsided about 6 m across the fault that corresponds with the submarine cliff along the western margin of the abraded terrace. This Post-Roman faulting occurred in two phases: one during Early Byzantine time, and the other near the end of Mamlukian time (a few hundred years ago). The Early Byzantine phase is indicated by an early sixth-century letter from the theologist Procopius of Gaza (Raban et al. 1976, 20) to Caesar Anastasius complaining that Caesarea Harbor was not functioning anymore as a protected anchorage, and adding that ships had been sunk in it by storms. Both phases of faulting are believed to be assocated with renewal of massive supply of quartz-sand from the Nile River. Both tectonic phases caused subsidence of the downthrown block on which the Herodian harbor is situated. The net amount of vertical shift across the second fault is about 13m, most of which occurred in Pre-Roman times, probably during the Iron Age. On the other hand, the upthrown block across the first fault was subjected to oscillatory (down-and-up) movements that occurred sequentially, perhaps even twice in Post-Roman times as indicated by the positions (relative elevations) and ages of marine beach and swamp deposits (Neev et al. 1978a). However, the net amount of movement on the upthrown block is small.

The history of the water supply system to Caesarea throughout Roman and Crusader times (Reifenberg 1951; Olami and Peleg 1977; Nir 1985) suggests the involvement of small vertical tectonic movements. The High Level Aqueduct, leading from the southeastern flank of Mt. Carmel to Caesarea contains three separate channels: A, B, and C. Channel A was built by King Herod in the first century BC. Channel B was constructed during Hadrian's time (137–138 AD) to double or more the water supply, but also to support and repair damages to Channel A caused by a strong earthquake in 130 AD. Channel C later was erected atop the rubble-filled Channel B in order to raise its level 2.5 m at the northern approach to Caesarea. The carrying capacity of Channel C was only ten percent of the original capacity of the then defunct Channels A and B. We concur with one of the rationales suggested for the construction of this new and higher channel, which is the occurrence of a "Tectonic subsidence of the whole areas" (Nir 1985, 187). Perhaps Channel C was built during the first phase of the Byzantine oscillatory movement between the fourth and sixth centuries AD when the Caesarean harbor and apparently also the onshore belt did subside.

Another aqueduct, the Low Level Aqueduct, was constructed mostly east of the High Level one sometime during the Byzantine period to carry water from near Maagan Michael (Fig. 1) to Caesarea. Although Olami and Peleg (1977, 37) assumed that it was erected during the fourth century AD, it is quite likely that it was built somewhat later (during the fifth or sixth centuries AD) to supplement the High Level Aqueduct. The capacity of the Low Level Aqueduct was estimated to have been 2500 cu. m per hour, more than the combined capacities of aqueducts A and B at their best. We doubt that Channel C functioned until Crusader time, as suggested by Olami and Peleg (1977), because the water resources of Caesarea during the 12th and 13th centuries were in the great swamps east of it (Reifenberg 1951). The flooding by swamp water of extensive areas including Roman and Byzantine structures (such as the Hippodrome east of the city) is inferred by Neev et al. (1978) to have occurred during the first stage of subsidence. Also the desertion of Caesarea during the 14th century was not just because of intentional destruction by man (Reifenberg 1951; Ayalon 1964), but also because of effects of Post-Crusader tectonic movements, according to evidence from the harbor (Raban et al. 1976).

3. *Michmoret* (N32°24'08" E34°51"54"). A Persian Age structure excavated by Dr. J. Porat at the inner bay of Michmoret (Fig. 1) just above present sea level is overlain by an extensive layer of dark-brown loam (swamp deposit) that forms an elevated (about +4 m msl) terrace a few meters thick (see II B 6, last paragraph). Interbedded in the upper part of this loam unit are lenses of naturally-deposited *Glycyimeris* sp. shell. Thus, we suggest that sometime after the Iron Age this site was subjected to an oscillatory movement. Relatively thick accumulations of loose shells also were found atop Persian to Roman structures that had been built on elevated (now a few meters above msl) abraded terraces at both ends of the bay.

A 4-m deep water well 25 m east of the shoreline was re-dug by Nir and Eldar (1986c, 1987) to its paleowatertable, which now is at -1.4 m msl. They noted a slight eastward tilt of its walls that they related to instability of the water-logged underlying sandy layers. We suggest, instead, that the tilt may have been produced by the rebound part of an oscillatory tectonic movement (see Synopsis—IV A 4). Similar eastward tilts occur elsewhere across the coastal cliff (see, for example, our Fig. 18 and Neev et al. 1978a, fig. 11; as well as III D 6 and III E 2 below). Nir and Eldar (1986b) related the present low elevation of the well's paleowatertable to a Post-Persian eustatic rise of sea level (see our doubts in that respect in IV A 6).

4. *Netanya* (N32°19'40" E34°50'45"). Recording of uninterrupted seismic reflection profiles across the coastline of Israel involves difficult geophysical operations. A rare case where good results were obtained is demonstrated by Telseis profile No. 80-M-25 (Fig. 4D,E) about 7 km south of Netanya. Reliable data were recovered in this profile from about 7 km offshore to about 0.5 km east of the coastline, although the shooting line actually ended about 1.5 km inland. Supplementary seismic and well log data, however, are available both north and south of this site on land as well as offshore.

We interpret the compiled data as indicating three successive major phases of rejuvenated normal faulting across the present coastline since Miocene: (i) The earliest was just prior to the "M" Horizon (a time equivalent of the Messinian event, ten to seven million y BP). The bundle of reflectors that characterises that horizon (Fig. 4D,E) onlaps a pre-existing, nearly 300-m high morphological step across the coastline. Its depth east of the coastline is 1.2 sec (or about 1.2 km), whereas west of the coastline it is identified at 1.5 sec (or about 1.5 km). This jump of about 300 m occurs in a relatively short horizontal distance (perhaps 200 m but not more than 500 m in an east-west direction), which is equivalent to a gradient of not less than 35 degrees. Thus, it may reflect a cumulative throw of 300 m of normal faulting since Miocene. (ii) The second event or phase is indicated by the contact of the Kurkar and Saqiye groups. This surface extends nearly horizontally in the offshore westward from the coastline to a distance of 6 km (Fig. 4A). At the Item No. 1 drill hole, it is at a depth of about 400 msec (about 300 m) below msl (Fig. 4A,B,E). Starting about 1 km west of the coastline, this surface tilts upward to the east, straightening again to a nearly horizontal attitude about 0.5 km offshore. Its depth at the coastline is about 150 m (Shachnai, 1974, cross sections SH 44, 45, 47; our Fig. 4A,B). The difference of 150 m in a distance of 0.5 km is equivalent to a gradient of not less than 16 degrees. On shore, this unconformable surface, which apparently was nearly horizontal when formed, now tilts westward 0.5 to 1 degree. A cumulative 150 m of normal faulting across the coastline is implied since early Pleistocene. (iii) The third and youngest event is indicated by the difference in elevations of the early Holocene Calcarenite Bank (Unit 5a) including its underlying Epipaleolithic Hamra Layer (Unit 4a) across the coastal zone (see Stratigraphy—above; and Fig. 4A,B,C). On land, these rock units are at elevations of +30 to +50 m along the coastal cliff, whereas 800 to 1700 m west of the coastline (at shallow offshore drill holes No. N–21 and N–23) they are at depths of -20 to -30 m. Considering the nearly horizontal gradient of the seismic reflectors in the upper Kurkar sequence west of shot point 70 and east of shot point 60 (Fig. 4D,E), the break in elevation of the Kurkar's offshore and onshore reflectors should have occurred along a distance of about 500 m. A vertical difference of 50 to 70 m in a distance of 500 m equals a gradient of at least 6 degrees. This means a total of more than 50 m of normal faulting during the past 6000 years.

It appears likely from the above observations that the Hof Hasharon coastal segment was subjected to an east-west differential movement as well as to rejuvenation of north-south arching activity. We consider that post-Jurassic to pre-Cretaceous normal faulting across the coastal fault at Caesarea (see above) was an earlier phase of activity along the same fault. The mutual genetic relationship between these three different tectonic activities (the north-south arching, the east-west normal faulting, and the general Holocene upwarp of more than 100 m) should be elaborated further.

An indicator for a late Holocene oscillatory movement across the coastal fault between Michmoret and Tel Aviv is the presence atop the coastal cliff of northeastward-elongated lobes of dune sand (see the Hadera Sand Dunes—II B Unit 7a and Fig. 8). In addition, a thin and patchy carpet of inconsistently oriented single *Glycymeris* sp. shells, flat but well-rounded pebbles of kurkar rock fragments (to 5 cm in diameter), and rounded pottery sherds of different ages is extensively scattered atop the coastal cliff region. Although the assembly has a uniform affinity (all formed in marine-littoral environments), it was not described as a separate unit in Chapter II (Stratigraphy), because it is devoid of sedimentary structures that could identify its mode of deposition. Yet its characteristics lead us to suggest that it was deposited by a transgressive sea. The site where this carpet is best expressed is a few km south of the Netanya beach (just north of the Soldier's Home) near the type locality of the biostromal burrowers of the Calcarenite Bank (Unit 5a). The carpet covers a broad westward-tilted (about 5°) abrasional terrace that truncates the Nof Yam clayey sand unit (II B 6) and underlies the Hadera Dune Sand (Unit 7a). Presumably, this abrasional-depositional event represents an oscillatory movement that occurred sometime between 5000 and 3000 years ago.

5. Ga'ash (N32°13'40" E34°49'05"). The sheet of dune sand a few meters thick overlying a Byzantine site atop the coastal cliff (+30 to +40 m high) at Ga'ash (Figs. 1, 16A; II B, Unit 7a) suggests that the last phase of sand supply to the now-elevated Hof Hasharon segment (Fig. 8) is younger than 1500 y BP. An oscillatory movement that caused the land side to subside to approximately the present sea level and then to rise again had to occur to enable the sand to encroach inland.

6. Apollonia (or Tel Arshaf) (N32°11'42" E34°48'20"). The harbor facilities (breakwater, etc.) of the Crusader fortress of Apollonia are presently too shallow (0.5 to 1.5 m) to be useful. Moreover, the outlet of the tunnel that originally enabled a safe approach from the harbor to the fortress is now at an anomalously high elevation of about +6 m above water level (exposed entrance). In addition, all of the structures within this site appear to have gone through severe destructive tilting. These data suggest that the site was uplifted by a few meters during Post-Crusader times. If this movement was oscillatory, like the contemporary movements at Caesarea and Ga'ash, the amount of rebound of the upthrown block at that place exceeded that of the preceding downwarp. The coastal fault (Fault 1 of Caesarea) may lie along the western edge of the abraded terrace, and a now-submerged part of the harbor may lie beyond that fault.

7. Tel Michal (N32°09'38" E 34°47'35"). The Tel Michal site (Figs. 1, 5, 9, 17; II B Unit 7f) is 6.5 km north of the Yarkon River and 3.5 km south of Apollonia atop the coastal cliff at an elevation of +26 m. It was first settled about 3700 years ago, when a square-shaped structure of Middle Bronze II b age was built (Fig. 17). The western part of this settlement is underlain by Kurkar Sandstone (Unit 1 or 3), whereas its eastern part is built upon a 4- to 6-m thick artificial earth ramp (Herzog et al. 1978; Herzog 1981; Herzog, personal communication). The faces of this square platform are diagonally oriented to the north-northeast trending coastline. In a catastrophic event prior to Late Bronze I (between 1600 and 1570 y BC), the western section of the platform abruptly collapsed and disappeared. The platform was rebuilt by Late Bronze I people who extended the earth ramp farther southeastward. The same sequence of events was repeated when the western part of the new platform collapsed. It was rebuilt during the Late Bronze II period by a further eastward extension of the earth ramp (Fig. 17). This time a stone wall was put into the platform as a support. The Late Bronze II cultural occupation continued until the end of the 14th Century BC, when the site became deserted. These two or even three destructive events probably were caused by renewed tectonic activity along the coastal fault system, perhaps genetically correlated with a long tectonic phase in the Aegean Sea and Western Anatolia that included the catastrophic eruption of Santorini (Thera) about 3500 years ago (see also II B Unit 7c) and a sequence of destructive earthquakes that led to the decline of the Late Bronze Greek and Hittite civilizations in the eleventh Century BC.

At Tel Michal, there are no indications of younger similar catastrophic events. However, several cultural breaks, which are reported to have occurred in later times, may have been induced by natural destructive processes: (i) between Late Bronze and the tenth or eleventh century BC; (ii) in the late eighth and the entire seventh century BC; (iii) at the middle of the fifth century BC; (iv) throughout the Byzantine period (between Late Roman and Early Moslem times); and (v) after the thirteenth century AD (Mamlukian time).

Gifford et al. (in press) reported a 495 ± 70 year-old vermetid reef (radiocarbon date for whole rock sample) developed as a biogenic crust atop an abraded terrace that now is about 100 m off Tel Michal in a water depth of 1.5 m. These authors concluded that this terrace subsided by that amount during the historical past. Raban and Tur-Caspa (1979) traced this terrace from about 20 m east of the coastline (practically from the base of the seacliff) to about 150 m west of it. At that point, the abraded terrace drops abruptly at a north-south trending line. Toward the east, the terrace rises from −2.5 m to −1.5

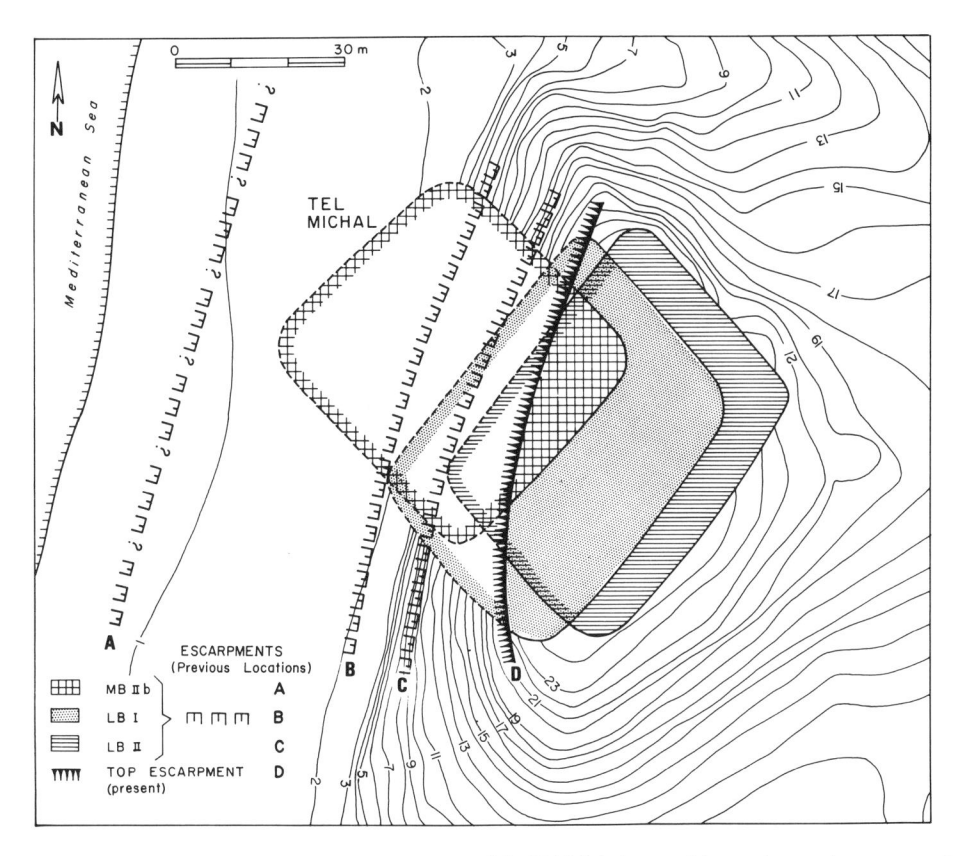

Figure 17. A 1-m contour interval topographic map of the Tel Michal area with superimposed reconstructed configurations of Middle Bronze II b, Late Bronze I, and Late Bronze II rectangular earth ramparts (modified from Z. Herzog, in preparation, by permission). These man-made structures built probably for defense purposes were destroyed twice between about 1600 y BC and about 1300 y BC, apparently because of repeated collapse of the coastal cliff. These events may be related genetically to tectonic-volcanic eruptions of Santorini and associated tsunamis. The cumulative distance which the top of the coastal cliffs escarpment has receded during that phase is about 60 m. Recession since then is negligible. This Middle to Late Bronze tectonic phase also may have been associated with a strong oscillatory tectonic movement (see III D 2 and 1).

m at the foot of the coastal cliff, whereas on the west it is at a depth of -6.5 m. These authors suggested recent 4-m westward normal faulting along the north-south trending line. We infer the presence of at least two coast-parallel stepfaults. The eastern one (of 1.5-m throw) is at the base of the cliff and occurred in Late Mamlukian time, whereas the western one is about 150 m off the coast and could have occurred during the same phase or sometime earlier, during the Byzantine or Persian phases. Such a history is analogous to that reported for Caesarea (see above, and Neev et al. 1978a). The only indication for an oscillatory type of movement of the upthrown block at the Tel Michal site and the coastal segment between Netanya and Yavneh Yam is supplied by the Post-Byzantine and/or Post-Crusader dune sands that lie atop the coastal cliff. Only traces of shell beds were found atop the cliff of the Hof Hasharon segment.

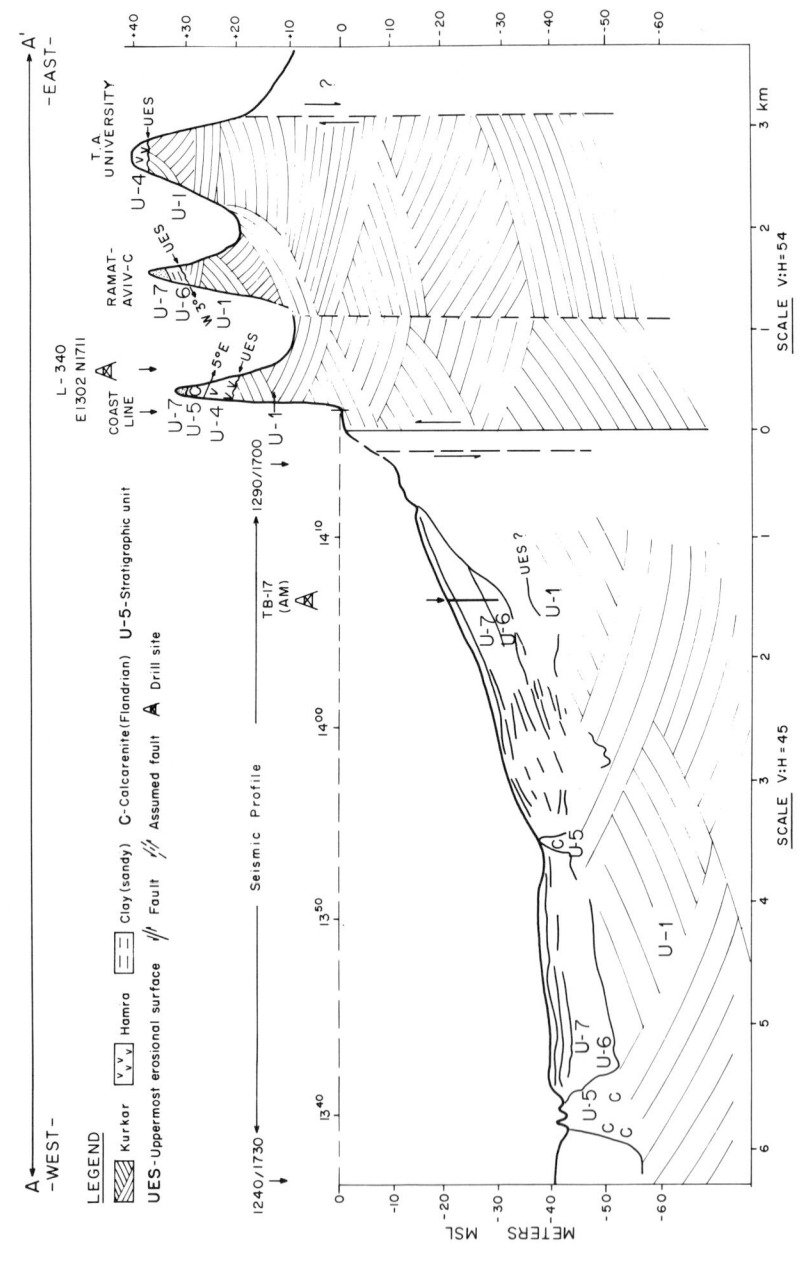

Figure 18 An east-west geological cross section (offshore part based on seismic profiles and drillings) between Tel Baruch and Tel Aviv University. For positions of its three segments see Figure 19 A-A'. The Calcarenite Bank (Unit 5a) at the offshore kurkar ridge is from its occurrence at the TA-12 drill site off Yafo (II Unit 5a, III C 10, Figs. 19 and 21). Note changing dip directions measured on Uppermost Erosional Surface (UES) across the kurkar ridges on land.

A probing transect along the beach and across the trend of Nahal Gelilot also was made by Gifford et al. (in press) a few hundred meters north of Tel Michal (see Fig. 8 where the channel of Nahal Gelilot is marked as Drainage). The trough of this channel was detected at a depth of 6 m below the backbeach surface. The landward extension of this channel (Nahal Gelilot from the coastal cliff eastward) is now "hanging" at an elevation of more than 10 m above the beach. It forms an east-west linear feature for about 1 km across the now-elevated paleoswamp plain that stops the northeastward advance of sand dunes. This linear east-west segment of Nahal Gelilot may express another transverse fault. The wadi then gradually curves northeastward for another kilometer where it intersects the second kurkar ridge (Fig. 8). The channel crosses that ridge through a tunnel dug by the Romans or Byzantines to drain the swamps farther east. Gradients along both segments of the Nahal Gelilot channel east and west of the second kurkar ridge are negligible, in contrast with the steep (several degrees) gradient across the coastal cliff between the paleoswamps and beach.

8. Tel Baruch (N32°07′35″ E34°47′04) **and Ramat Aviv C** (N32°07′25″ E34°47′25″). The existence of a coast-parallel fault off Tel Baruch is suggested on the basis of an offshore seismic profile and sampled jet drill hole TB17 (Figs. 18 and 19; Bakler 1976) as well as onshore information (Gophna, 1977; Ritter-Kaplan 1979). The offshore kurkar ridges, 3 and 6 km off the coastline, may consist of the early Holocene Calcarenite (II B Unit 5) similar to the kurkar ridge off Yafo. The 12-m sedimentary sequence penetrated at drill hole TB17 (about 1.5 km west of the coastline, N32°08′22″ E34°46′15″) consists of low-energy gray marine clayey sand (Unit 7b) that overlies a more compact dark gray-black clay layer containing brackish-water ostracodes. The age of this compacted clay layer is estimated to be middle to late Holocene (Unit 6). A seismic profile (Bakler 1976) indicated that the littoral belt (at least to 3 km off the coastline) is tilted westward. On land a 5-degree eastward tilt of the depositional contact between the Hamra beds (Unit 4a) and Calcarenitic Bank (Unit 5a) is recognized across the +30-m high coastal cliff about 3 km north of the outlet of the Yarkon River (Neev et al. 1978a, fig. 11). One or more coast-parallel faults are implied between the offshore and onshore areas. The post-middle Holocene throw across this fault zone is estimated to be about 50 m.

Similar examples of eastward tilting due to tectonic activity are noted at several other onshore sites along the coastal cliff and are interpreted by Neev and Bakler (1978) as having been formed during one of the late Holocene oscillatory movements (see Synopsis). Eastward projection of the 5-degree dip for a distance of about 1 km puts the contact between Units 3 and 4 at an elevation of about −50 m. Unfortunately, no subsurface data are available from the morphological trough between the coastal cliff and the first kurkar ridge east of it. On the other hand, sandstones of Unit 1 (and possibly also of Unit 3) crop out at the crest of the adjacent kurkar ridge on the east at an elevation of +30 m. The top of this kurkar at the eastern ridge attained a nearly perfectly flat surface probably by marine abrasion prior to deposition of Unit 4a (the Netanya Hamra). This abraded terrace now is tilted westward about 4 degrees. A 2-m sequence of Early Bronze swamp deposit (see Unit 6) overlies the kurkar near the top of this easternmost kurkar ridge (Ramat Aviv C) at an elevation of about +30 m msl. The geological cross section

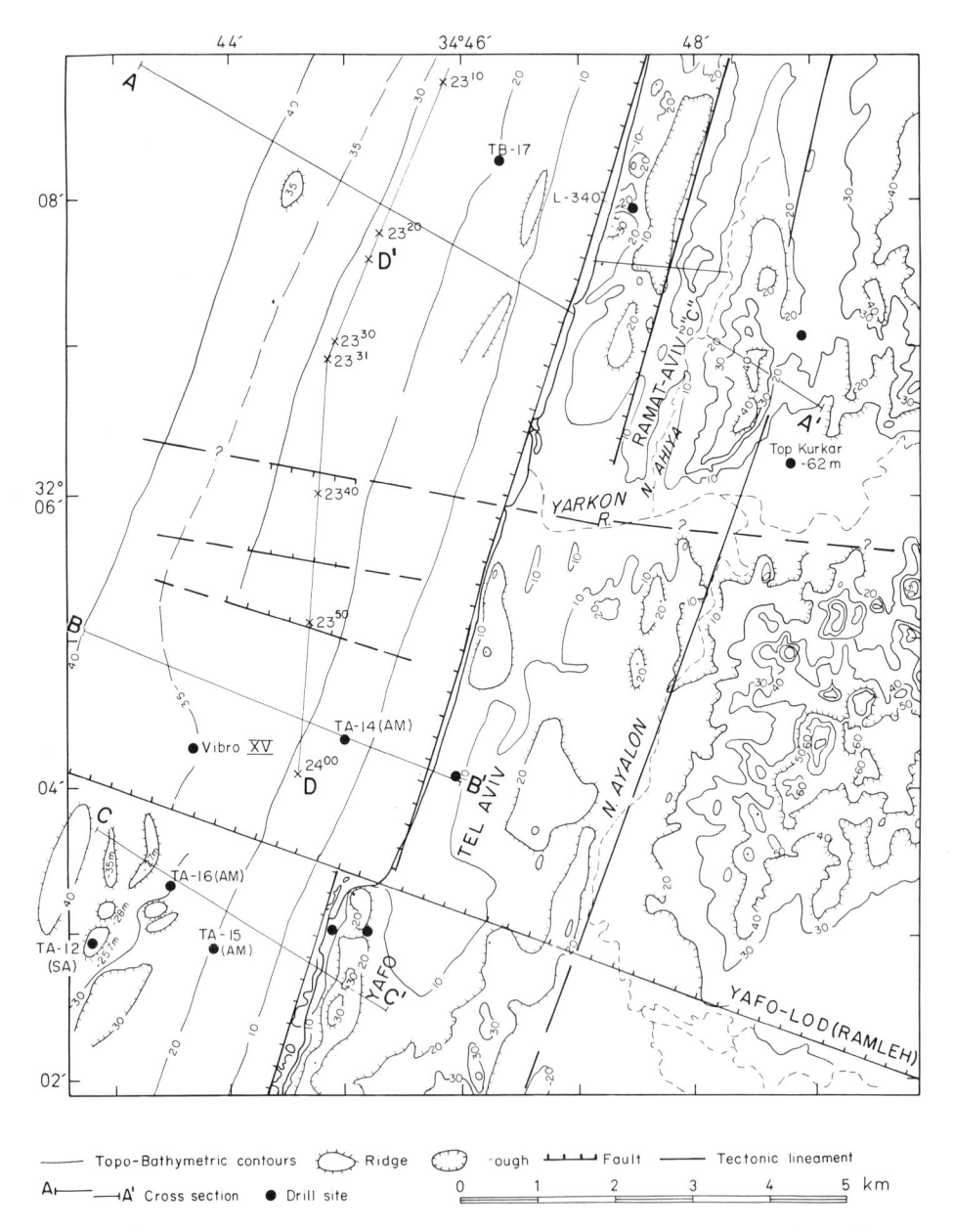

Figure 19. Map of tectonic elements, bathymetry, and topography (in m) in the Tel Aviv—Yafo area. It includes geological cross sections, the coast-parallel Uniboom profile, and drill holes.

across the coastal belt (Fig. 18) suggests a system of coast-parallel tectonically tilted blocks separated from each other by faults. It also implies that the part of the coastal zone now on land was subjected to a tectonic uplift of about 30 m that may have been associated with an oscillatory type of movement. This event must have occurred sometime after Early Bronze time and may represent a rejuvenation of an older faulting process.

9. The North-South Trending Ayalon Fault. Support for tilting of the coastal belt comes from comparison of present and past gradients of the Yarkon River. The bottom of the alluvial sequence that fills the gorge of the late Pleistocene Yarkon River at its intersection with the Ayalon River (Fig. 19) about 3 km east of the coastline is at an elevation of -62 m msl. However, the maximum depth of the top of the Kurkar (Unit 1 or 3) along the coastline between the outlet of the Yarkon River and Yafo was identified in numerous drillings at depths that do not exceed -35 m msl (Issar 1968). Such a relationship is anomalous, because the base level of erosion at the time of entrenchment of the Yarkon River's gorge was west of the present coastline, so that the erosional trough across the coastline should have been deeper than upstream (eastward). The most reasonable explanation for this inverse relationship is upward tectonic movement during Holocene of the coast-parallel belt on land between the coastline and the eastern flanks of the third (Tel Aviv University—Fig. 18) kurkar ridge that has a horst-like structure. Another coast-parallel fault along the eastern edge of the first kurkar ridge between Tel Baruch and Ramat Aviv C is suspected (Fig. 18).

The third (easternmost) fault (Figs. 18, 19) is expressed by the north-northeasterly segment of the Ayalon River and, together with its northern extension just east of Tel Aviv University (at Ramat Aviv C), it forms an extremely straight 8-km long lineament exactly parallel to the coastline. Extension of this lineament farther north is traced on LANDSAT images as well as on available topographic maps along the route of the Tel Aviv—Haifa railroad. This feature was marked as a "lineament on ERTS imagery" in figure 4 of Bartov et al. (1977).

The uplifting process that affected the coastal zone both on land and in the offshore since early Holocene also may explain the absence of any deltaic or trench extension of the Yarkon River in the present littoral belt.

10. Geological Cross Sections across the Tel Aviv—Yafo Coast. A 4-m core sample was obtained off southern Tel Aviv in a water depth of 37 m (Vibrocore No. XV, N32°04'15" E34°41'44"; Figs. 19, 20). Most of it (the upper 3.6 m) consists of low-energy marine sediments (a dark gray clayey sand layer, Unit 7b). This sequence overlies at least 40 cm (to the bottom of the core) of light yellowish well-sorted clean quartz sand. The lower unit represents a high-energy (beach) environment and contains large *Glycymeris* shells, whose radiocarbon age is 4595 ± 230 y BP (A. Geyh, Hanover, Germany, personal communication). As sea levels since the Bronze Age have been relatively near those of the present, it is implied that during this time span the sea floor at this site tectonically subsided from the beach level to below the high energy zone. Cumulative subsidence since then is estimated to be more than 30 m.

Another 12-m drill hole (TA14) is in a water depth of 12 m (N32°04'17" E34°45'00") along the same east-west trending cross section. Although it was only jet sampled, a fairly reliable stratigraphic sequence was established there (Bakler 1976, figs. 2c, 5b, 14). The upper part of this sequence consists of a 3-m dark gray clayey sand layer. These relatively low-energy marine sediments overlie a 2-m layer of brown to black clay of swamp origin. The latter is underlain in turn by a more than 7-m reddish hamra layer within which this drill hole bottomed. An angular pottery sherd coated with yellowish

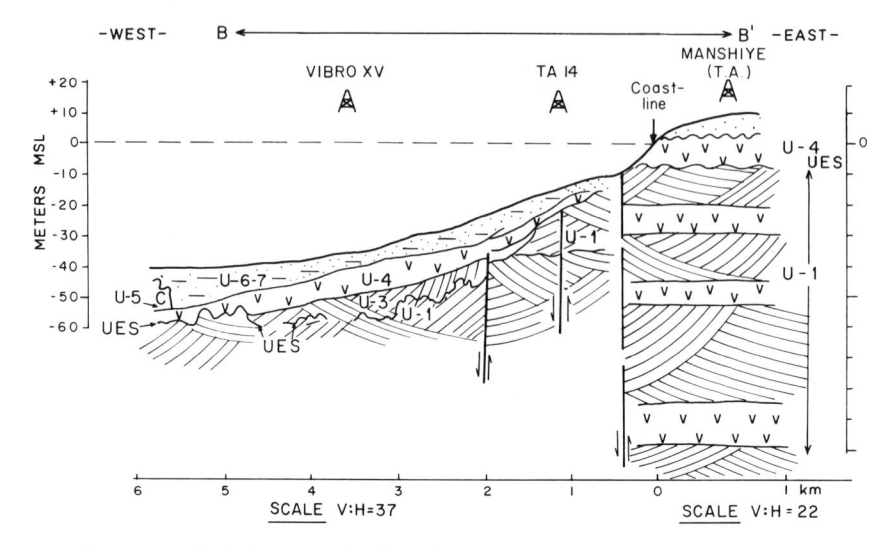

Figure 20. East-west geological cross-section through the coastline at Manshiye (southwestern suburb of Tel Aviv). The concept of a transgressive facies change from high-energy to low-energy regimes across the littoral belt during the past 4500 years was established mainly on the basis of Vibrocore holes such as No. XV.

glaze (typical of the Mamlukian culture of 700 to 500 y BP) was found within a sample from the swamp sediments. These findings may indicate that, during Mamlukian times, this site was on land at or just above sea level and that afterward it tectonically subsided by slightly more than 12 m.

Off Tel Aviv, the uppermost erosional surface (UES in Fig. 20) slopes moderately to the west in correspondence with the bathymetric gradient. This pattern characterizes the littoral belt of the coastal segment between Caesarea and Tel Aviv. Across the littoral belt of Yafo, however, the relationship of the UES to the bathymetric gradient is somewhat different (Fig. 21). A flat horizontal and relatively strong seismic reflector, approximately separating Units 6 and 7, extends eastward from a submarine kurkar ridge cropping out at a depth of 30 to 40 m to near the coastal fault. The bathymetric gradient is similar to that across the littoral zone of the Tel Aviv—Caesarea segment. The pattern off Yafo is typical of all the southern segments as far as Gaza (Neev et al. 1976, fig. 11, profile 25.3; Bakler 1976, figs. 2b, 5b, profile I-I).

Off Yafo, the sedimentary apron above the horizontal seismic reflector to the sea floor consists of a low-energy gray sandy clay sequence that accumulated during the past 4000 years (Unit 7b). The average grain size at the eastern fringe of this apron, where its thickness is about 30 m, is appreciably coarser than farther westward. At the western periphery, the relatively thinner sedimentary sequence onlaps the submerged kurkar ridge composed of the early Holocene Calcarenitic Bank (Unit 5a). Locally, the UES can be traced as a moderately westward-sloping reflector beneath the horizontal seismic reflector (Fig. 21). Its elevation near the coastal fault probably is deeper than −30 m msl, whereas on land at the Yafo promontory it is higher than +40 m msl. Therefore, a

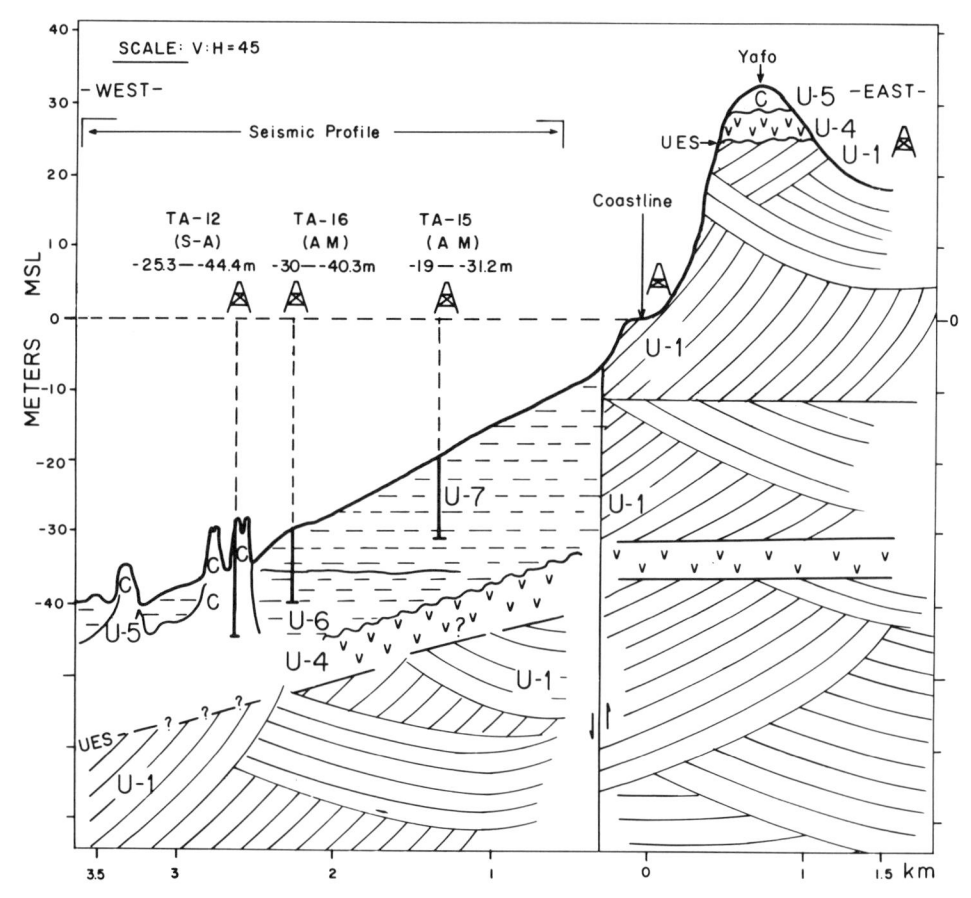

Figure 21. East-west geological cross-section through Yafo Harbor. Nearly horizontal dips were noted within Unit 7 and possibly also Unit 6 on all seismic profiles across the littoral zone south of Yafo. Radiocarbon ages of shells sampled to the bottom of both TA-16 and TA-15 drill holes are younger than 4000 years. Feeble westward dips are at somewhat greater depth along the UES.

displacement of more than 60 m is implied across the coastal fault zone at the Yafo promontory.

11. Transverse (East-West) Faults Across the Tel Aviv—Yafo Coast.

The UES is expressed as a shallow rather horizontal reflector in a coast-parallel Uniboom profile that follows the approximate 30-m isobath between Caesarea and Yafo (Hall 1976; Fig. 19). A unique anomalous feature is present near the southern end of this profile from off the Reading power station (the 2330 hrs time mark at the northern bank of the Yarkon River outlet) and southward along a stretch of about 1 km (Fig. 22). A sequence of strata that is truncated by the UES there is abruptly downwarped and tilted to the south. At the southern periphery of this tilted block (at the 2340 hrs time mark), the strata appear to have been dragged downward even more. Farther south (to the 2345 hrs time mark), another 1-km-long southward-dipping block is present. A third tectonic block is recognized

64 Holocene Tectonic Histories

along a stretch of about 0.5 km (to the 2350 hrs time mark), where the sedimentary sequence between the UES and sea floor is tilted northward. From there to the southern end of the profile (the midnight time mark), the apparent orientation of the UES is horizontal again (although the true dip is to the west, as indicated on the transversely-trending seismic profile and geological cross-section—Fig. 21). The existence of three transverse faults across this coast-parallel seismic profile is interpreted (Figs. 19, 22) as indicating that the downthrown side across the southern fault is on its north, whereas across the two others it is on their south. The patterns of tilt, truncation, and bending taken together suggest a north-south compressional mechanism where the southern flank is overriding and even overthrusting the northern one. The northern fault may extend eastward along the trend of the Yarkon River, in agreement with the idea that the Yarkon basin is a tectonically disturbed area more or less perpendicular to the coastal fault (Ritter-Kaplan 1979).

Still another transverse (WNW-trending) fault, the Yafo—Lod (Ramleh) line (Fig. 19), is implied by: (i) the abrupt northward terminations of the coast-parallel kurkar ridges both on land (the coastal ridge) and in the offshore area. This termination occurs along a west-northwest trending line just north of the Yafo promontory; (ii) the east-southeast alignment of the Ayalon River between Yafo and Lod (Fig. 19). This trend is interpreted by Kallner-Amiran (1950–51, 58, figs. 2, 3) based also on the concept of Sieberg (1932) as an "axis of major seismic intensity extended NW-SE from Jaffa through Ramleh to Jerusalem." Sieberg further suggested the existence of a minor epicenter at the junction of the Yafo—Ramleh line with the coastal fault line. "The inferred line explains the

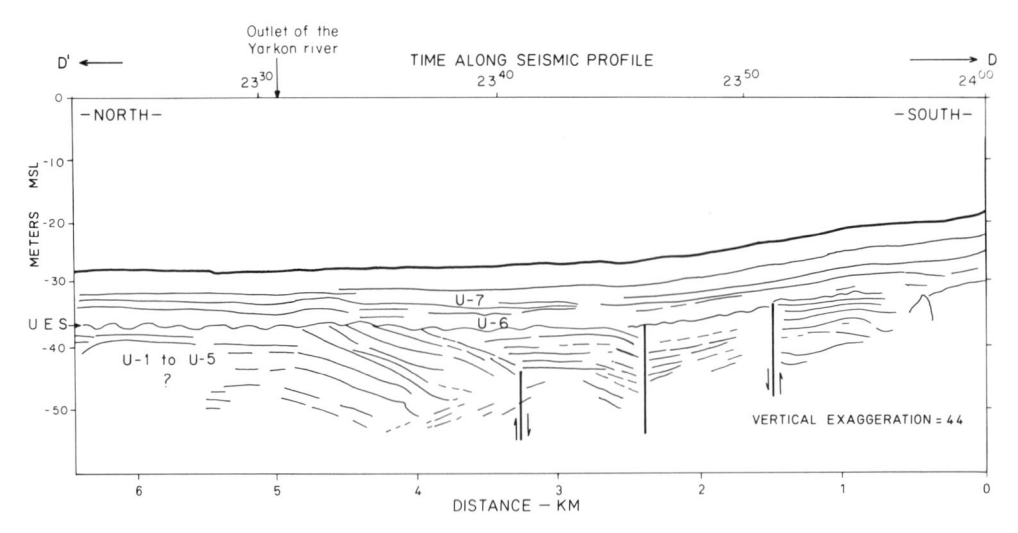

Figure 22. Geological cross section hand drawn from a coast-parallel seismic (Uniboom) profile off Tel Aviv. Three transverse faults off Tel Aviv (between the Yarkon River and Yafo) are suggested. The last phase of activity across these faults was during late Pleistocene (pre-Unit 7 and perhaps also pre-UES). Apparently, the southern block suppressed and overthrust the northern ones. The Yafo—Lod (Ramleh) transverse fault (which is beyond this figure; see Figure 19) is the southernmost (and main?) element within this disturbed zone. The time marks along the top of the figure also are indicated along the D'-D profile in Figure 19.

origin of the coastal bend at Jaffa, an outstanding singularity of the coast of Israel" (Kallner-Amiran 1950–51, 60). Physiographic indicators in the Yafo area suggest that the downthrown side of this fault is on its north. In the same area, Klang and Gvirtzman (1983, fig. 1, based on seismic correlations of Triassic, Jurassic, and mid-Cretaceous reflectors) show the existence of segmented west-northwest to east-west trending faults that extend both onshore and offshore. Nevertheless, the downthrown side of the faults within this area is mostly to the south. Klang and Gvirtzman also marked the existence at depth of three other transverse faults in the offshore farther north of the Yafo fault. These faults may correspond with the three late Pleistocene faults between the Yarkon River Fault and the Yafo Fault (see our Figs. 19, 22). They relate the following affinities to the transverse faults of that region: (i) The faults are clustered in elongate assemblages that are 15 to 70 km long and consist of short and small individual faults that together form a major shear belt. (ii) The downthrown sides along these faults vary and in some instances it is not clear which side is up thrown. Only a discontinuity or a disturbance in the regularity of the reflecting horizon that can be traced long distances indicates the presence of these faults. Although Klang and Gvirtzman (1983, 16) considered that these transverse faults are Miocene in age (22–5 my), they believed that slow motion could have continued along them even later, probably affecting subrecent tectonic features. The existence of a belt of late Pleistocene transverse faults is corroborated, but we found no indication in the late Pleistocene and younger sequence to support Klang and Gvirtzman's concept of recurrence of a 6 to 7 km sinistral shift along the Yarkon Shear Zone.

D. Southern Coastal Segment (Yafo to Rafiah)

1. Yavneh Yam (N31°55'20" E34°41'35"). Two Roman to Byzantine floors crop out a few meters above msl along a coast-parallel low escarpment at the coastline about 300 m north-northeast of the Yavneh Yam promontory (Figs. 1, 23). Apparently, both floors were used as wine presses, as suggested by two in situ fluid collectors (jars) fixed at their centers so that fluids could flow across the floors toward them (E. Ayalon 1981). The northern part of the lower floor, which is about 2 m above msl, appears to have been slightly tilted to the east, in accordance with the dip of the underlying abraded surface of the kurkar. A layer about 80 cm thick of coarsely bedded rubble composed of kurkar, sand, and pottery sherds separates the lower floor from the upper one. However, a 20- to 5-cm shell bed overlain by a few cm of dark brown (swamp) clay covers the rubble layer just beneath the upper floor. This shell bed is thickest at the south end of the 10-m long outcrop, where it contains three separate horizons. These horizons gradually thin and wedge out northward where the remaining single thin shell bed is patchy. The shells are dominantly concave downward, closely packed, and imbricated (nestling textures). These features indicate that the shell bed was deposited in a natural marine (beach) environment (see Unit 7 d i above). This conclusion disagrees with that of Arad and Wachs (1976) who considered the same shell bed to be "obviously man made . . . that was used as the foundation of a building" (their p. 1 and fig. 1). They based their conclusion on

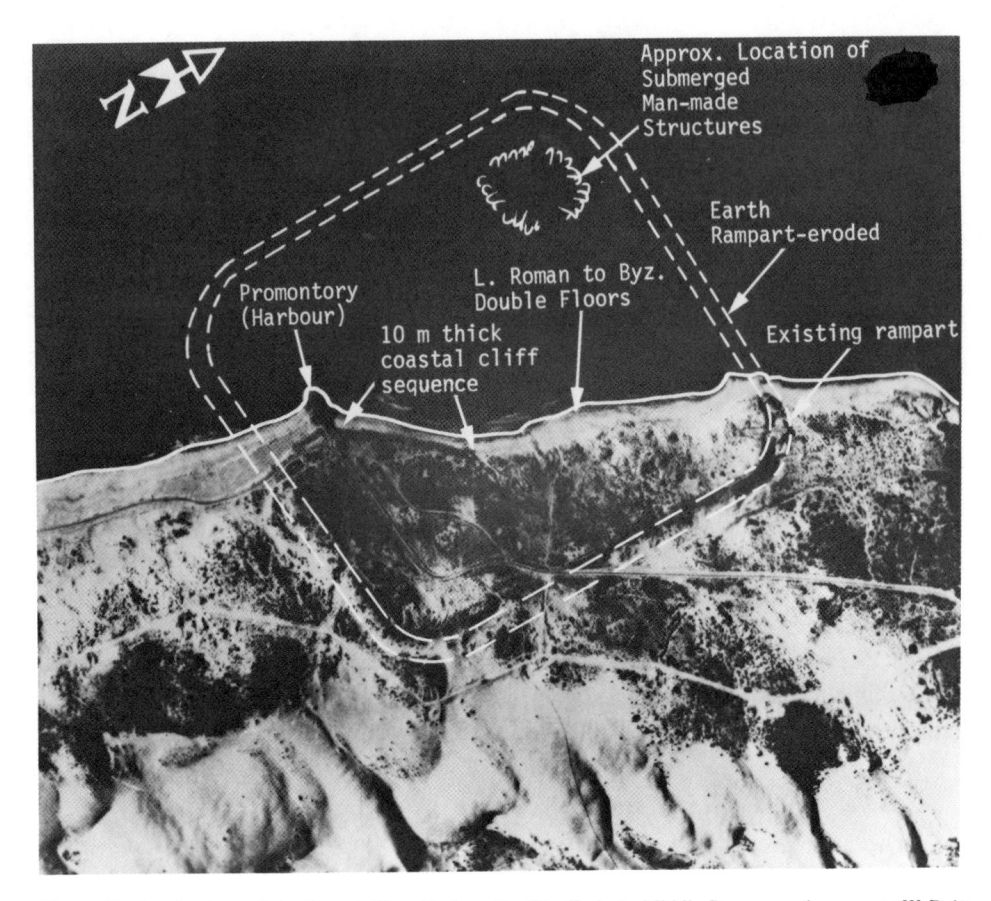

Figure 23. An air photo of the Yavneh Yam Harbor site. The Early to Middle Bronze earth rampart (III D 1) forms a square enclosed fortified structure. The now abraded offshore part of that wall is redrawn, (modified from Kaplan, 1978). This structure was catastrophically destroyed and abandoned during the same tectonic phase of Santorini, Tel Michal (III C 7), and Tel Haraz (III D 2)

the opinion of Ronen (1980, 168, table 2), who wrote that "the valves in these artificial structures must have been deliberately turned over [to a concave downward position—authors], more carefully in the latter [Yavneh Yam—authors] than in the former locality [Tel Shiqmona—authors]." Based on our conclusions that this shell bed was naturally deposited, we infer that this site was subjected to at least a 4-m oscillatory (down-and-up) tectonic movement prior to building of the upper floor, sometime during the Byzantine period. Results of excavations made at a nearby site (about 200 m southeast of these floors) suggested that a cultural break occurred between the Hellenistic (and perhaps even the Roman) period and the fifth Century AD (Vitto 1984).

An up-to-10-m sedimentary sequence in which pottery sherds are abundantly scattered is exposed along the coastal cliff from the Yavneh Yam promontory to about 100 m farther northward (Fig. 23). These sediments appear to have an aquatic origin, as suggested by their cyclic, graded, and regularly (horizontal and long) bedded nature; the presence within them of long lenticular gray-brown clay layers; the presence of dirty sand layers and lenses some of which exhibit graded and flaser bedding similar to those in Figure 12; and the presence of shell lenses in which the shells are imbricated (nestling textures) and are dominantly concave downward. Textures and orientations of the shells within these lenses look exactly like those underlying the Late Byzantine floor but are not associated directly with any man-made structure. We suggest that this 10-m sedimentary sequence was deposited in a restricted marine (beach) environment. Although the Yavneh Yam area is known to have been occupied intermittently between Early Bronze and Medieval times, it was hitherto not thoroughly investigated archaeologically (R. Gophna, personal communication). The implied marine environment of deposition indicates that the area east of the promontory was tectonically uplifted during late Holocene and that the latest occupation of the promontory itself was during Crusader time. An indication that this site is being uplifted tectonically even at present was found by Tzur and Safriel (1978), who studied the environmental factors that limit the development of *Vermetus* encrustation at the rims of fringing reefs (the abraded terraces atop the kurkar ridge) in Israel. The only sites along the coastline of Israel where this reef is barren of the *Vermetus* crust are at Yavneh Yam and, according to A. Raban (personal communication), at Ashqelon. Absence may be because present uplift there is too rapid for the vermetids to keep pace. Possibly, the rebound of the upthrown block had not yet reached its level prior to the latest tectonic event.

The remains of a square enclosure formed by artificial earth ramparts were excavated and studied by Kaplan (1978) at Yavneh Yam (Fig. 23). This rampart-enclosed structure, the areal extent of which is 800 m × 800 m, was built during Middle Bronze II (about 4000 y BP) and was maintained until the beginning of Late Bronze I (about 3500 y BP). More than half of this enclosure has been eroded by marine abrasion (Kaplan 1978). Such a constructive-destructive history is analagous to that of the first phase of settlement within the Tel Michal site (see III C 7, and Fig. 17). Both sites could have been destroyed by the same tectonic movement along the coastline of Israel at the time of the eruption of Santorini about 3500 y BP.

Submerged features that appear to be man-made exist on the sea floor in water depths of about 10 m just off the Yavne Yam site (Z. Ben-Avraham, personal communication). Such massive features that survived marine erosion could be structures of Bronze or younger age.

2. Tel Haraz (N31°52'35" E34°40'25"). Various sedimentological, mineralogical, and geochemical criteria applied in the study of the Tel Haraz sequence (see II B Unit 7c) suggest that the coastal zone of that site was subjected to an oscillatory tectonic movement sometime during about 3500 y BP. Consequently, the two kurkar coastal ridges (Fig. 24) were downwarped about 30 m, submerged, and then emerged in a rebound-like movement to about their present postitions. The importance of the Tel Haraz findings is in the use of different criteria for determining environments of deposition of its sedimentary sequence, as compared with most other sites discussed in this article.

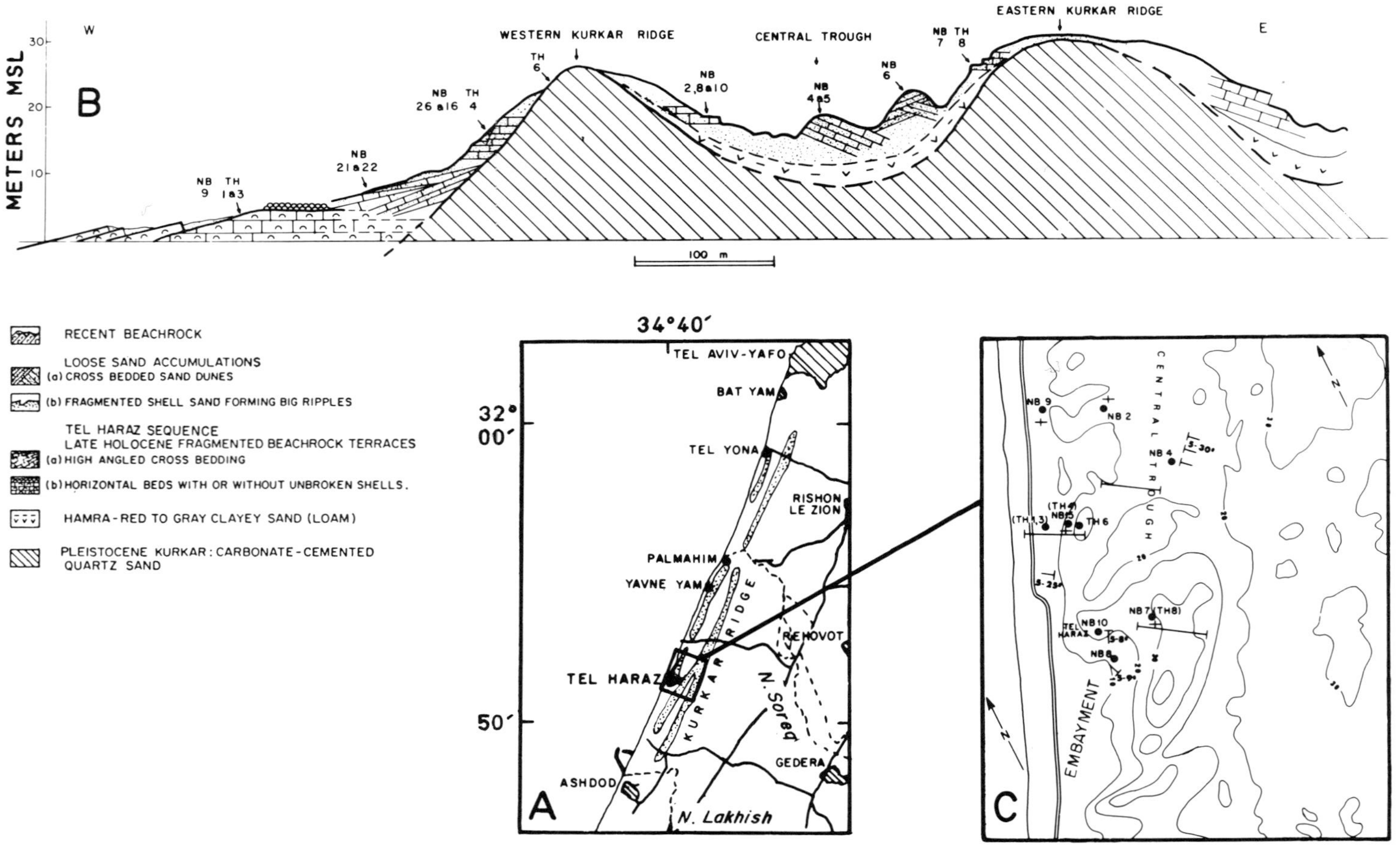

METERS MSL
30
20
10
W
B
NB TH
9 1a3
NB
21a22
NB TH
26a16 4
TH
6
WESTERN KURKAR RIDGE
NB
2,8a10
CENTRAL TROUGH
NB
4a5
NB
6
NB TH
7 8
EASTERN KURKAR RIDGE
E
100 m
RECENT BEACHROCK
LOOSE SAND ACCUMULATIONS
(a) CROSS BEDDED SAND DUNES
(b) FRAGMENTED SHELL SAND FORMING BIG RIPPLES
TEL HARAZ SEQUENCE
LATE HOLOCENE FRAGMENTED BEACHROCK TERRACES
(a) HIGH ANGLED CROSS BEDDING
(b) HORIZONTAL BEDS WITH OR WITHOUT UNBROKEN SHELLS.
HAMRA - RED TO GRAY CLAYEY SAND (LOAM)
PLEISTOCENE KURKAR: CARBONATE-CEMENTED QUARTZ SAND
34°40′
32° 00′
50′
TEL AVIV-YAFO
BAT YAM
TEL YONA
RISHON LE ZION
PALMAHIM
YAVNE YAM
KURKAR RIDGE
REHOVOT
TEL HARAZ
N. Soreq
GEDERA
ASHDOD
N. Lakhish
A
CENTRAL TROUGH
NB 9
NB 2
NB 4
(TH4)
(TH1,3) NB13
TH 6
NB 7(TH8)
TEL HARAZ
NB10
NB8
EMBAYMENT
N
C

3. Ashdod——Ashqelon Area. Intensive oil exploration activity in the area of Ashdod—
—Ashqelon (both onshore and offshore) yielded a better stratigraphically controlled understanding of the geological history of this segment of the coast as compared with other segments. Yet the results of these studies emphasize the great complexity of the coastal zone along which repeated tectonic movements have occurred since at least the Triassic. Some highlights (Greenfield and Neev 1983; Greenfield 1984; Neev and Greenfield 1984) are summarized below, because they are relevant also to the geological histories of other coastal segments:

(i) The top Jurassic reflector in the Ashdod 1 Well is at a time-depth of about 2.1 sec (equivalent to about 2500 m) but occurs at a distance of 12 to 14 km off the coastline at a depth of more than 4.5 sec (near 7 km). Moreover, the Late Jurassic sequence (Tithonian—Kimmeridgian) that is missing at Ashdod 1 Well was found offshore beyond 12–14 km (based on the analyses of seismic profiles that were tied to the Delta and Til offshore wells). The presumed 4.5 km difference in structural elevations between these two points represents a westward gradient of more than 20 degrees.

(ii) The well-known peneplain-like top Jurassic unconformable surface on land was traced westward in most of the offshore seismic profiles to a distance of 12–14 km offshore (Fig. 25). The integrated shape of this limit forms a rather linear coast-parallel line that probably is the top of Jurassic base level (JBL). The unconformable peneplain-like surfce east of it, when abraded by the sea of that time, must have been nearly horizontal. The more than 20-degrees westward gradient, therefore, must have been formed by a later westward tectonic tilt, much of which occurred sometime between the end of Jurassic peneplanation and the end of Early Cretaceous.

(iii) The JBL is considered to be a tectonic feature, perhaps an ancient left-lateral shear that subparallels both the coast of Israel and the Pelusium Line (Neev 1975). It is associated with compressional features throughout its entire length and width: four large anticlines having a pronounced asymmetry to the southeast (and even thrusting at depth) are en echelon to it on its east between points off northwestern Sinai and off Palmahim (Greenfield 1984; Neev and Greenfield 1984). The most intensive folding phase across these four structures occurred during Triassic—Jurassic. During Early Cretaceous, the belt along the JBL subsided to become a coast-parallel trough and a depocenter. Asymmetric folding was rejuvenated during Late Cretaceous. The position of the new folding axis exactly corresponds with the axes of the older folds.

(iv) The post-Jurassic large-scale westward tilt was associated with several coast-parallel faults, both off shore along the littoral zone (the belt between the JBL and the coastline) and on shore along the coastal plain (Greenfield and Bino 1974). Figure 26 describes the fault pattern that was detected across the Top Jurassic unconformable surface (after Greenfield and Neev 1983). It also traces several coast-parallel photolineaments (after

◁——————————————————————————————————

Figure 24. The Tel Haraz east-west geological cross section (Figure 24B) from the coastline eastward through the first and second kurkar ridges; the cross-section consists of segments shown in Figure 24C, which is an enlargement of part of the area on Figure 24A, from Bakler et al. (1985, fig. 1). The approximately 3500-year-old Tel Haraz marine sedimentary sequence transgressively onlaps both ridges, thereby indicating a more than 30-m oscillatory tectonic movement perhaps associated with the Santorini volcanic eruption. By permission of Earth and Planetary Science Letters, Amsterdam.

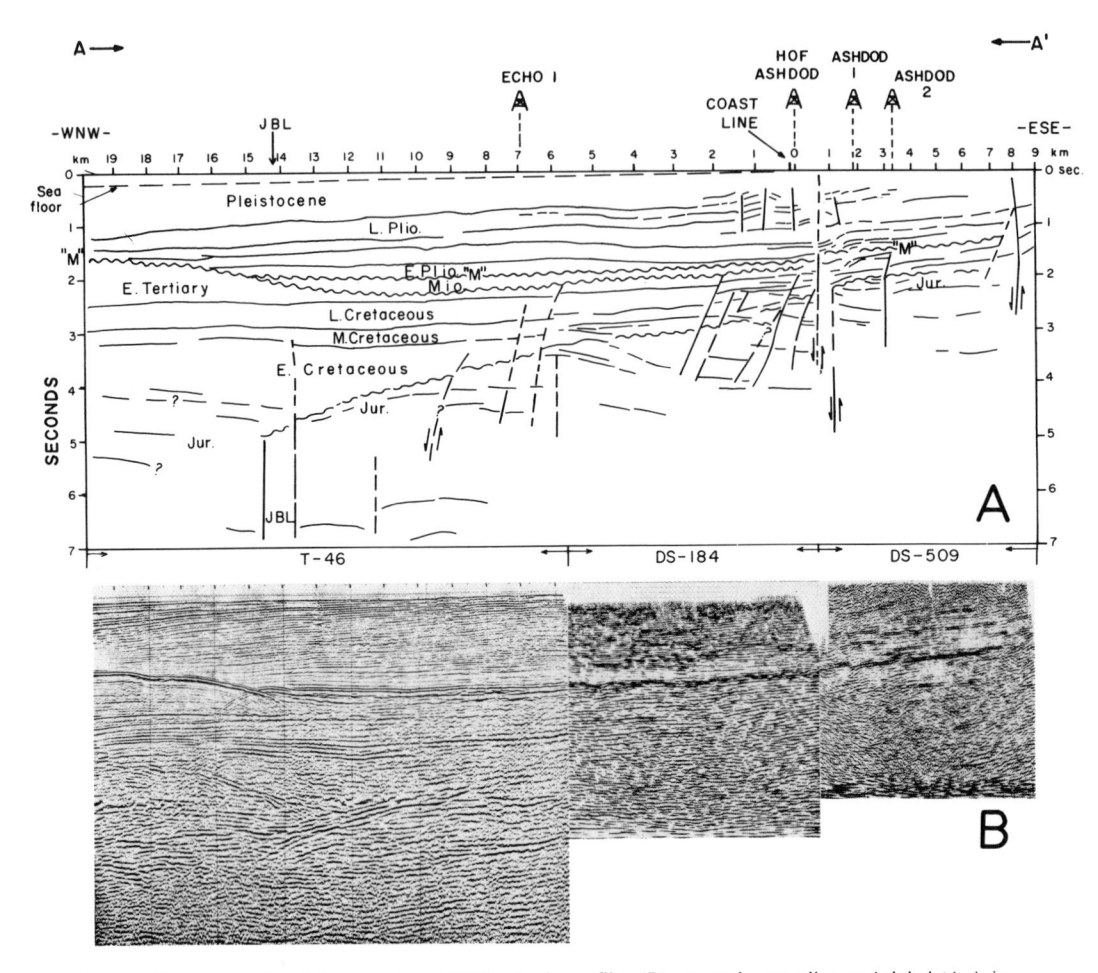

Figure 25. A composite of three west-east CDP seismic profiles (*B*) across the coastline at Ashdod (A-A in Figure 26). (*A*)—an accompanying geologic hand-drawn (uncorrected to depth values) cross-section. The most important features are: (i) the coastal fault zone that was rejuvenated recently, (ii) the western limits of the top Jurassic peneplaned surface, indicating that the base level of that time was about 14 km west of the present coastline, where (iii) an important coast-parallel tectonic element (shear?) named JBL corresponds with this top Jurassic base level (*A* is modified from and *B* is from Neev and Greenfield 1984).

Bartov et al. 1977) as well as a small segment of a post-Tyrrhenian (younger than 100,000 y BP) coast-parallel fault that was detected at the Nizzanim area by detailed stratigraphic analysis within the kurkar sequence (Parchamovsky 1981). The position of this fault corresponds rather well with that of a photolineament mapped at the same site and also with a coast-parallel topographic trough east of the second kurkar ridge (about 2 km east of the coastline). The vertical displacement across this fault is 27 m at the Pliocene—Pleistocene contact (the Top Saqiye), 14 m in the middle of the Kurkar Complex, and fades out towards the top of this unit.

Another coast-parallel fault probably exists between the Ashdod No. 1 and the Hof Ashdod wells (Fig. 25), a few hundred meters east of the coastline, where the "M"

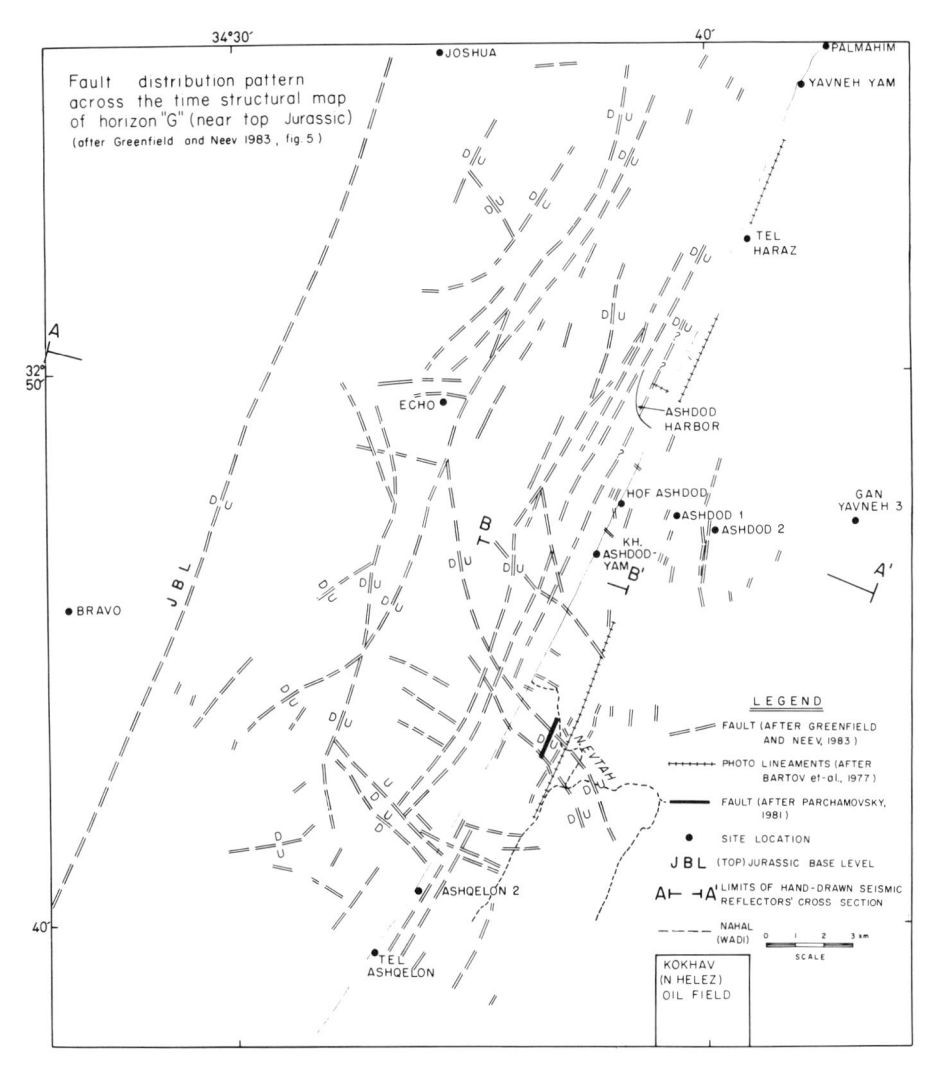

Figure 26. Map of tectonic elements across the Palmahim Ashdod—Ashqelon area. Offshore ones were mapped on the G reflector (near top Jurassic).

Horizon (the Messinian unconformity) is displaced by about 100 m. Rock salt was found within the Mavki'im (Messinian) Formation at the Hof Ashdod well (at the coastline), whereas it is absent at the Ashdod No. 1 well about 2 km farther eastward. The top of Jurassic there is at a depth of about 2900 m, or about 400 m deeper than at Ashdod No. 1. Steepness of the dips measured by a dip-meter survey in the Hof Ashdod well (Shomrony 1983) gradually increases from about 15 degrees southward at a depth of 2700 m to more than 40 degrees southeastward between depths of 2780 and 2830 m. Dips decrease appreciably again to the bottom of the hole. Such a pattern suggests continued movements along a coast-parallel fault plane through which this well penetrated.

Post-Roman faulting activity across the present coastline is indicated at Ashdod Harbor by the presence of a 4100 ± 380 year old peat layer at a depth of 2 m (msl) within the P–2 drill hole just east of the coastline. Another analysis yielded an age of 1940 ± 420 y BP for cuttings from a peat layer sampled at a depth of about 18 m below msl in a water depth of 5 m in a drill hole within the harbor (Fig. 27) a few hundred meters west of the coastline (N31°40′45″ E34°38′30″). These peat fragments were within a fine-grained beach-sand layer that directly overlies the Kurkar sequence (Unit 1 or 3), but they were absent higher in the sequence. Irregular dips of seismic reflectors were noted within the Pliocene—Pleistocene sequence near the coastline in Figure 25.

A summary of the offshore-onshore Holocene structural-stratigraphic relationships in the Ashdod—Ashqelon area is illustrated by a hand-drawn profile (Fig. 27) that is based on shallow-penetration seismic profiles, shallow drill holes, archaeological excavations, and surface mapping. It is an east-west geological cross section (Fig. 27; Neev et al. 1968) that crosses the ruins (khirbat) of Ashdod Yam (N31°46′50″ E34°37′15″) and a series of coast-parallel faults as well as a 30- to 40-m sequence of post-UES sediments

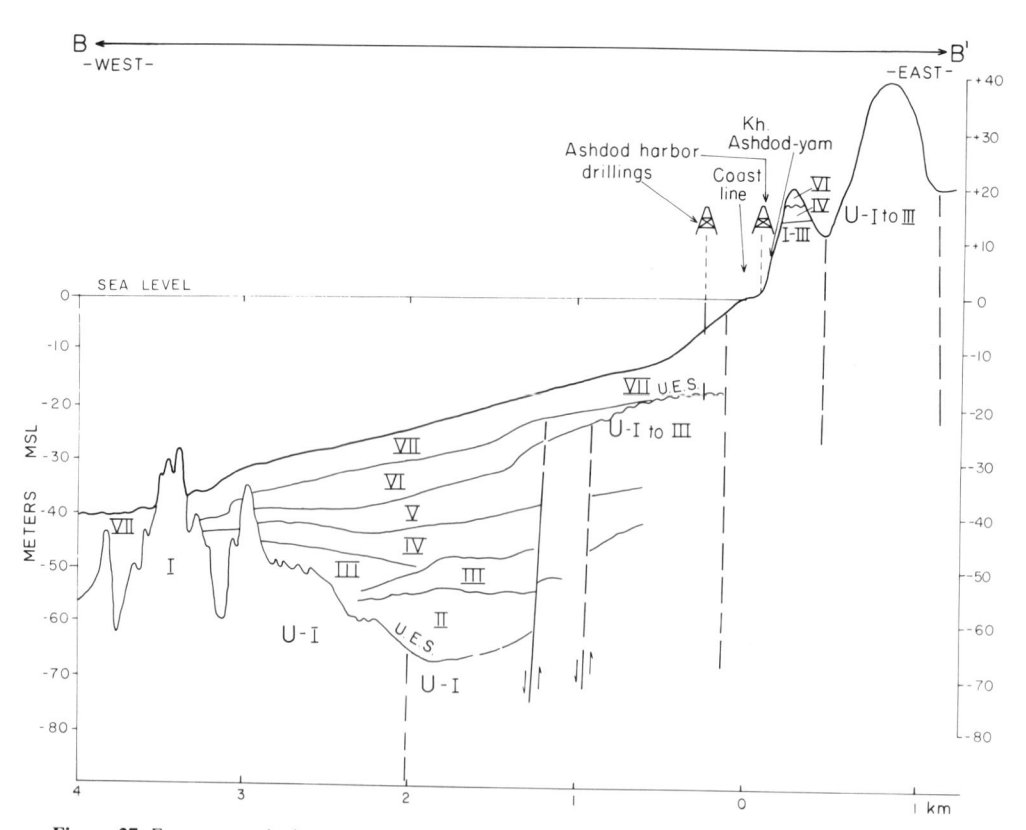

Figure 27. East-west geologic cross section across Ashdod Yam (Kh—ruins of the ancient site). Based upon shallow seismic profiles and drill holes made offshore as well as surface mapping and archaeological stratigraphic data on land and extrapolated to offshore. Note the eastward dips across the eastern flank of the offshore kurkar ridge which were preserved despite the westward tilt. Roman numbers = stratigraphic units (Chapter II B).

(overlying the uppermost erosional surface that formed during latest Pleistocene). The different reflectors represent the time-stratigraphic Units 2 to 7 that presumably exist along the axis of this coast-parallel trough. These units wedge out gradually to the west, toward the first offshore kurkar ridge, but they terminate rather abruptly eastward probably because of a post-Unit 5 (Post-Chalcolithic) faulting phase. This conclusion is based on the assumption that the late Neolithic (about 7000-year old) dark brown clay layer (aquatic environment) that is onshore at Nahal Evtah (at about +10 m, N31°44'20" E 34°36'15", see Fig. 27; II Unit 5d; and Yeivin and Olami 1979) was deposited from the same freshwater body that filled the nearby offshore trough. The present elevation of the offshore equivalent of the swamp deposits of Unit 5 is expected at about -40 m. Another perhaps similar tectonic phase could have occurred even earlier between Units 4 and 5 (between Epipaleolithic and Neolithic times—about 10,000 years ago). This possibility stems from the fact that the top of Unit 4 on both banks of Nahal Evtah underwent erosion and channeling prior to deposition of Unit 5 (Yeivin and Olami 1979, fig. 4), whereas, in the seismic profile across the nearby offshore basin, this contact appears to be conformable and smooth.

Another set of five coast-perpendicular shallow-penetration seismic profiles was made 15 to 20 km southwest of Khirbet Ashdod Yam, at Zikim, along the terminal segment of the Elat—Ashqelon oil pipeline. One of them (Profile D) is presented in Figure 28 (From N31°39'22" E34°30'05" to N31°38'25" E34°31'20"). In both Ashdod and Zikim profiles, the structural-stratigraphic pattern across the littoral belt (from the coastline to bathymetric contour of about 25 m) is similar to that expressed in all other seismic profiles across the entire central coastal segment south of Yafo (Fig. 21) and differs from that which characterizes the central segment (north of Tel Aviv). Technically, the Zikim profile (Fig. 28) is unique, as it extended eastward into water depths as shallow as 3 m (Levy et al. 1968). At 5 to 7 m water depth the recent marine clayey sand layer (Unit 7) onlaps eastward the steep flank of a submerged kurkar ridge. This contact is interpreted as due to the fault plane.

Based on the above, it appears that this segment of the present coastline is tectonic in origin. Moreover, it belongs to a coast-parallel system of faults that occupies a belt between a few km inland and about 12 km offshore. According to Neev and Greenfield (1984), this conclusion applies also to the rest of the coast of Israel from at least Mount Carmel to northwestern Sinai.

4. Ashqelon (N31°39'50" E34°32'40"). Tel Ashqelon was intermittently inhabited since Neolithic times. In 1270 AD it "was finally destroyed by the Mamluk Sultan Beibars, never to rise again" (Avi-Yonah and Ephal, in Avi-Yonah and Stern 1976). In fact, it was inhabited until 1948 by a small Arab village, El Jora. The deliberate nature of the Mamlukian destructive operation, which also applied to most other coastal settlements along the Syrian—Palestinian coastline, is well documented (Ayalon 1964). This policy was initiated by Salah ad Din al Ayoubi in the twelfth century AD and was maintained until 1322 AD in order to hinder a new crusade. Many of the destroyed coastal cities were revived and reconstructed a few hundred years later. At that time, the most heavily

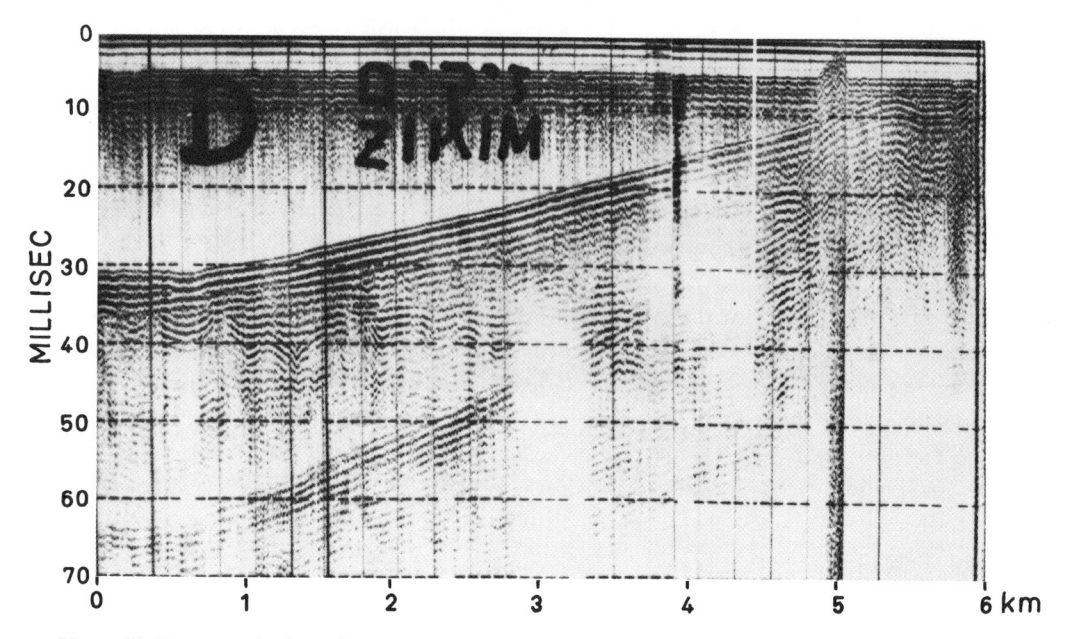

Figure 28. East-west seismic profile off the Zikim Oil Pipeline Terminal (17 km south of Ashdod Yam). Note (i) westward and eastward slopes across the buried kurkar ridge (at a depth of about 45 msec), and (ii) reflections and side reflection from nearly vertical western limit of a submerged coastal kurkar ridge (at depths of 10 to 23 msec), probably indicating the coast-parallel fault.

destroyed segment of this eastern Mediterranean coastline was between Sidon and El Arish. Nevertheless, our findings suggest that desertion of the coastal sites was not only because of human activities but because of natural events as well. This conclusion is supported by the sedimentary cover on the entire area of Tel Ashqelon. A good example is the fill within a medieval structure at Tel Ashqelon that involved natural aquatic (marine) depositional processes (see II B Unit 7d i and ii; Figs. 11A, C, D and 12). As this fill now is at an elevation of about 10+ m msl, the entire site must have been subjected to an oscillatory vertical tectonic movement sometime after its destruction in 1270 AD. Perhaps desertion of the coastal zone by the local population after the man-made Mamlukian destruction could explain at least partly the fact that the tectonic event which followed was not reported by contemporary goegraphers and historians.

Another naturally deposited shell bed more than 1 m thick of the same age was reported by Neev et al. (1973) to be a few hundred meters farther north-northeast along the coastline at an elevation of +12 to +13 m msl (N31°40′12″ E34°32′58″). This terrace was excavated and the archaeological as well as sedimentological aspects of its origin were reexamined thoroughly by Ronen (1980) and Ronen and Zemer (1981). Our comments on their analyses and conclusions were discussed earlier (II B Unit 7d i and ii). The following remarks refer to points of disagreement that relate directly to this specific terrace: (i) The age of the shell bed: pottery sherds of medieval age, although very few, were among sherds that are imbricated within this shell bed and were identified twice and independently by experienced archaeologists (M. Dothan and R. Gophna, personal communications). It is possible that these younger sherds were so scarce that they were overlooked during the analysis made by Ronen and Zemer (1981). It could happen, however, that a mistake was made by the other two archaeologists, as the edges of most sherds were rounded by wave abrasion. In such an event, this shell bed could have been deposited during the Byzantine tectonic phase and not during the Mamlukian one.

(ii) Two amphorae were found by Ronen (1980) at the lower part of the 1.10 m shell layer A, in a mouth-to-mouth position and in a coast-perpendicular orientation. If such cylindrical-shaped vessels were carried by waves and currents along a westward sloping beach, the chances that they would become stabilized and covered by sediments perhaps are better when they are oriented coast-perpendicular than coast-parallel. In fact, we found a coast-perpendicular oriented Persian jar of similar configuration that is well cemented within a beachrock layer at the coastline of Atlit (Neev and Bakler 1978). Therefore, we are doubtful about Ronen's statement (1980, 166), "it is impossible that the waves could have laid them [the jars—authors] in the position in which they were found [coast perpendicular—authors]."

(iii) The underlying layer C (1.50 m beneath the top of the terrace) that consists of angular pottery sherds resembles a mosaic pattern and, therefore, is considered by the above authors to be an artificial pavement. Our observations indicate, however, that parts of large vessels, when broken to smaller sherds under the load of overlying sediments or another kind of a pressure, form similar patterns.

(iv) Although we sought a rationale to explain the investment of such a large effort involved with piling up of this artificial shell accumulation at that place (rather than an origin by natural deposition), we did not find one.

Based on these observations, we suggest that the coastal cliff of Ashqelon was subjected to an oscillatory type of tectonic movement during the past. This could have occurred once (sometime during the medieval period) or twice (also during Byzantine times). It is possible that the upward rebound movement of the continental block at the Ashqelon site has not yet reached its pre-movement elevation (the one prior to its being downwarped and submerged during Mamlukian time). This possibility is based on the fact that the bottom of the fortified western Crusader wall is still beneath present sea level.

5. *Gaza Area*. Gaza (approx. N31°30′ E34°28′) was inhabited at least since the Late Bronze (1469 BC; Ovadiah 1976), and it functioned since then (although interruptedly) as an important administrative center. It is on the older inland (Neev and Friedman 1978) coastal route, about 3 km east of the present coastline. In this respect, its history is analogous to that of Tel Ashdod, which also is remote from the coastline (about 4 km inland). Some leads for inferring the history of alternating constructive and destructive cultural stages in the Gaza—Ashdod area during the Chalcolithic to Roman interval can be deduced from brief descriptions of archaeological excavations made by Kenyon (1979). These include Tel Ajjul at the mouth of Nahal Besor or Wadi Gaza (10 km south of modern Gaza—see Fig. 30), Ashdod and Ashqelon. The descriptions may be divided into four stages.

(i) An almost uninterrupted succession of settlements is noted from Chalcolithic to Late

Bronze time. The peak of this stage was reached during the Middle to early Late Bronze when the coastal belt of Israel was inhabited by the Hyksos (a Semitic-Asiatic nation that invaded and ruled northern Egypt during the 18th century BC—during Middle Bronze). (ii) A major event of destruction, apparently caused by natural processes because resettlement was by people of the same culture, terminated the Late Bronze II stage. This destructive event may correlate with the oscillatory tectonic phase at Tel Haraz, Yavneh Yam, and Tel Michal, as well as with the Santorini volcanic eruptions and the sequence of earthquakes that may have terminated the Minoan culture. (iii) The Philistines, or Sea Peoples, invaded this already culturally declined region during the twelfth century BC. Sometime during the Early or Middle Iron Age (twelfth to eighth century BC) Gaza had "a decadent period in the city's Philistine history, a period that seemed to the excavator [Phythian-Adams 1923] to have closed with a disaster and, at least on part of the site, to have ended with desolation and perhaps total abandonment" (Ovadiah 1976). This event could have been contemporaneous with the tectonic destruction at the coastal site of Deir el Balah (see below and Unit 7e,g). The biblical story of Samson and the collapse of the Philistine temple at Gaza (Judges 16:29–30) also may have been associated with these events. During the eighth and seventh centuries BC, this region twice was conquered and destroyed by the Assyrians and Babylonians. It gradually revived again during the Persian rule and reached another cultural peak during the Hellenistic to Roman interval.

During the Roman (or even Early Byzantine) period the city of Gaza extended westward to the seashore and was named Maritima Gaza-Constantia Maiumas Neapolis (Ovadiah 1976). Industrial installations (including dye works, a street, and a house, the age of which is late fourth or early fifth century AD) were excavated on the seashore of Gaza a few meters above msl and about 300 m south of the present harbor (N31°31'30" E34°25'40"). This complex was destroyed by fire and overlain by a 2.5 m layer of finely laminated silty sand. During the early sixth century AD, a synagogue was built atop this sandy layer, to be destroyed or abandoned shortly after the Arab conquest (early seventh century AD).

A naturally deposited thin lense of concave-downward oriented shells is interbedded within medium grain size clean sand (beach type) layer at an elevation of about +10 m a few hundred meters south-southeast of the synagogue. The seaward edge of this sand layer forms a terrace that curves inland, roughly following the +10 m topographic contour in the shape of an embayment. The estimated radiocarbon age is about 500 y BP, as deduced from the 97.2 ± 3.3 per cent modern carbon content of a few charcoal fragments imbricated within shells (A. Kaufman, personal communication).

It is implied from the above that the Gaza region underwent a destructive event that may have been tectonic in origin more than 3000 years ago. Later, the coastal cliff of that region records a succession of two oscillatory (down and up) movements: the first phase during the Early Byzantine period, and the second one in Late Mamlukian time (early fifth and fifteenth centuries AD).

6. *Deir el Balah.* (between N31°24'40" E34°19'10" and N31°25'05" E34°19'45"). The stratigraphic-environmental data for Units 7d(i,iv),7e,7g imply that the Deir el Balah Site underwent an oscillatory movement sometime during the Iron Age (Fig. 29). The magnitude of this movement is estimated to have been about 20 m, although possibly its downward part was somewhat smaller than the upward rebound.

The physiography of the coastal ridge segment between Tel Qatif and Nahal Besor (south of Gaza, Figs. 1 and 30) is similar to the Hof Hasharon segment between Tel Baruch and Nahal Poleg (south of Netanya, Fig. 1). Main points of similarity are the very narrow (less than 50 m) beaches and the active wave erosion at the foot of the coastal cliffs. The top of the cliff gradually rises from a few meters above msl at Tel Qatif to almost +25 m at Deir el Balah. Dark brown and tan loams of Unit 4e (Epipaleolithic) now fill steep valleys that had become entrenched during the latest glacial epoch, and they onlap the Kurkar strata of Units 1 or 3. This unit is overlain by a few-meter-thick sequence of tan and reddish brown loam layers. Epipaleolithic to Byzantine archaeological sites were identified within this sequence (Y. Gilad and E. Oren, personal communications), thereby indicating it to belong to Units 4 to 7 (Unit 5a, the Calcarenite Bank, is absent south of Yafo).

Relics at least five meters high of Iron Age mud-brick walls were found at two nearby sites atop the coastal cliff south of the Deir el Balah beach at elevations above +20 m msl (Figs. 29A and B—their coordinates are in the captions). These relics were exposed following piratical quarrying by local farmers of both the overlying loams and the mud-brick walls. Apparently, these two sites were part of an extensive Philistine settlement about 3000 years ago. Sediments (Unit 7) that onlap the walls cover the top of the coastal ridge and extend (and apparently also thicken) toward the trough at the east. Lateral facies changes are recognized within this sequence; fine-grained well-sorted to muddy sands onlap the mud-brick walls, whereas dark brown swamp loams and green-gray to reddish brown marls of evaporitic (lagoonal) origin occur elsewhere (see Unit 7e for more detailed description and discussion). Shell lenses 10 to 20 cm thick (mostly of *Glycymeris* sp.) that were naturally deposited in beach environments (see Unit 7d for criteria) are interbedded mostly within the swamp loams. Some lenses occur twice in an outcrop, being separated vertically by one or two meters of dark brown loam. An especially extensive accumulation of such shells is atop the cliff between the two sites. They form a layer to 20-cm thickness over an area of several hundred square meters, covering like a carpet a slightly eastward tilted terrace at an elevation of more than 20 m. It is worth mentioning here that the experienced geologist, L. Picard, (personal communication) considers that this outcrop provides especially convincing evidence for a natural marine (or beach) environment of shell deposition. The shell carpet resembles the one at the +2 m to +4 m terrace at Tel Haraz beach (Fig. 24) where there is no doubt about a natural mode of deposition.

Archaeological studies made at Tel Qatif (N31°23′45″ E34°18′12″ at the coastline 3 km southwest of the Deir el Balah Site) excavated a Persian site that probably functioned as a military stronghold along the Via Maris coastal route (E. Oren, personal communication). After being deserted, this site became covered by a few meters of reddish-brown well-bedded hamra-like sediment. We consider this type of sediment to have been deposited in a mudflat aquatic environment (see Unit 4a). At the crest of the tel remains

Figure 29. Mudbrick structures buried under marine sediments (for position, see Figure 30) *A.* 5-m high relicts of an Iron Age (early first millenium BC) mudbrick structure. The site is on the coastal cliff of Deir el Balah (N31°25′03″ E34°19′45″) at a present elevation of +23 m, (see II B Unit 7e, and III D 6). It is covered by shallow marine-related lagoonal sediments. An oscillatory movement of at least 20 m is suggested to have occurred during the Iron Age. *B.* Another mudbrick structure of the same age and dimensions as A. It is just a short distance (a few kilometers) south of A on the coastal cliff (at +20 m msl N31°24′40″ E34°19′10″). It is overlain by the same sequence in which evaporitic sediments as well as the shell lenses of II B Unit 7e are interbedded.

of tan to green-gray mud-brick walls are overlain by the reddish-brown well-bedded sediments that are rather horizontally oriented, but along the eastern slope they are tilted 4 to 5 degrees southeastward. Similar examples of southeastward-tilted strata (their strike parallels the coastline) occur elsewhere along the coastal cliff between the Deir el Balah site and Tel Qatif, as well as at Tel Baruch (III C 8). These dips mean that this segment of the coastal ridge had another (after the Iron Age one) oscillatory movement sometime after the Persian period. The event could have occurred either during the Byzantine or the Mamlukian tectonic phases. The southeastward tilt may be due to a higher or a more abrupt rebound part of the oscillatory movement (see also Neev et al. 1978a).

E. Coastal Segment of Northwestern Sinai

From a hydrological point of view the northeastern limit of the northwestern Sinai segment should be placed at Nahal Besor (Wadi Gaza) and not at Rafiah (Figs. 1 and 30). At present, the entire mountainous region southeast and south of that segment (south-central Negev to Sinai) drains into the Mediterranean Sea by just one river—Wadi El Arish. Formerly, at least four other rivers drained the same catchment area (Neev et al. 1982). Most changes of hydrological pattern were due to stream capture caused more by tectonics than climate change. Although most of this subject is beyond the scope of the present work, we describe and discuss the following items because they are related to recent tectonic activity along the coast.

1. Hydrological Pattern Between Nahal Besor (Wadi Gaza) and Wadi el Arish. (a) The drainage pattern of Wadi Silka (within the Deir el Balah area, Fig. 30) provides supporting evidence for both the tectonic nature of the coastal ridge there and for very recent movement along it. Wadi Silka exhibits a regmatic drainage pattern in which the kurkar ridges are being breached by transverse parts of the stream. Topographic relief at the main breaching site, about 5 km southeast of the Deir el Balah coastline, is 30 to 40 m in a distance of 1.5 km. Even the lower part of this wadi near Kefar Darom is relatively deeply (a few meters) incised into the now-elevated mudflat plain that fills the broad interridge trough. The erosional process continues within this segment of the wadi during occasional vigorous floods. Therefore, it is surprising that this wadi terminates rather abruptly a km inland from the coastline at an elevation of about +10 m. A recent tectonic uplift along the coastal ridge to its present elevation of about +20 m could explain this enigma.

(b) A more than 25-km long and rather narrow (about 1 km) linear topographic depression extends subparallel to the coastline along the inland boundary of the coastal ridge, between Sheikh Zuweid (N31°13′15″ E34°06′20″) and Bir Jaradi (N31°09′15″ E33°55′40″; Fig. 31). Six- to 15-m high recent sand dunes overlie a sequence of alternately bedded hamra-like clay sediments and eolian sands along the coastal ridge (II B Units 3 and 4). Elevations at the crest of the coastal ridge vary from +30 m to +50 m, whereas those along the trough of the adjacent depression vary from about +10 m in the west-southwestern segment to +20 m east-northeast of Sheikh Zuweid (to +40 m west of Rafiah at its east-northeasterly extreme).

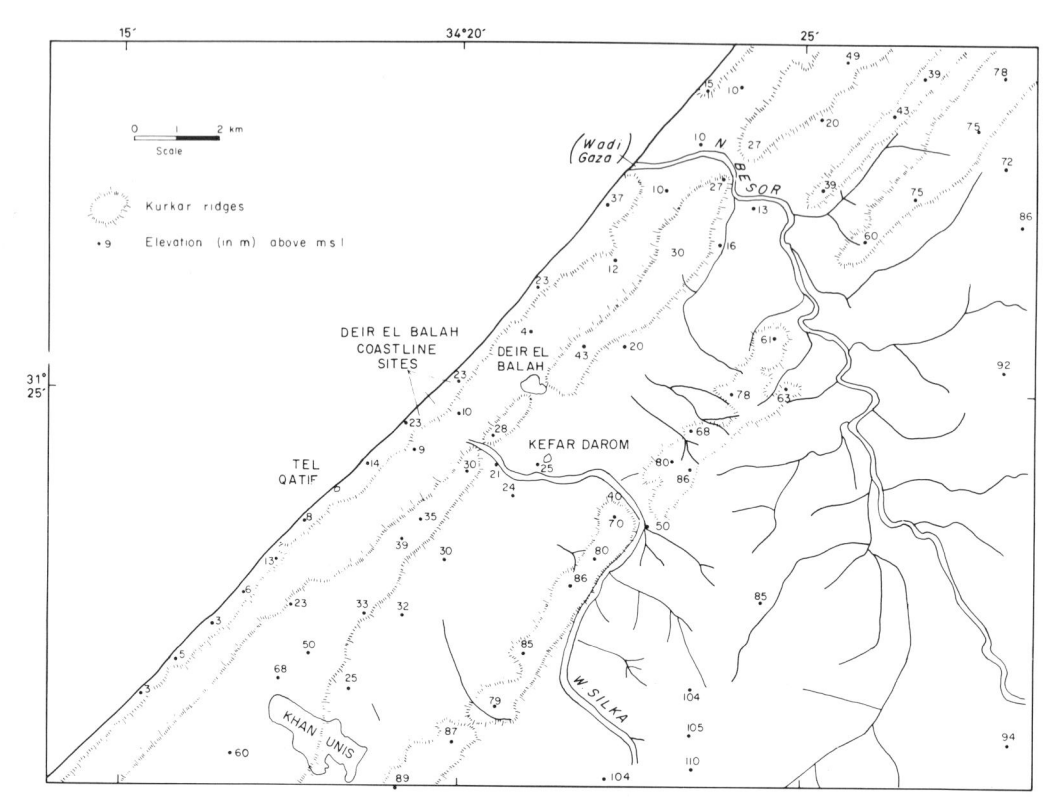

Figure 30. Drainage pattern (hydrographic map) and coast-parallel ridges (mostly kurkar) of the southern part of the southern coastal segment (III D 6). Wadi Silka, a dry wash that often flows torrentially during winters but dissipates within the trough between the coastal cliff and the first onshore kurkar ridge, probably because of the last (less than a few hundred years ago) upward rebound of the upthrown (eastern) side of the coastal fault. Originally, this wadi reached the sea through one of the saddles (now hanging valleys) in the coastal cliff.

A very shallow evaporitic water body occurs within the 3-km long Sabkhat e Sheikh (Sheikh Zuweid—Fig. 31) about to 2 km inland at an elevation of about +20 m. It must be hydraulically detached from the nearby sea. The existence of such a water body is not easily explained, because the seaward gradient of nearly 0.5 degree measured along the Pliocene—Pleistocene contact across the coastal plain of Israel (see Fig. 4A) apparently is present also across the coastal plain of northwestern Sinai (A. Issar, personal communication). A tectonic rise along the seaward rim of the coast-parallel topographic depression (Fig. 31) is required to explain the presence of the sabkha. Unfortunately, sufficiently detailed subsurface data to check this hypothesis are not available.

The tectonically active nature of the coastal segment between Sheikh Zuweid and El Arish is suggested on the basis of the following observations: (i) The pattern of the reflectors across the coastal zone within some of the coast-perpendicular shallow water seismic profiles in this segment (profile numbers DS, 178, 179, 180, 186—OEL property) appears to express a tectonic disturbance. (ii) A low seacliff (Emery and Kuhn 1982) is being abraded at present into the elevated terrace of hamra-like sediments. Date trees planted on the latter occasionally collapse and fall into the sea. (iii) The top of the hamra unit occurs at various elevations from +10 to -30 m (Fink 1969). Gentle dips in different directions (many to the southeast) were observed within the bedded hamra sequence that crops out at the coastline and farther inland (see also Unit 4d). Environment of deposition of the hamra was that of mudflats in hydraulic equilibrium with the nearby sea (see Unit 2c); therefore, these beds originally were nearly horizontal and flat.

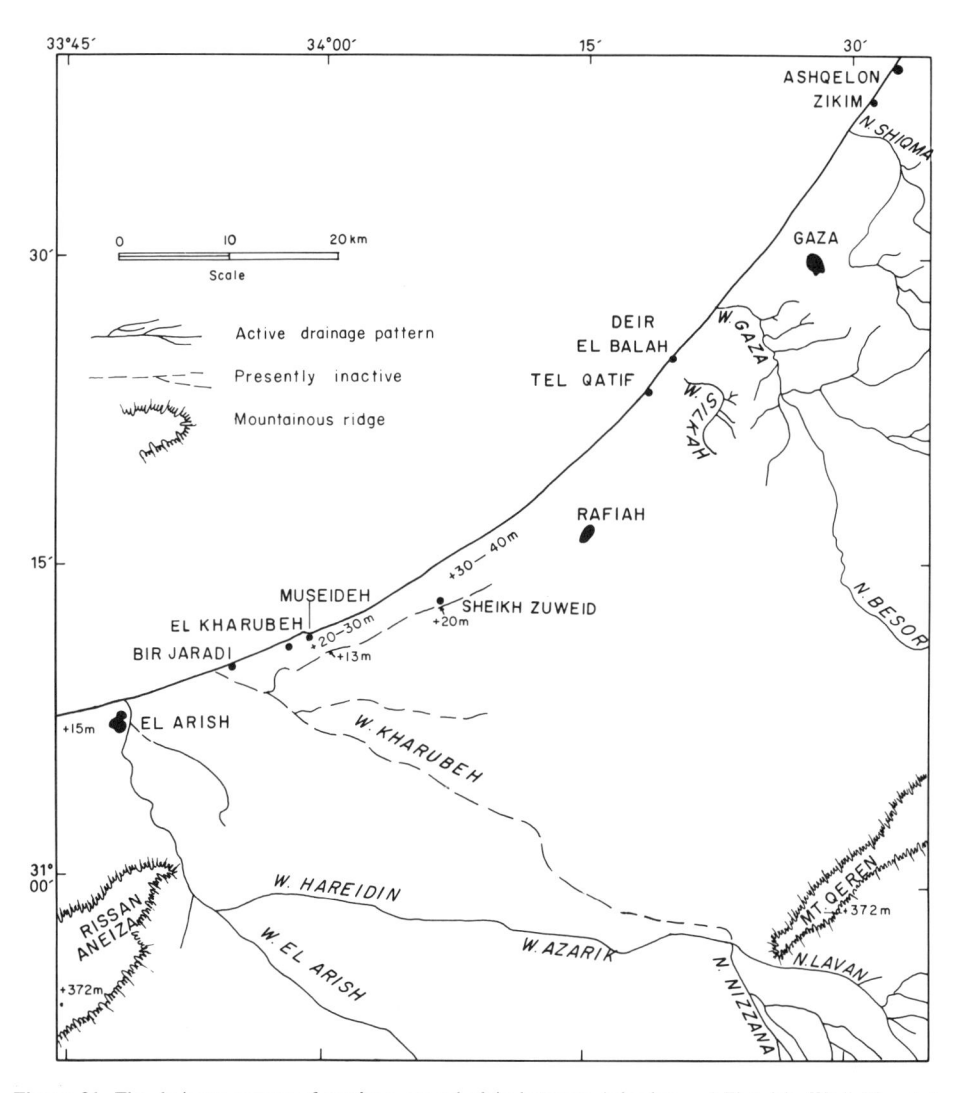

Figure 31. The drainage pattern of southern coastal plain between Ashqelon and El Arish. Wadi Kharubeh was captured into Wadi El Arish in Post-Byzantine times (sometime during the past 1500 years) by a rejuvenated uplift of the Mt. Qeren structure and possibly also by additional fracturing and subsidence along the transverse east-west trending belt of tectonic lineaments. This belt extends eastward from the Rissan Aneiza region along and parallel to the track of Wadi Hareidin-Azarik (see also Figure 32).

(c) Wadi Kharubeh abruptly terminates about one km inland from the coastline at El Jaradi (Fig. 31). This situation is rather similar to the terminaton of Wadi Silka (see above—a). Nevertheless, there is a basic difference between the two: at least until Byzantine time, the west-northwesterly trending Wadi Kharubeh drained a significant part of the mountainous central Negev area. Sometime afterward, it was captured at the junction of Nahal Lavan and Nahal Nizzana to flow westward and join Wadi el Arish at Bir Lahfan. Since then, Wadi Kharubeh has been abandoned (Dan 1977). Our additional observations indicate that the capture was due to a very recent uplift of Mount Qeren, whereby the southwestern periphery of its plunge was tilted to the south. The new track of the wadi (Wadi Azarik—Wadi Hareiden; Fig. 31) follows east-west tectonic lineaments along which linear dunes were superimposed (Neev et al. 1982). Moreover, even today at the crucial site of capture, the old abandoned channel is not being dammed by the dunes. We, therefore, disagree with Dan (1977), who considered the drifting dunes as the only factor responsible for capture.

Based on the arguments above (a and b), the abrupt termination of Wadi Kharubeh a short distance before reaching the coastline must be due to recent uplift of the coastal ridge.

2. Post-Pleistocene Tectonic Rise of Coastal Segment Between Tel Qatif and El Meidan.
Hamra-like sediments rather than dune sands (kurkar) appear to have been the dominant facies within the Middle Paleolithic to Late Neolithic coastal sequence between Tel Qatif and Al Kharubeh (see II B Units 2c, 4d, and 5d). Although actual close association of these aquatic sediments with the nearby sea level is indicated just once (during the Middle Paleolithic Unit 2c), it is probable that all of these mudflats were in hydraulic equilibrium with the sea. Therefore, their elevation when deposited during the low stand of sea level of the past glaciation was more than 100 m below present sea level. Their present elevation of about +20 m msl indicates a tectonic rise of this site by more than 120 m.

Analogous relationships appear to exist just west of El Arish (Unit 4e; Fig. 31), where three environmental changes within the sediments occur at the +15-m msl elevated terrace. The sequence of these three environments is as follows from bottom to top: a freshwater settling basin, a high-energy river, and mudflats and estuaries. These changes may correlate with fluctuations of sea level beginning with late Würm (latest glaciation) and ending just before the Chalcolithic (7000 to 6000 years ago). Despite the environmental changes within the sequence, an uninterrupted aggradational regime (no hiati or unconformities) is recognized. Based upon the analogies at Akhziv, Dor, Caesarea, Netanya, and Mount Casius (Units 5 and 4), it is suggested that this site was tectonically uplifted more than 100 m since the end of glaciation. The latest phase of that tectonic rise (to about +15 m msl) occurred during Post-Chalcolithic time. Similar conclusions are reasonable for the two elevated lumachelle terraces at the El Meidan and Bardawil railroad stations (see Unit 5b) (Fig. 32).

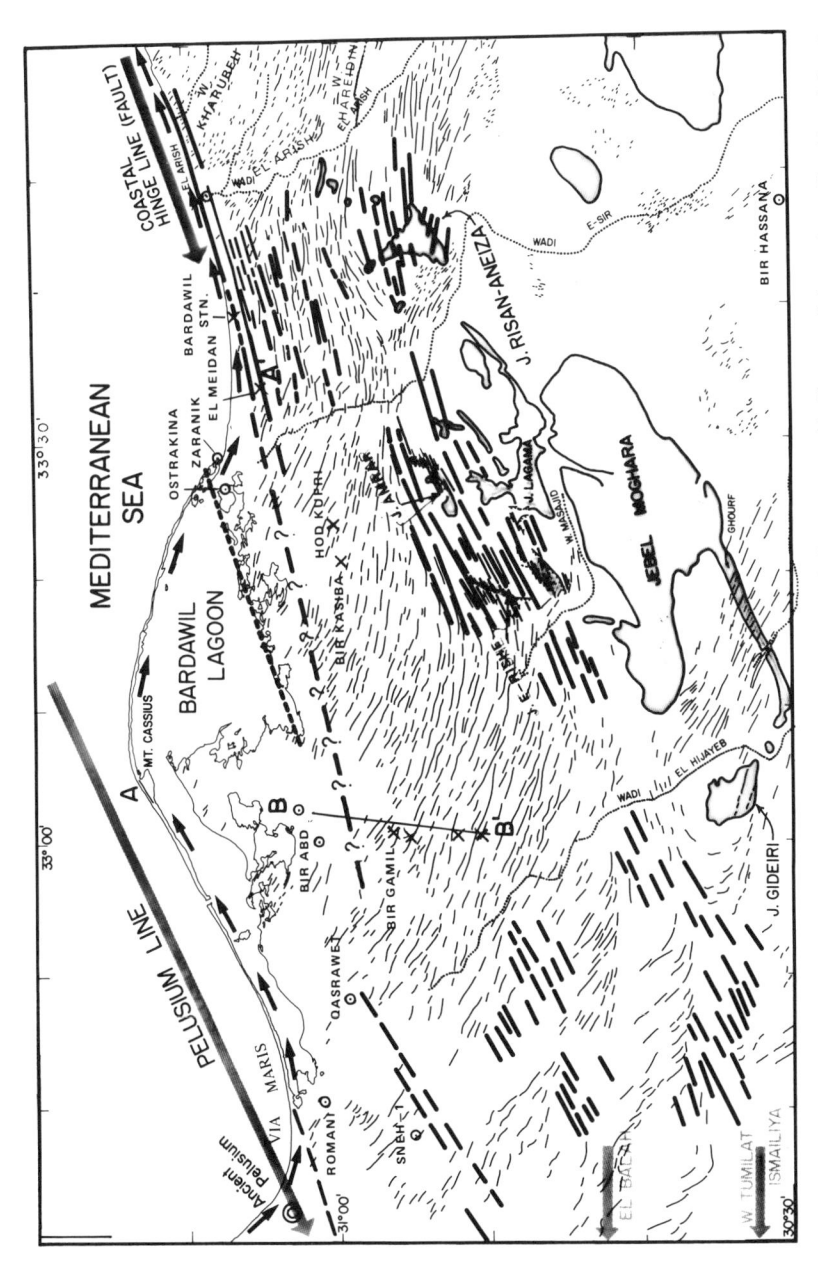

Figure 32. Distribution patterns of linear sand dunes (narrow lines), tectonic lineaments (wide lines), and the main wadies (dotted lines) across northwestern Sinai (modified from Neev et al. 1982, fig. 3). Positions of profiles B-B' (Figure 33) and A'A' (Figure 34) also are shown. The four X marks south of Bir Jamil along the B-B' profile show positions of late Pleistocene freshwater algal limestone outcrops. Wadi E-Sir and Wadi Masajid, were captured toward Wadi El Arish, whereas Wadi El Hijayeb was captured toward Wadi Gafgafa (beyond this map) probably because of an additional upward tectonic movement of the Jebel Moghara—Risan Aneiza range, which occurred recently (in Post-Byzantine or even Post-Mamlukian times). The now-abandoned courses of these three captured wadies could not be traced beyond (north of) the El Arish—Bir Jamil tectonic line (the inland extension of the coastal hinge line).

Two uncertainties are present in the above arguments and conclusions: absence of precise dating from within the sediments and indirect nature of evidence implied when continental sediments (although of aquatic environments) are associated with the level of the nearby sea.

3. Inland Extension of the Coastal Fault. The west-southwest trending coastline to a few kilometers west of El Arish apparently is fault controlled, as indicated by the extension of the elevated terrace on its south side. This terrace plunges westward and disappears near the Bardawil Railway Station. Beyond that point and as far as Mount Casius, the clockwise curvature of the coastline increases, and it trends about east-west (Fig. 32). A sequence of now-abandoned berms that converge counterclockwise is recognized along that last coastal segment between Ostrakina and Bardawil Railway Station, thereby emphasizing its prograded nature. Nevertheless, the west-southwest trend of the coastal fault is maintained by the inland extension of a set of photolineaments from the Bardawil Railway Station for at least 30 km. This linear feature marks the boundary between lowlands and sabkhas on its north-northwestern side and a more elevated territory on its south-southeastern side. This boundary extends farther westward as far as Bir Jamil—Bir Abd and even beyond. The southern province also is structurally elevated, as implied by the elevations and ages of several early Holocene lumachelle terraces (such as at Bardawil and El Meidan railway stations—Unit 5b) and of the late Pleistocene freshwater algal limestone banks (at Bir Jamil and the four sites south of it, as well as at Hod Kufri—Unit 2d, and Fig. 32).

The following additional conclusions are inferred from these data (when plotted on geological cross-sections with corresponding values of total gravity—Figs. 33 and 34): (i) The boundary between the southern and northern provinces is a tectonic hingeline that is an extension of the one along the coastline farther northeast (Fig. 32). (ii) In this region the hingeline extension lies between the basin of the Bardawil Lagoon and the Moghara—Lagama—Risan Aneiza chain of structures (Fig. 32; Lapidoth 1972). (iii) Another structural high rises from the Bardawil structural trough toward Mount Casius in the west-northwest, thereby closing the Bardawil Lagoon on its northwestern side. (iv) An important phase of the vertical differential tectonic movement that separates the structurally high area on the south from the trough of the Bardawil Lagoon occurred along this hingeline in Holocene times (during the transition into the Holocene and throughout it). These data corroborate our conclusion about the regional tectonic rise of the continental province and subsidence of the oceanic one that occurred during the transition from Pleistocene into Holocene across the central and northern coastal segments of Israel (see above: Akhziv, Akko, Dor, Caesarea, Netanya).

It should be noted that the El Arish—Bir Abd segment of the overland route (or the ancient military road) between Egypt and Canaan in the Early Bronze Age roughly corresponds with the relevant segment of the coastal hinge line (Fig. 32; Oren 1973; Neev and Friedman 1978; Chapter IV).

4. Ostrakina (or Felusiat—N31°07'22" E33°25'50'). The several sites that are scattered over an area of a few square kilometers near the eastern end of Bardawil Lagoon were

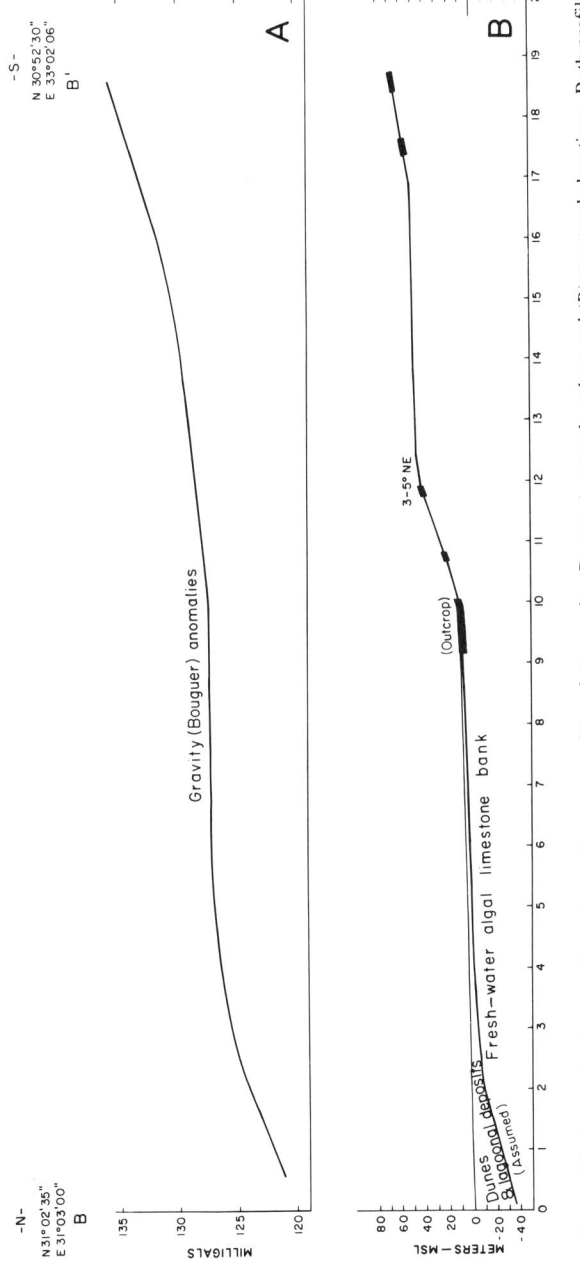

Figure 33. Twenty-km long north-south trending twin profiles of (A) gravity (Bouguer) anomaly values and (B) structural elevations. Both profiles correspond with B-B′ in Figure 32. The structural profile (B) is based on present elevations of widely scattered outcrops (relicts) of a nearly 35,000 year old freshwater algal limestone bank (II Unit 2d). It is assumed that these algal limestone beds originally were deposited at the bottom of an extremely flat and shallow lake. The northern half of this profile was extrapolated on the basis of its gravity profile (A).

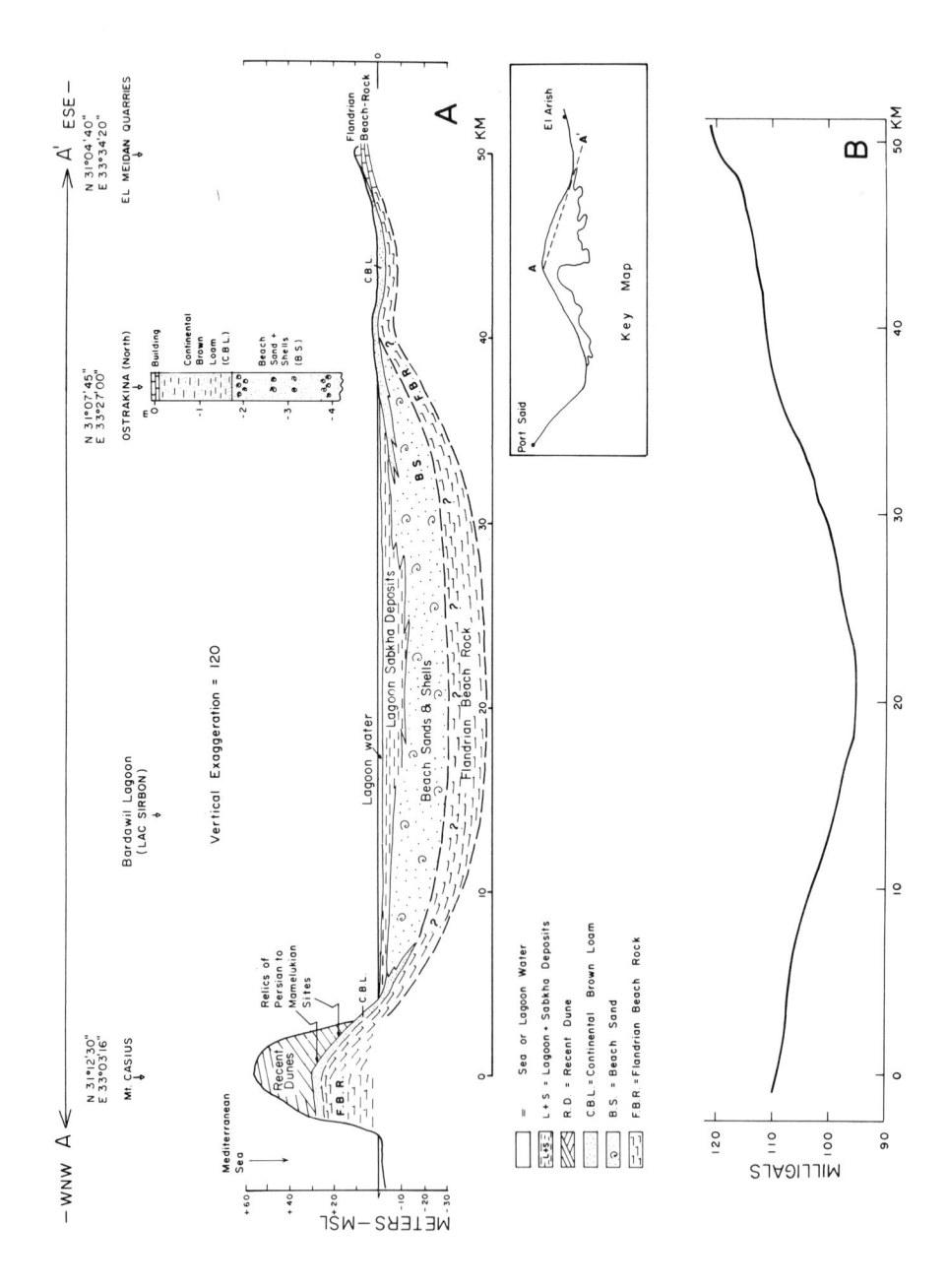

termed Ostrakina during Hellenistic to Byzantine times. This group of settlements served as an important caravan station on the Via Maris (Fig. 32) and was a major industrial center between the first and early seventh centuries AD. Five Byzantine churches served inhabitants and travellers who camped at Ostrakina, demonstrating the intensity and type of demographic activity there. A large population existed in spite of a severe shortage of drinking water, through use of very few shallow wells that tapped the thin freshwater lens floating atop the subsurface seawater. At present, all of these wells are silted and yield only seawater. The area continued as a caravan center throughout Moslem, Crusader, and Early Mamlukian times until it finally was destroyed and deserted after an earthquake in 1302 AD (Oren 1977). This earthquake may be the same one that badly damaged St. Catherine Monastery in the Sinai (N28.5° E34.0°) before dawn on 1 May 1312 (Nektariov, 1660, 197–198; Ben-Menahem 1979). Perhaps the same earthquake is dated 1 May 1302 by Rushdi Said (Cairo Univ., personal communication to KOE in 1969); and 8 August 1303 by N.N. Ambraseys (personal communication to KOE in 1972). Confusion may arise because of different conversions into the modern calendar system. According to Said, the earthquake also did serious damage at Hermopolis and Alexandria in Egypt, Cyrenaica, Tunis, Sicily, Cyprus, and Constantinople.

    Geological observations and data recovered from shallow drillings made by Neev at Ostrakina (Unit 7g; Fig. 34) outline the recent geological history. Tectonic subsidence occurred during the Early to Middle Iron Age (about 3500 to 2500 y BP), as indicated by rapid accumulation of high-energy beach sand (more than 2 m thick) that contains abundant shell lenses. It is assumed that the early Holocene lumachelle layer that crops out at El Meidan (Fig. 34) also exists beneath the beach-sand layer across the entire basin of Bardawil Lagoon. These beach sands grade upward into a hamra-like layer overlain by dune sands that originally accumulated to an elevation of several meters above msl. The latter are topped by a 20–40 cm layer of lagoonal sediments. Such a sequence appears to express three alternating tectonic phases: active (high rate of subsidence), quiet (low rate), and another tectonically active phase of subsidence and submergence. The eastern half of the bar that closed Lac Sirbonis (later named Bardawil Lagoon) was one of a system of northward-prograding bars and spits. Nevertheless, there always was an opening between the eastern end of the spit and the coastline at Ostrakina. The present opening at Zaranik (Fig. 32) cleans itself every winter during storms. The self-cleaning mechanism is fed by the piling up of Mediterranean water that overflows the bar, thereby producing a violent eastward current within the lagoon that seeks an outlet at the eastern end. The presence of numerous sand terraces that contain interbedded pebbles of pumice and also tar (recently brought by Mediterranean currents) along the inland shores of the lagoon at elevations of a few meters above msl indicates both the intensity and height of the piling up and overflow. The Zaranik opening is the only permanent and natural one along the

◁——

Figure 34. A west-northwest 50-km long geological cross section between El Meidan and Mt. Casius across the eastern fringes of Bardawil Lagoon *(A)*. It is tied to outcrops at Mt. Casius and El Meidan and to a 3-m deep drill hole at Ostrakina. Interpolations between these sites are supported by the configuration of the gravity (Bouguer) profile *(B)*.

bar of Bardawil Lagoon. A pattern of prograding bars recognized on both sides of Zaranik resembles ones at the outlets of rivers. Consequently, this opening has migrated about 3 km north of Ostrakina since Late Roman times.

The northernmost site of the Roman to Byzantine town originally was atop the stabilized dune layer. Apparently, during the second century AD, this site (Tabba Felusiat, or Site 153 of Oren) was at the coastline and served as an important port, as indicated by remains of storage facilities that have been excavated (Oren 1977). Moreover, some of the Late Roman buildings at Ostrakina's harbour are now partly covered by lagoonal muds and tilted northwestward about three degrees. These facts appear to indicate tectonic subsidence of this site toward the trough of the syncline within the lagoon between Ostrakina and Mount Casius (Fig. 34). The subsidence may have occurred in two phases: one at the end of Byzantine time and the other at the end of the Mamluk regime.

5. Mount Casius (N31°12'30" E33°03'16"). A gradual regional tectonic uplift at Mount Casius (northern shore of Bardawil Lagoon, Fig. 32, 34) during the transition from Pleistocene until middle Holocene is deduced from the dominance of aquatic-lagoonal environments that prevailed throughout the relevant stratigraphic sequence (Unit 5c). Folding and uplifting of the Mount Casius peninsula during late Holocene is suggested by the structural configuration of the hamra-like layer (continental brown loam in Fig. 34) that was deposited above the early Holocene aquatic sequence.

Indications for a Post-Persian, or even a Post-Roman, tectonic phase were found along the southern coastline of the Mount Casius peninsula. A low (about +4 m msl) WSW-ENE trending seacliff was formed at the southern shore of the lagoon (N31°12'11" E33°04'18"). This cliff faces southeastward, toward the lagoon, and is protected from intensive abrasion by the open sea. Lenses of naturally deposited shells with imbricated rounded pottery sherds are interbedded at the top of this terrace. At least one of the abraded pottery sherds was identified as Persian. The top of this terrace is slightly tilted to the northwest, implying a tectonic uplift. In addition to its local implication, this finding corroborates our interpretation about natural marine deposition of the similar elevated shell-bed terraces along the coastline of Israel, because in the protected lagoon a displacement of shells to high elevation by storm waves (as suggested by some) cannot have occurred. The WSW-ENE trend of this terrace agrees with the trends of several other linear features in this area: (i) a low sandy ridge a few hundred meters north of this terrace; (ii) the western half of the bar that closes Bardawil Lagoon on its north; and (iii) the northern coastline of the Bir Abd peninsula (at Mat Iblis about 3 kms south of the low seacliff).

The oldest pottery sherds found across the Mount Casius peninsula are Persian (sixth century BC, E. D. Oren, personal communciation) or somewhat older (Iron Age—Oren 1973). Therefore, we deduce that this may have been the first time during the Holocene that the peninsula became connected with the mainland. The connection was made either along the bar or across the strait separating Mount Casius from the Bir Abd peninsula that is south of it. Possibly the following citation from Strabo made during 23 BC approximately (Hamilton and Falconer 1854, 174, v. 3), describing the geological event at

Mount Casius, fits our model of the oscillatory tectonic movements that occurred several times along the coastline of Israel during the past 3000 (or even 4000) years: "A similar phenomenon took place at Mount Casium in Egypt. The ground, to a considerable distance, after a violent and single shock fell in parts, at once exchanging places; the elevated parts opposed the access of the sea, and parts which had subsided admitted it. Another shock occurred, and the place recovered its ancient position, except that there was an alteration (in the surface of the ground) in some places, and none in others. Perhaps such occurrences are connected with periodical returns the nature of which is unknown to us." The above appears to describe faithfully a tectonic event of oscillatory nature that occurred at Mount Casius sometime during the Roman period. A slightly different translation was provided by Ambraseys (1962). The event was distinctly different from the description in Strabo's next previous paragraph of another phenomenon that occurred on the shore between Tyre and Akko. Apparently, a tsunami is described, as the paragraph mentions "a wave from the sea, like a rising tide, overwhelmed the fugitives; some were carried out to sea and drowned, others perished in hollow places; then again the ebb succeeding, uncovered and displayed to sight the bodies lying in confusion among dead fish." The only common denominator between these two lively descriptions is the fact that both were coastal events associated with tectonism that caused the sea to flood the land and then regress. Perhaps the two events were confused by Striem and Miloh (1975) because their description of the event at Mount Cassius is close to that which occurred between Tyre and Akko.

6. On-Land Segment of the Pelusium Line. The western half of the bar that separates Bardawil Lagoon from the Mediterranean Sea differs from the eastern half mainly in two ways. Physiographically, the western half is more narrow and more linear, and traces of washover fans on the lagoonal side are rare. These fans are formed by flows of seawater that pile against it during heavy storms. In contrast, washover fans are abundant along the eastern half of the bar. Secondly, the average elevation of peaks along the western half of the bar is greater than along the eastern half (+4 to +6 m versus +1 to +3 m msl). Moreover, large patches along the broad crest of the western half of the bar are paved by fragments of a thin layer of beachrock to diameters of 1 m. Similar features were not observed along the eastern bar.

A prominent photolineament (Neev et al. 1982, fig. 4) extends southwestward from the western tip of Bardawil Lagoon to at least Qantara on the Suez Cannal. This lineament is a direct continuation of the western half of Bardawil bar (Neev et at. 1976). Its extreme linearity (Fig. 32) suggests tectonic origin and indicates recently rejuvenated activity. It was named the "Pelusium Line," a term coined after the industrial city and harbor of Pelusium (or Tel Farameh, N31°02'40" E32°32'30") that is about 3 km northwest of the photolineament and about 4 km south-southwest of the present Mediterranean coastline. The partly submerged position of this site below water table (which is at sea level), as well as of Burge et Tineh (the Mamlukian harbor installations about 2.5 km west-northwest of the site of Pelusium on the northern rim of the now-defunct Pelusiac branch of the Nile Delta) corroborates the conclusion about recent (within the last 500 years or so) renewal of tectonic activity across the line.

The site of Pelusium (Fig. 32) was inhabited first during Persian times (sixth to fourth century BC), when it long served as the main entrance to Egypt (it was used by the fleet of Alexander the Great to invade Egypt). It existed as a flourishing industrial and agricultural center until its submergence during Late Mamlukian time, after which its vicinity became a salt desert and the course of the Pelusiac Branch was silted.

Two experimental geophysical surveys were made across this segment of the Pelusium Line. Both were along a profile between the drill hole site of Sneh No. 1 and the site of Pelusium: (i) A 12-km long seismic reflection profile was run southwestward from Sneh No. 1 (Fig. 32) to about 2 km beyond the photolineament of the Pelusium Line (Ginzburg and Amitai 1968, line G1-DD in their fig. 2 and sections 4 and 10). A general pattern of seaward (northwestward) dip of the sequence between the surface and a depth of about 3.5 sec is present along this cross section. Three or four reflectors are recognized and the intervening sedimentary units also thicken northwestward. Unlike the upper two reflectors, which are easily detected at the northwestern end of the profile, the third reflector abruptly stops about 3 km beforehand, near the point where the profile crosses the photolineament. This reflector dips northwestward from a depth of 2.1 sec at the Sneh No. 1 well to a depth of 3.2 sec where it disappears. Systematic reversals of as much as to 10 degrees to the southeast occur from this point of disappearance throughout the entire unit between the third and the second reflectors. At that site the depth to the second reflector is 1.6 sec. (ii) The second experimental survey consisted of six magnetotelluric soundings along a 20-km long northwesterly profile. This profile extends about 6 km beyond the photolineament (Rotstein et al. 1978). Results indicate that the upper crust in the area is divided to a depth of 40 km into three resistivity layers: the upper two thicken to the northwest across the Pelusium Line and, based on correlation with the stratigraphic log of Sneh No. 1, are interpreted as follows: an upper unit having a resistivity of 1.5 ohm-m consists of mostly Pleistocene loose sands thickening from 360 m at Sneh-1 to 500 m at the northwestern end of the profile. It is underlain by a Tertiary shale unit, the resistivity values of which are 0.27 to 0.47 ohm-m. This unit thickens from 1350 m near Sneh-1 to 3500 m at the northwest. Resistivities of the third layer are very high (20 to 200 ohm-m—much higher than could be determined accurately by the magnetotelluric method), and its total thickness is more than 40 km. The top of this layer, which consists of Early Cretaceous limestones, also dips northwestward. The basement-sediment interface could not be detected either in this survey or in other magnetotelluric surveys along the coastal plain of Israel and northwestern Sinai.

The distribution of Bouguer gravity values in northwestern Siani indicates the existence of a gravity trough along the Pelusium Line (Lapidoth 1972). Gravity values across the profile between Sneh-1 and Pelusium drop from +122 mgls at Sneh to +110 mgls along the axis of the trough at Pelusium and at the Bay of Tineh, and they rise again to almost +130 mgls at Port Said.

The Pelusium Line extends both northeastward as a submarine geosuture (Neev and Greenfield 1981) and southwestward as a transcontinental megashear across Africa (Neev 1977; Neev et al. 1982). Here, it forms a tectonically disturbed zone and a trough along the eastern limit of the Nile Delta.

7. Sand Supply into Northwestern Sinai During Holocene. The small erg of sand dunes south of the coastline between El Arish and the Suez Canal is younger than late Pleistocene. This is indicated by the approximately 35,000 y BP age of the chalky freshwater limestone that underlies it (see Unit 2d). The following data and other considerations suggest the depositional history of this erg: (i) Although we found no evidence of Unit 3 (30,000–20,000 y BP) dunes, the presence of Unit 3 dunes along the coastline of Israel probably required contemporaneous dunes to have been present along northwestern Sinai. (ii) The same line of thinking means that we should not expect extensive dunes along the coastal plain of northwestern Sinai during the Epipaleolithic (the time equivalent of the Unit 4 mudflat hamra deposits that are extensive along the coastal plain of Israel). (iii) Considering the presence of a rather thick beach and lagoonal quartz-sand sequence of Neolithic to Chalcolithic age (or 9000 to 6000 y BP) at Mt. Casius (see Unit 5c), we believe that some of this sand migrated landward as dunes. Moreover, a northward increase of the detrital carbonate component within the Calcarenite Bank (Unit 5a) along the coastline of Israel led us to assume that, along the coast of northwestern Sinai, the equivalent sand bank consists of almost clean quartz grains. Numerous Early Bronze I–II settlements along the overland route between Egypt and Canaan (Oren 1973, 200–201), as well as the fact that most of them were built atop stabilized (but sterile) dunes, suggest that during this period the sand supply to the coastal plain of northwestern Sinai had considerably decreased. This process of stabilization could have been during the transition between the Chalcolithic and Bronze periods.

(iv) Although we found no evidence of an increase in the rate of landward sand supply to northwestern Sinai in pre-Late Bronze time, we believe that such a change occurred. This belief is based on the assumption that a phase of landward quartz-sand supply occurred along the coastal zone of Israel in pre-Late Bronze (about 3700 y BP) and post-Early Bronze (see Unit 7a) times. As the northwestern Sinai coastal zone is nearer the source of these sands (the Nile Delta), an even more intensive sand ingression should have occurred there. Archaelogical remains of the period from the Early Bronze Age III to the end of the Middle Bronze Age are relatively more scanty in northwestern Sinai (Oren 1973).

(v) Renewal of human settlements along the coastal plain of northwestern Sinai during the Late Bronze Age through the Persian—Hellenistic and Early Roman periods suggests diminution of sand import and stabilization of the dunes. A later phase of sand ingression into northwestern Sinai between the late second and early fourth centuries AD is supported by archaelogical findings at Qasrawet (about 20 km southeast of Romani, N30°56′30″ E32°49′00″). An important Nabatean caravan station and temple existed at this site between the second century BC and the end of the second century AD. It finally was deserted after a period of decline caused by unstable political and economic conditions in Egypt (Oren 1982). This desertion also was associated with an intensive phase of sand supply, as indicated by the fact that the 6–8 m high relics of Nabatean structures were completely covered by a thick layer of dune sand prior to resettlement of this site during the early fourth century AD. This last settlement that functioned as a Late Roman military stronghold was deserted by the end of the fourth century, possibly again because of the joint effect of political unrest and excessive traffic difficulties created by encroachment of sand dunes, among other causes.

(vi) Another phase of sand stabilization associated with extensive human settlement along the coastal plain of northwestern Sinai occurred between the Early Moslem period and the Early Mamlukian period (Oren 1973; and personal communication). The segment of the Via Maris between Port Said (or Tenis—the ancient industrial center and port, the relics of which are now mostly submerged under the lagoons about 10 km south of Port Said), through Mt. Casius to the Bardawil Railway Station (Fig. 32) was deserted during the late Mamlukian Period (or during its transition to the Turkish Period). Some parts of this segment now are flooded by the lagoons and others are covered by dune sands (Fig. 32). Many Mamlukian sites along or adjacent to the overland route between the Nile Delta (Qantara) and southern Israel (at least as far as Ashdod) also were covered by dune sands. This event occurred during Late or Post-Mamlukian time. In that respect, it is interesting to quote Jarvis (1943, 95–96): "it is difficult to date the inroad of sand that now stretches from the Mediterranean coast some twenty-five to thirty miles inland, but there is one stretch of dunes that has recently invaded the Hassana area [at the southeastern part of Fig. 32—authors] and which has advanced a mile and a half in ten years, covering a wide gravel expanse that a decade ago was entirely free from sand. If the dunes on the seashore have advanced at the same rate, one may assume that the sandy belt is not more than five hundred years old or possibly considerably less, which explains the ease with which armies crossed and recrossed what is now a veritable barrier." The above deduction could be related just to the last significant phase of the beach-sand ingression to northwestern Sinai (the Post-Mamlukian one).

IV. Synopsis

A. Tectonics

1. Contemporaneous Upwarp of Continental Crust and Subsidence of Oceanic Crust in Eastermost Mediterranean Region since Late Pleistocene. The data at Akhziv, Akko, Dor, Caesarea, Netanya, Nizzanim, El Arish, Bir Jamil, and Fadda 1 (see II Unit 5 C for description of the latter) imply that the coastal belt of Israel and northwestern Sinai was uplifted appreciably since the end of glaciation. This uplift appears to have been rather steady at least until the climatic optimum about 6000 years ago. It paralleled the eustatic rise of sea level due to deglaciation; otherwise, the lagoon and swamp environments at Akko and Dor could not have been maintained while sea level rose by about 130 m.

The recent tectonic rise of the coastal belt may be part of a regional post-Pliocene upwarp that involved the entire continental block east of the Mediterranean Sea. The Judean Upwarp (Picard 1943) or the Structural Backbone of Israel (Neev 1960) is part of this block that is sub-parallel to the coastal hinge line. This continental block rose and subsided isostatically several times since Triassic and perhaps even earlier (Neev et al. 1985).

Some recent observations by Neev in northern Sinai near the Biblical site of Qadesh Barnea (about 80 km southeast of El Arish) indicate that the structural backbone of Israel continues to undergo a Holocene rejuvenation of uplift. Late Pleistocene lake sediments extensively blanket basinal areas along the drainage pattern of Wadi El Arish. These sediments consist of yellowish-brown finely laminated silts and sands in which greenish marl and whitish chalky layers are interbedded (the latter are more abundant in the upper part of the sequence). At El Quseime (N30°40'00" E34°22'40") at an elevation of about +300 m msl, the sequence includes a dense lenticular algal (travertine-like) limestone layer that overlies the sandy silts. A radiocarbon age of this limestone is 33,500 ± 800 y BP (J. C. Vogel, personal communication—Pta-2795). At Wadi Qudeirat, near Qadesh Barnea about 4 km southeast of El Quseime (N30°38'50" E34°24'20") at an elevation of about +350 m msl, these lake sediments contain a few meters of yellowish-brown silty marls that crop out on both banks of the wadi. A lenticular layer rich in disintegrated charcoal and Late Paleolithic flint implements (O. Bar-Yosef, personal communication) is interbedded on the southern bank of the wadi. The radiocarbon age of a NaOH extract of this charcoal sample (Pta-2819) is 33,800 ± 940 y BP, whereas that of the NaOH residue (Pta-2818) is 28,212 + 2748 − 2064 y BP (J. C. Vogel, personal communication). The aggradational regime near Qadesh Barnea persisted until at least Late Epipaleolithic time (about 11,000 y BP; O. Bar Yosef, personal communication). This is indicated at a site of that age interbedded within the uppermost part of the sequence across the now-dissected terrace and a short distance downstream. Four layers, each about 20 cm thick, taste salty and have a darker hue (suggesting a higher content of hygroscopic water-soluble salts, thereby resembling the evaporitic layers of Deir el Balah—see Unit 7e above). They are interbedded within the lower part of this marl sequence across the wadi just north of the Late Paleolithic site. Twelve samples from these four layers were analysed for their water-soluble salt contents, that ranged between 0.5 to 1.0 per cent of dry sample weight. Some ionic ratios computed from these 12 analyses help infer the origin of the mother brines. These are listed in Table 5, together with ratios in the seven samples from Deir el Balah evaporites and in the oceans (see Tables 1 and 2). Comparison of results suggests that geochemically the Qadesh Barnea brines are similar to the Deir el Balah ones. On the other hand, they have an entirely different affinity than that of dissolved salts in a freshwater spring of Qadesh Barnea (which are carbonates).

Unlike at Deir el Balah, the Qadesh Barnea deposits are geographically remote from the Mediterranean Sea as well as from the Bardawil Lagoon that served as a recent analogue to the Deir el Balah brines. The following tentative conclusions are suggested: (i) The waters of the late Pleistocene lakes in northern Sinai were not of the purely freshwater type, but were brackish ones. (ii) Their dissolved salts may be related genetically to the ocean ones. (iii) These lakes went through several (cyclic ?) events of partial dessication, when their dissolved salts reached high degrees of concentration. (iv) It is assumed that the brine-soaked sediments when deposited at Qadesh Barnea were topographically lower than the El Quseima algal reef. At present, they are about 50 m higher than the El Quseima site. (v) No relict of a barrier or a sill that could have blocked or restrained flow from a "hanging" water body at Qadesh Barnea toward the lake at El Quseime could be identified along the route between these two sites. The present northwestward gradient of about 0.75 degree between the two sites may have formed by a subsequent westward tectonic tilt. Such a tilt may have been caused by an additional rise of the structural backbone of Israel during the Holocene. Perhaps a quantitative estimate can be made of the total amount of post-Pleistocene upwarping or westward tilting on the basis of similar studies along the entire length of the Wadi el Arish paleolake.

Table 5
Composition of Source Salt Beds

Ionic Ratios (equivalents)	Qadesh Barnea (12)	Deir el Balah (7)	Oceans
Na/Cl	0.25 – 1.271	0.47 – 0.82	.86
Ca/(HCO$_3$ + SO$_4$)	0.36 – 5.2	0.64 – 7.1	0.34
SO4/HCO$_3$	0.7 – 4.0 *10.7*	0.1 – 0.6	23.3
Ca/Mg	1.0 – 8.7 *21.0*	3.7 – 7.5	0.2
Cl/(HCO$_3$ + SO$_4$)	0.5 – 26.0	0.7 – 3.3 *143*	9.6
Cl/HCO$_3$	1.0 – 49.0	0.8 – 22.3	233.0
Cl/SO$_4$	0.8 – 65.5	4.2 – 41.0	10.0

1. Parens—number of analyses.
2. Italics—exceptional ratios.

It is assumed that this post-Pleistocene tectonic rise of the continent was contemporaneous with "the main phase of subsidence of the eastern Mediterranean (which) occurred rather abruptly during the Pleistocene and Holocene" (Neev et al. 1976, 48). Both movements appear to have been controlled isostatically and related genetically. Late Pleistocene submerged terraces, which are common elsewhere, could not be detected along the outer shelf and slope off Israel perhaps because of very recent westward tilting and downwarping.

Similar types of vertical differential movements are known across coasts (that function as hinge lines) in other parts of the world during the same time span and are due to isostatic weighting of the continental shelf by returned glacial meltwater (Bloom 1963; Chappell et al. 1982)

2. Nature and Magnitude of Coastal Fault System. The data described in the present study have led us to conclusions regarding throw or vertical differential movement across the coastal belt: (i) Post-Jurassic (during the past 141 m.y.): Across the 14-km wide faulted littoral zone along the entire coast of Israel, the cumulative throw amounts to 3 to 4 km (about 2.5 seconds). (ii) Post-Messinian (during the past 7 to 5 my): A throw of about 300 m across a few hundred meter wide faulted zone occurred along the central coastal segment (at Netanya); a throw of 100 to 200 m occurred along the southern segment (at Ashdod and Gaza). (iii) Post-Pliocene (during the past 1.8 my): Total throw of 150 m was across the central coastal segment, but only 17 m at Caesarea. (iv) Post-early Holocene (during the past 6000 years): A throw of 40 to 60 m occurred across a few hundred meter wide faulted belt along the central and southern coastal segments; a maximal throw of 15 m was along the northern and the Hof Hacarmel segments.

Due to the nature of the data (mostly subsurface information across the land-sea contact), we were unable to further narrow the belts across which the differential vertical movements actually occurred. Cumulative values of the post-Messinian movements probably would be larger than those quoted above if measured across a wider belt (across the 3-km inner littoral belt where the sea-floor gradient is appreciably steeper than farther west). Cumulative values are due to both faulting and westward tilting.

The coastal fault should be interpreted as a huge and old growth fault. Nevertheless, its linearity and strength have led many to investigate an association with wrench-faulting mechanism as well. Gvirtzman (1969) rejected such a possiblity, at least since late Miocene, based on the smooth and direct extensions of Neogene transverse river systems across the coastline. In a recent abstract Herzog and Horowitz (1976) suggested that Tel Michal (Fig. 1) was rotated about 37° with respect to the present coastline trend during the past 4000 years (but mostly during the Middle Bronze) as a result of strike-slip movements. The direct and smooth seaward extension across the coastline of the transverse Yafo—Lod fault, as well as its adjoining northward facing escarpment (III C II and Figures 19 and 22) do not favor such a possiblity.

3. Sequence of Oscillatory Tectonic Movements Across the Coastal Fault System during Late Holocene. Phase 1. The first indication for rejuvenation of relief across the present coast during the Holocene is along the Hof Hasharon (central) segment (III C) where the Calcarenite Bank (II B Unit 5a) wedges out and disappears a short distance (few hundred meters) east (landward) of the shore. Similar indications of such a relief also are present: (i) across the Khirbet (ruins) Ashdod Yam—Nahal Evtah—Nizzanim coastline (III D 3) and (ii) just west of El Arish (III E 2), although at that site we do not have data from the littoral belt. The above features suggest an embryonic rejuvenation of the differential vertical movement sometime between the end of the Epipaleolithic and the beginning of the Chalcolithic periods (10,000 to 6000 y BP). Across many other sites, both in the northern segments (III A and B) and in the southern ones, lagoonal to swamp conditions have uninterruptedly prevailed on both sides of the coastline until the transition between Early and Middle Bronze (about 4000 y BP). Nevertheless, uplift and emergence of the second kurkar ridge (east of the coastline) apparently occurred about 6000 years ago. This conclusion is implied from the stratigraphic sequence at Tel Akko (III A 2), but probably it is not unique to that site.

Phase 2. By Middle Bronze II b time (about 3700 y BP), the coastline already had been sculptured to a cliff-dominated configuration resembling the present one. This implies transformation of coastal physiography from a flat lagoonal-swampy one on both sides of the coastline into an elevated land block on the east side bounded by a very narrow beach. The cultural gap within the stratigraphic sequence at Tel Akko between the Early Bronze I and Middle Bronze II layers occurred probably because of this tectonic phase.

Phase 3. The transition between the Middle and Late Bronze periods about 3500 y BP was marked by a catastrophic event of tectonic nature that apparently was even more severe than that during the former transition. The traces and results of this event are recognized at Tel Michal, Yavneh Yam, and Tel Haraz (III C F and III D 1 and 2, respectively). The sedimentary sequence at Tel Haraz represents the oldest well-established evidence for oscillatory tectonic movements along the coast of Israel. The beginning of this phase may correspond with the Santorini catastrophic eruption, thereby suggesting regional dimensions to this tectonic event.

Phase 4. Another phase of tectonic activity that left its imprint on the history and physiography of coastline occurred sometime during the transition between the Late Bronze and the Iron Age. Its traces were recorded at Tel Michal and Tel Abu Hawam (III C, F, and III A 3, repectively). Based on data from Tel Abu Hawam, this movement may have had an oscillatory nature, but its magnitude was relatively small.

Phases 5 and 6. Depositional and cultural histories of the Deir el Balah coastline (III D 5) clearly indicate another oscillatory movement across the southern segment of the coastline sometime during the Early or Middle Iron Age (between the twelfth and eighth centuries BC, as inferred from corroborative evidences recorded at Tel Gaza—III D 4).

The Via Maris (the coastal traffic route) started to function during the sixth century BC, the Persian Period. This also was when the city-harbor of Pelusium was built for the first time and when the Pelusiac branch of the Nile River started to flow (Sneh and Weissbrod 1973; Oren 1977; and Neev and Friedman 1978). These cultural and physiographic changes probably resulted from tectonic activity. It is not yet clear whether they should be incorporated within Phase 5 or whether they belong to a separate somewhat younger phase (Phase 6 during Persian-Babylonian time, 2700 to 2500 y BP).

Phases 7 and 8. Late Byzantine and Late Mamlukian (or about 1500 and about 500 y BP, respectively). Difficulties involved with precise identification of dates of movements are greater in the study of the last two phases than of earlier phases. For example, it is easy to say that the oscillatory movements at Akhziv and Dor (III A 1, and B) were during Post-Roman time. However, it is not yet clear whether they occurred during Byzantine or Late Mamlukian phases. There also are the facts from Ostrakina (III E 4) and the desertion of the Via Maris segment that extends between Tenis and El Arish (III E 7; Neev and Friedman 1978). Consequently, we now are convinced that there were two separate phases of oscillatory movements across the coastline of Israel. This conclusion helped us to sort out several problems that previously were not satisfactorily explained. A good example is the date of the partial subsidence of the Caesarea harbor breakwater as inferred from a sixth century AD letter (Raban et al. 1976; see also III C 2). Another example is the finding of Early Moslem graves dug on the coast-parallel sand ridge south of the Crusader wall at Caesarea. Beach sand, shell beds, and swamp deposits are interbedded within this sand ridge that, in turn, overlies a row of Late Roman storehouses (Neev et al. 1978a).

Distinction between these two phases as separate entities does not mean that tectonic activity completely ceased between the phases. For example, the oscillatory type of movement described by Strabo at Mt. Casius (III E 5) probably was rather close to his time, the Middle Roman period between the Persian and the Byzantine phases.

Another example is the sand supply to the top of the cliff along the Hof Hasharon segment. The mechanism for such a process is better understood now than earlier (Neev et al. 1973), because additional convincing arguments have accumulated for both Late Byzantine and Late Mamlukian oscillatory movements (Fig. 8; II Unit 7a; III C 5; etc.). The most convincing arguments for Post-Crusader encroachment of dune sand across the coastal cliff lie in the existence of a rather dense forest atop the ridge between Apollonia and Ga'ash (I Unit 7a) during Crusader time; deposition of a new blanket of sand on the ridge, perhaps associated with a short phase of submergence under seawater, may have killed this forest.

At least two new findings indicate that the onshore (eastern) side of the coastline of Israel is rising tectonically even at present. The first one was made by Tsur and Safriel (1978) and is briefly described for Yavneh Yam (III D 1). The second indication was found by Kafri and Karcz (1975), who compared two sets of precise leveling measurements made by the Geodetic Survey of Israel in 1961 and 1969. Their study indicates that the coastal zone of Israel was uplifted during the nine-year period at an average rate of 11 mm/year compared with the area east of it (which includes the Judean Mountains).

4. A Working Hypothesis on the Origin and Mechanism of Oscillatory Tectonic Movements. The mechanism and origin of the oscillatory type of movements along the coastal fault of Israel mentioned by Neev et al. (1973) and Neev and Bakler (1978) are illustrated by Figure 35. Contemporaneous upwarp of the continental crust and subsidence

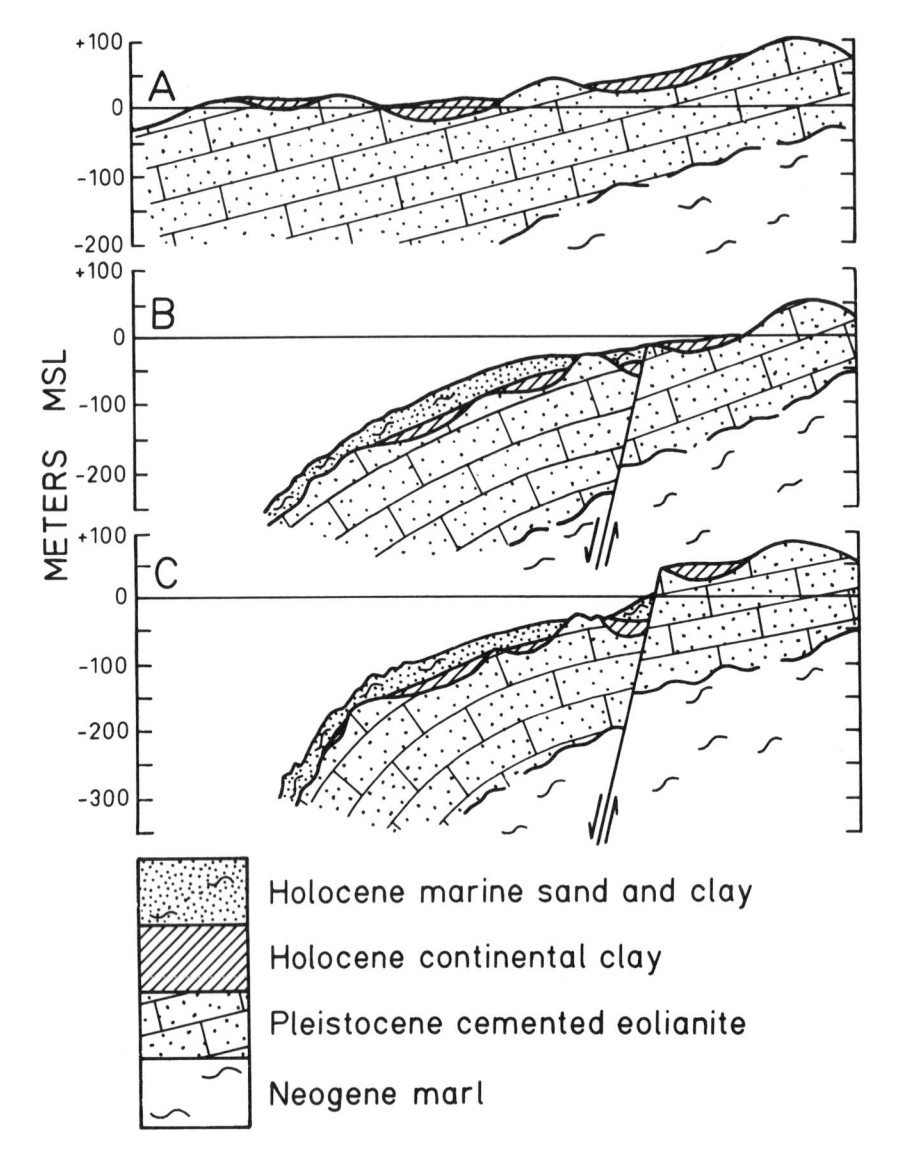

Figure 35. Sketch diagram describing a proposed mechanism for the three stages involved with the generation of each of the oscillatory movements across the coastal fault of Israel that have occurred repeatedly during late Holocene (modified from Neev and Bakler 1978, fig. 3). *A.* Early Holocene—A 100-km broad coastal plain extended rather uniformly both east and west of the present coastline and was slightly tilted to the west. The coastline of that time was along the western fringe of this belt. *B.* Post-middle Holocene—The 100-km wide belt was then downwarped to the west, because of increased subsidence of the Levantine Basin. As the coastline stabilized, the adjacent strip of land at its east became submerged. *C.* Post-middle Holocene—Faulting activity was rejuvenated across an old coast-parallel fault that corresponds with the present coastline. This fault also corresponds with the apex of the downbuckled arch, where the tension accumulated was greatest. The upthrown (eastward) side thereby rebounded to release the tension and re-emerged to return to nearly its pre-downwarping elevation.

of the oceanic one in the easternmost Mediterranean region formed a structural and morphological arc. The width of this arc is about 100 km. Its axis along the present coastline is known to be an ancient line of weakness that corresponds with a buried ancient fault. Probably maximal tensional as well as compressional forces caused by bending of the arc are concentrated along its axis. These forces should increase with an increase in differential vertical movement across the width of the arc. If the marine side of the arc is downwarped more than the continental side, the coastal belt may be dragged downward more intensively and become submerged. Additional tensional force across the arc may tend to be released in an upward movement of the continental side. Eventually, the continental side may rise to its original elevation or locally even somewhat above it. In such an event, the continental side may become tilted landward by a few degrees, as has been recorded just north of Tel Baruch (see Neev et al. 1978a) and along the Deir el Balah—Tel Qatif segment (III D 5). Such a complicated type of movement may not involve earthquakes, because at least part of the movement could be as slow creep.

Although field evidence for similar oscillatory movements elsewhere is scarce, the movements across coasts near convergent plate boundaries may not be unique. For example, two such movements, each lasting about 30 years, were reported by Thatcher (1984) from tide-gauge records of the past century in Japan. The maximum amplitudes along the coast were 2 m, but the net movement for a complete cycle seems to be about zero. Based on the ideas of Imamura (1929) and Fitch and Scholz (1971), these coastal crustal movements may be related to convergence activity at the subduction belt about 150 km offshore and that "the slow interearthquake oceanward tilting and coastal subsidence . . . represented elastic strain buildup, while the abrupt movements of roughly opposite sense that occurred during great earthquakes signaled the release of the accumulated strains" (Thatcher 1984, 3087). Cumulative uplift along the coast of Japan since 1890 correlates well with the distribution of Late Quaternary or Holocene uplifted marine terraces. These oscillatory movements also are associated with marked permanent subsidence that occurs farther inland (see for analogy the sections on Tel Baruch and the Yarkon River, III C 8 and 9).

It can be argued that the continental margin off Israel is a passive one (Garfunkel and Derin 1984; Ginzburg and Ben-Avraham 1986) and the mechanism that generates the oscillatory movements there cannot be compared with that across convergent plate boundaries (such as off Japan, Peru, or Washington-Oregon). This argument may not be valid because oblique collision is postulated to occur along the Pelusium Line, which is a left-lateral megashear located off and subparallel to the coastline of Israel (Neev 1975; Neev et al. 1985). It also is the contact between the Sinai subplate and the African plate. The effect of such an activity (oblique collision), together with northward underthrusting of the African plate at Cyprus and Crete, is to depress the floor of the easternmost Mediterranean basin, thereby bending seaward the arc along the continental margin of Israel with results similar to those along convergent plate boundaries.

5. *History and Rhythm of Tectonic Movements*. The latest glaciation (from about 30,000 until 10,000 y BP) may have been a rather quiet tectonic period; at least sea-level changes were due more to eustatism than to tectonism. Moreover, if fluctuating climatic and sea level changes of the Pleistocene also were associated with isostatically controlled movements, the latest period of glaciation could have been in a trough of a sinusoidal curve of tectonic activity.

If regional vertical differential movement was renewed during the transition from Pleistocene to Holocene, it apparently began with a fast rate of activity that gradually decayed toward the end of middle Holocene (toward the end of the Early Bronze Age, or about 4000 y BP). This break marks the transition into tectonic and climatic regimes that apparently differ in their characteristics from those of the previous period. The change involved an increase in rate and amplitude of movement and the introduction of a new type of movement—an oscillatory one that can be compared with jerks or convulsions of the Earth's crust. The movements repeated themselves in several phases, perhaps having a cyclic or rhythmic nature. Westward downwarping (subsidence of the Levantine Basin) probably has had a more important role in the generation of these young phases than the counterpart regional upwarping of the continent. At least three of these late Holocene oscillatory movements were associated with changes into more humid climates.

6. Contradictory Concepts about Holocene Tectonics near Coastline. An unfavorable reception for the concepts and conclusions expressed here was expected even before the first relevant article was published (Neev et al. 1973). A list of opposing published articles is included in the Introduction—I A. Arguments are especially vigorous with respect to late Holocene oscillatory movements, although they also concern the absolute rate of differential movements since late Pleistocene. The skepticism concerning young oscillatory movements was well expressed by Mazor (1974, 149) as follows: "The notion that the mighty cities of Ashqelon and Caesarea were submerged below the sea a few hundred years ago may well be a nightmare for the present planners and builders of cities, harbors, and industrial plants along the coast today. Relief may be found, however, in the following observations that seem to indicate that the portion of Mediterranean coast under discussion has been, in fact, stable at least since Roman times." The effect of such a subjective, although understandable, human approach is discussed again by us (IV A 9, below) with respect to the probability of eustatic sea-level variations versus local vertical land movements. Mazor and the other opposing colleagues included in their arguments alternative interpretations with respect to some of our crucial finds, such as shell beds, lagoonal (evaporitic and brackish) and freshwater (swamp) clays, and sand dunes, all of which now are on or above the coastal cliff. Most of these controversies are discussed in the text above (II B Units 5a,7c and d; III D 1,2,4) as well as in Neev et al. (1974, 1978b).

The finds of Nir and Eldar (1986a,b, 1987) support Mazor's (1974) conclusions. During their fascinating and dangerous study, they redug seven ancient water wells (some to depths of 20 m) along the coastline between Ashqelon and Dor (see Fig. 1) that originally were dug between Persian (2500 y BP) and Crusader (700 y BP) times. They imply that the Post-Persian paleowatertables in these wells were at elevations that are near mean sea level of the present (± 1.5m). Therefore, they concluded that the coastal belt east of the coastal cliff has been tectonically stable since about 2500 or even 3100 y BP (allowing for vertical shifts of no more than one meter).

Since our first relevant publication (Neev et al. 1973), we have repeatedly stated that the present structural elevation of the upthrown coastal block (east of the coastal cliff) is about the same as that of the pre-oscillatory movements (before 1000, 2000, or 3000 y BP). This conclusion was based on data similar to those of Nir and Eldar (1986b), Mazor (1974), and others. There is no conflict, therefore, between their finds and our concept. However, these data served as just part of the basis for our tectonic model (see Fig. 35). The other part includes sedimentological-stratigraphic data from both the onshore and offshore, as described in Chapters II and III. These data should not be ignored or dismissed, for they describe the environments at the sites between the times of original construction or deposition and the present. Moreover, we do not agree with alternative interpretations about the depositional environments supplied by some of our colleagues (see above). Our model, no matter how odd it may sound to subjective ears, tries to satisfy the entire scope of challenges posed by all the data hitherto found; therefore, we believe it to be correct until a more convincing alternative interpretation is supplied. Moreover, intriguing problems are left still unanswered with respect to coastal stability. Most important of these, of course, is a tendency by workers to overlook well based data that are not compatible with their conclusions.

We also consider as premature any attempt to plot the rate at which the eustatic curve of sea level changed since Persian time (the past 2500 years) from the seven wells of Nir and Eldar (1986a). An average rate of 2 mm/year of sea level rise is estimated by them for the 350-year period between Persian and Hellenistic times. This value is based on present elevations of paleowatertables at Michmoret (-1.40 m) and Yavneh Yam (-0.70 m), respectively (Nir and Eldar 1986b, 1987). However, the present elevation of paleowatertable in another well of Persian age is identical with present mean sea level. This well (Tel Qassila—no. 3 of Nir and Eldar 1986b) is 1.8 km inland of the coastline at the outlet of the Yarkon River (Figs. 8, 19). The +1.80 m elevation of the bottom (or paleowatertable) was projected westward to the coastline by Nir and Eldar in agreement with the regional westward gradient of slightly more than one per mil for the present watertable. Such a difference between nearly zero and -1.40 m for water wells that were dug during the same period (Persian) makes their basis for calculations doubtful.

The Roman paleowatertable at the Tel Mor well about 1 km east of the coastline at Ashdod Yam (Nir and Eldar 1986c, 1987) is now at an elevation of about +2.3 m (redigging bottomed at +1.8 m within the characteristic clay and pottery sherds that accumulated below the watertable). Projecting the one per mil westward gradient to the shoreline places the present elevation of the paleowatertable at +1.3 m msl. These data advocate the presence of a differential vertical tectonic movement rather than eustatic changes of sea level. The net cumulative difference in tectonic movement across the coastline approaches 3.0 m since Persian time (-1.4 to +2.0 m).

It should be implied from the above that we also doubt the validity of the eustatic sea level curves made by Raban and Galili (1985) and Raban (1986) for the past 10,000 years (see also III B 2). In his conclusions, Raban (1986, 104) stated that the coastline of Israel was rather stable, "with no evidence of tectonic offsets during historic periods". Although he sees "archaeological and topographic evidence for longshore fault lines several hundred meters in the sea at Caesarea and off Maagan Michael," he postulated a 2.5m eustatic oscillation of sea level between 2500 y BP and 800 y BP (peaked at +1.4 m msl during the eighth century AD and reached a trough at -1.4 m msl during the thirteenth century AD).

We hope that the Late Bronze water well at Tel Dor, just a few meters east of the coastline (Raban, 1983a as quoted by Nir and Eldar 1986b), and the nearby but now submerged Post-Roman well (see above—III B 3) will be redug to below the present watertable. Continuation of this study may provide more information about tectonism of segments of the coastal upthrown block (whether they still are rising). This is especially true with respect to the critical segment of the coastline between Michmoret and the Yarkon River where no ancient wells have been redug.

Mazor (1974), Flemming (1968), Flemming et al. (1978), Raban (1981, 1983b, 1986), Sneh and Klein (1982), and Nir and Eldar (1986a,b, 1987) discussed the tectonic stability of the coastline with respect to its longitudinal dimension. However, they ignored the transverse (east-west) dimension, across which evidence indicates higher rates of absolute differential movements (subsidence and westward tilting of the offshore inner littoral zone). These offshore tectonic movements occurred during latest Holocene, as indicated even by colleagues who oppose our approach, such as Raban et al. (1976) at Caesarea, and Gifford et al. (in press), and Raban and Tur-Caspa (1979) at Tel Michal. It also was shown by us that during the Holocene, as well as since the Jurassic—Cretaceous transition (see III D 3; Fig. 25), the coastline functioned as a hinge with respect to regional differential movement so that the western oceanic province subsided, whereas the eastern continental belt rose. Consequently, the cumulative vertical movements should increase with distance from the fault. For reasons not yet understood, since Late Bronze time, the relative tectonic rise of the continental side (close to the coastline) was very small (a few meters at most).

We believe that the combined effect of the broad data spectrum presented in this study is more convincing than the limited scopes of our previous publications. Yet we are intrigued by the fact that none of the Post-Roman tectonic events, and especially the Post-Mamlukian one just a few hundred years ago was desribed by contemporary writers. Perhaps the explanation for such a documentation gap should be sought in the cultural-psychological background. For example, if most of the discussed tectonic movements had the nature of a slow creep, one could hardly distinguish their overall effect throughout an entire lifetime. At the other extreme is the phenomenon described by Strabo (see III E 5) of an oscillatory type of movement at Mount Casius recorded during Roman time. Clearly, the presence or absence of a qualified but unprejudiced observer at the site and time of the occurrence is important.

7. Tectonic Origin of Kurkar Ridges. Data from the entire coastal belt of Israel, both onshore and offshore, indicate that the linearity of kurkar ridges is tectonically controlled. In addition, a number of extremely linear coast-parallel photolineaments are evident on the Geological Photomap of Israel (Bartov and Arkin 1975) along the southern coastal plain of Israel, suggesting association with tectonic elements and thereby corroborating the above conclusion. Such a conclusion is supported by the curving and convergence pattern of these ridges, into which the present coastline as well as the Foothill Geosuture are introduced (Fig. 3). Such a pattern fits well into the regional pattern of geosutures (Neev et al. 1985). Another feature that is common to the kurkar ridges and the regional tectonic pattern is the landward curving and the occasionally branching convergence pattern along the northern segments of the three offshore kurkar ridges on approaching Akhziv Canyon (Figs. 3 and 14). The latter is another transverse tectonic element (Neev and Greenfield 1981, 1984) associated with a curving convergence pattern along deeply buried and much older coastal elements off Israel.

The above conclusion about the origin of the kurkar ridges in Israel is not so easy to accept, because their origin as well as the origin of other coast-parallel sand ridges in other parts of the world long have been interpreted as coastal dunes or offshore bars of purely sedimentary origin (see Introduction, I B). A good example is the analysis by Shukri et al. (1956) of the coast-parallel sand ridges between Alexandria and El Alamein. Although the role of sedimentary process in the formation of these sand ridges in Israel and Egypt should not be ignored, it still is worthwhile to further discuss several aspects relevant to the problem of their origin:

(i) Relatively thick hamra (red loam) layers alternate with eolianitic quartz-sand units within the three coast-parallel kurkar ridges on the coastal plain of Israel. If our interpretation about the mudflat (aquatic) origin of the hamra beds is correct, the interbedded dunes originally must have been deposited as sand sheets and not necessarily as coastal dunes. Moreover, the patterns of occasional barchans along the coastal kurkar ridge of Israel (Fig. 5) indicate that they originally migrated northeastward (in agreement with the prevailing direction of southwesterly winter storms) diagonally to the trend of the coastline (see Fig. 8). We doubt that these kurkar ridges originally were linear coastal dune ridges and suggest that they are tectonically elevated ridges formed along pre-existing tectonic lineaments (such as was recorded for Ramat Aviv C; III C 8 and 9; Figs. 18 to 21).

(ii) All of the linear kurkar sand ridges between Alexandria and El Alamein (Fig. 36B), except for the recent coastal one, are terminated sharply upon approaching the inland (southward) extension of the bisector that crosses the curved coastline of the gulf just east of El Alamein (Shukri et al. 1956, fig. 1). This abrupt termination throws doubt upon the exclusiveness of their sedimentary origin as coastal beach dunes (or bars). Results of a lineament analysis made on two LANDSAT images from this area (Fig. 36B) support these doubts. Three sets of differently trending photolineaments were traced, although merging and adjusting features were noted at intersections. These trends are NE to ENE, WNW-ESE, and E-W. In fact, these same three sets previously were identified in this area by Neev et al. (1982) and in their more regional context by Neev (1975) and Neev et al. (1976). Lineaments of the first set directly extend the kurkar ridges toward the southwest and west-southwest from their previously known points of termination (see above) at least as far as the northern rim of the Qattara Depression. The northwesternmost lineament within this set appears to extend from the coastline toward and along the north-

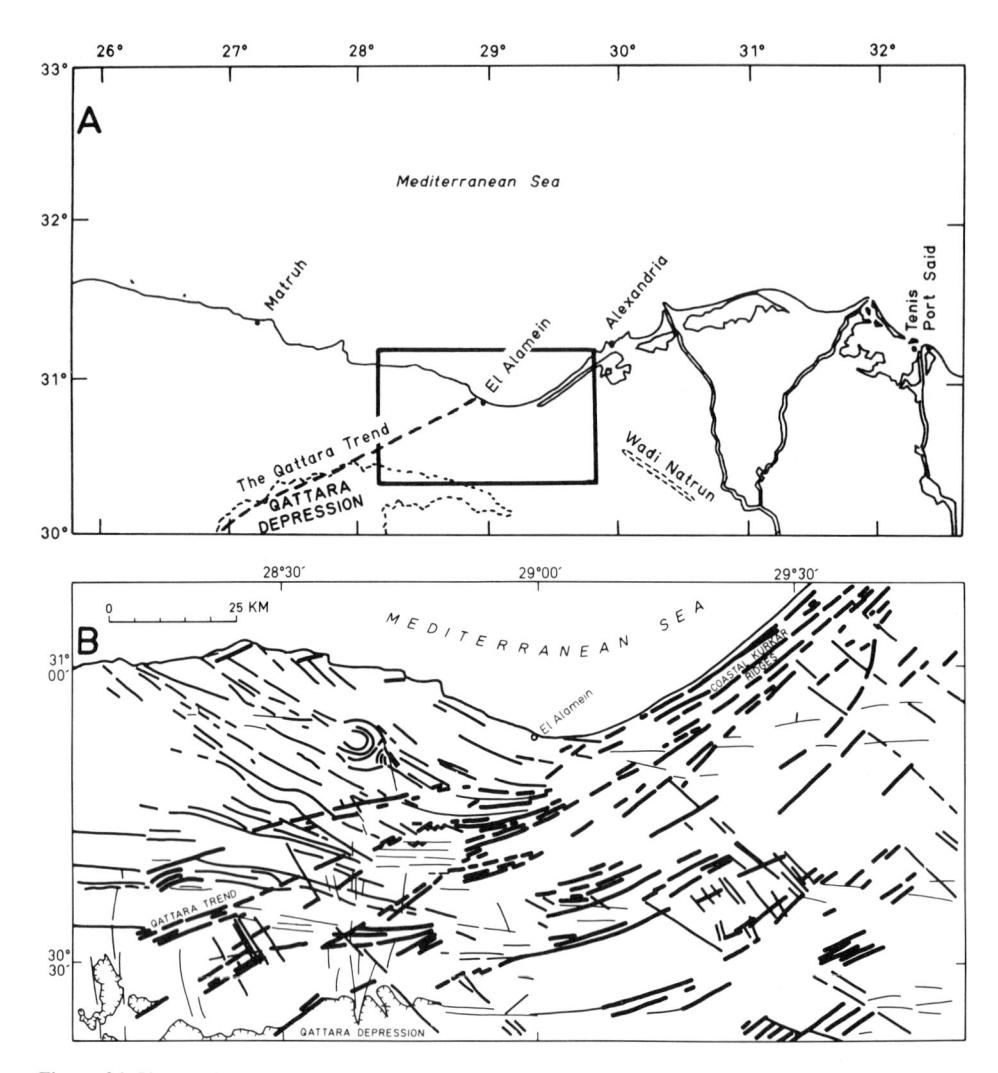

Figure 36. Photogeological study of lineaments across northwestern Egypt, made on two LANDSAT images (3 and 4 of 16 July 1984, 178/039 quadrants 1 and 2) in order to investigate the origin of coast-parallel kurkar ridges between Alexandria and El Alamain (Shukri et al. 1956, fig. 1). *A.* A reference map showing the broader scope and extent of some features noted on *B*, as inferred from additional geophysical and geological data. *B.* Photolineament map indicating coexistence of three different tectonic trends: (i) the Qattara trend (NE to ENE) and its extension along the Al Alamain—Alexandria kurkar ridges, (ii) the Tethyan trend (WNW and NW) that extends inland through Wadi Natrun to Cairo (see *A)*, and (iii) the equatorial (east-west) trend. At intersections of these three sets, some lineaments of one set curve and merge with others of a different set.

western rim of the Qattara Depression and beyond (Fig. 36A). It is considered by Neev et al. (1982, 1026, on the basis of the analysis of LANDSAT scene E-1149-08132-5 from 19 Dec. 1972) to be "the southwestward extension of the Qattara—Eratosthenes Shear . . . [and is] associated with indications of left-lateral offsets." Similar indications for left-lateral shifts also were noted on the satellite photographs analysed for the present study (Fig. 36B). The Qattara Trend (N45°–60°E) was described by Riad et al. (1983) mainly from analysis of their regional Bouguer gravity anomaly map. It extends as a gravity feature between the Qattara Depression and the coastline just west of El Alamein. Similarly, an isogammic contour that separates two provinces of magnetic anomalies appears to extend west-southwestward from the coastline just west of El Alamein and along the entire northwestern rim of the Qattara Depression (Meshref 1982; see also our Fig. 36A). This set of lineaments appears to converge slightly toward the northeast.

On the basis of the following observations we consider that the photolineaments of the second set (trending WNW-ESE) that dominate in the area northwest of the Qattara—El Alamein lineament (Fig. 36B) also may be tectonic in origin: (i) Linear trends and shapes of these lineaments suggest that at least some of them cross brittle rocks and form edges of cuestas. (ii) Angular offsets of the coastline at points where it is intersected by these lineaments suggest involvement of a tectonic factor. (iii) Tectonic lineaments that parallel the west-northwest trending coastline of Cyrenaica appear to extend inland beyond El Alamein toward the east-southeast through the narrow 50-km long depression of Wadi Natrun to end near Cairo (Fig. 36A).

The third set of photolineaments trends east-west and occurs mainly along the northern rim of the Qattara Depression (Fig. 36B). It also is present farther south as well as across the Cairo—Suez and northern Sinai districts (Neev et al. 1982).

The presence of three distinct sets of linear kurkar ridges in the region of the Nile Delta and the Qattara Depression suggests that the ridges are associated with tectonic lineaments either directly or by sand deposition along pre-existing topography

8. Seacliff Origin and Evolution. The presence of narrow kurkar ridges separated by broad plains means that changing relative sea levels of the past have produced a sequence of seacliffs from the outermost now-submerged ridge to the present cliff at the shore, with other ridges still on land awaiting their turn to become sites of seacliffs. Most steep slopes of these offshore ridges are on their eastern (landward) sides (Neev et al. 1966, figs. 2, 3, 4; Neev et al. 1976, figs. 9, 10, 12), but all of the original slopes may be obscured by their own debris left behind as sea level rose or the continental shelf subsided. Further burial and smoothing was provided by new marine sediments including remains of calcareous organisms.

Rapid rise of late Würm—early Holocene sea level probably produced only a thin bevelling of the now-submerged seacliffs, far less erosion than experienced by the present coastal kurkar ridge during the past 6000 years when sea level rose more slowly. Concentrated marine erosion could have begun even earlier along some coastal sections where uplift of the land kept approximate pace with rise of sea level. Vigorous wave attack augmented by uplift along the coastal fault produced the present seacliff with its steep slopes and exposed strata (Figs. 5, 9, 17, 18, 21, and 24). The most intensive seacliff recession in Israel may have been during Middle to Late Bronze time (about 3600 to 3300 y BP) because of combined local faulting and vigorous tsunamis (III C 7—Tel Michal). The longest stretch of modern high (to 40 m) seacliffs occurs between Netanya and Yafo.

North of Netanya this cliff gradually and irregularly decreases to only a few meters at Michmoret and Caesarea. High parts of the seacliff farther north and south mark local outcrops of hard kurkar (former high dunes). Between these higher places, the seacliff consists of gentle slopes cut in soft kurkar or hamra or low vertical cliffs in calcarenite. Locally, seacliffs are mantled and obscured by debris from weathering and erosion of the cliff. Regions of low seacliffs, particularly south of Yafo, also include stretches where sand blown from adjacent beaches has buried low cliffs so that no cliff may be visible. The close relationship between height of seacliff and its stratigraphic composition also is a function of the relative present activity of marine erosion along different parts of the coast.

Forecasting the future of seacliffs along the coastal kurkar ridge is difficult, as the process of recession is likely to be affected by future tectonic movements along the coastal fault and by possible faster rise of sea level. Where the ridge is narrow or composed of the most easily eroded materials, the seacliff should recede quickly and rise to its maximum height along the axis of the ridge. Further erosion would then lower the height of the seacliff and locally even remove it entirely to allow the landward side of the ridge remnants to become flooded by seawater. Thus, some seacliffs of Israel should progressively increase in height for a time, whereas others should progressively diminish.

At many sites, seacliff retreat during the past was slowed by construction of seawalls and later collapse of towers: Atlit, Dor, and Yafo by Phoenicians; Apollonia by Romans; Caesarea by Romans and Crusaders, and Akko by Crusaders. In these and other sites, earlier seawalls and shore structures were built by older cultures, and then repairs and new structures were made by younger cultures. In fact, some present municipalities along the coast have built the most extensive shore-protection structures of all time—detached breakwaters, groins, harbors, and seawalls that have protected some areas and exposed others to such severe erosion that even more structures are planned as remedies.

B. Comparison of Tectonics along Entire Coast

Criteria, evidence, and recognized dates of tectonic movements at about 30 geological-archaeological sites along the coasts of Israel and northwestern Sinai were discussed in detail within Chapter III. The essence of the relevant data plotted in Figure 37 includes 14 diagrams made for individual sites or closely associated groups of sites along the coast. In each of these diagrams, present elevations of indicators of past relative sea levels were plotted against their ages for the period between 19,000 years ago and the present. The diagrams show relative sea level changes that appear to be extreme in dimensions and abrupt in time. Changes are not necessarily contemporary at different sites. Such a pattern is similar to that of relative sea level (land level) changes throughout the world as revealed by tide-gauge records (Emery and Aubrey 1985; Aubrey and Emery 1986) and by radiocarbon dates (Newman et al. 1980). Their variation means that base level changes are due not only to eustatic variations of sea level but that they especially reflect local vertical movements of land levels (the land to which the tide gauge is attached). Changes in mean annual relative sea level and the annual average position of the shoreline are functions of differences in movement of ocean surface and ocean floor. It is only human desire for stability that leads one to believe intuitively that the solid land is more stable in long-term level than is the undulating water surface. Investigations of tide-gauge records to date, however, indicate that during the past half century annual average movements of the land in the coastal belt commonly are at least ten times the amplitude of the changes in mean annual sea level.

The data for each point on the relative sea (land) level lines of Figure 37 are derived from the previous text and are indicated only briefly on the diagrams and figure caption. Some of the jaggedness of connecting lines comes from inability of either geological or archaeological evidence to provide more precise levels of the sea during the entire time that diagnostic sediments were being deposited or when man-made structures were being attacked by wave erosion. Dates of activity are limited to the times that recognizable and now-exposed deposits were formed or that buildings happened to be close enough to the shore to be able to retain the imprint of marine erosion or submergence and yet not become totally lost by erosion.

The record, imperfect as it is, tells a story of tectonism if we are able to translate what is recorded into history—a job that is neither easy nor simple. One of the most striking parts of the record is the difference between the elevation history of the general onshore and general offshore belts. As indicated by almost all profiles of Figure 37, where data are available, the offshore belt has predominantly dropped, whereas the onshore one has predominantly risen. This difference, as well as oscillatory (down-and-up) movement of the onshore, is attributed to vertical movements of the coast on either side of the coastal fault or faults through the mechanism suggested by Figure 35.

Secondary variations in level are better recorded on land than on the sea floor because of far greater intensity of geological and archaeological exploration on land. The best way to generalize these differences and to subdivide the region into segments that have had somewhat similar tectonic histories is to plot the data separately for segments that appear to have behaved similarly. This method also provides more continuity with time than do individual sites where observations are discontinous due to chance of recording, chance of discovery, and chance of ability to determine dates of past events. By this means the northern one-fifth of the coast (Akhziv to Michmoret) is shown by Figure 38 to be related in that recorded onshore uplift during the past 15,000 years was limited to about 20 m and offshore downdrop was mainly only about 10 m, but some sites that are more than 9000 y BP reached 40 m. In contrast, the next one-fifth of the coast (between Netanya and Nizzanim) experienced extreme onshore uplift and offshore downdrop, both commonly to 40 m for sites older than a few thousand years. Again in contrast, the southwestern three-fifths of the coast (between Gaza and Pelusium) records only uplift and to less than 30 m with no data prior to about 10,000 y BP. The absence of recorded offshore downdrop in this region (off Sinai) may simply be due to far less submarine geological and archaeological exploration than off Israel. Within each of the three coastal segments are smaller coastal units that have recorded differential tectonic movements, as indicated by Figure 37.

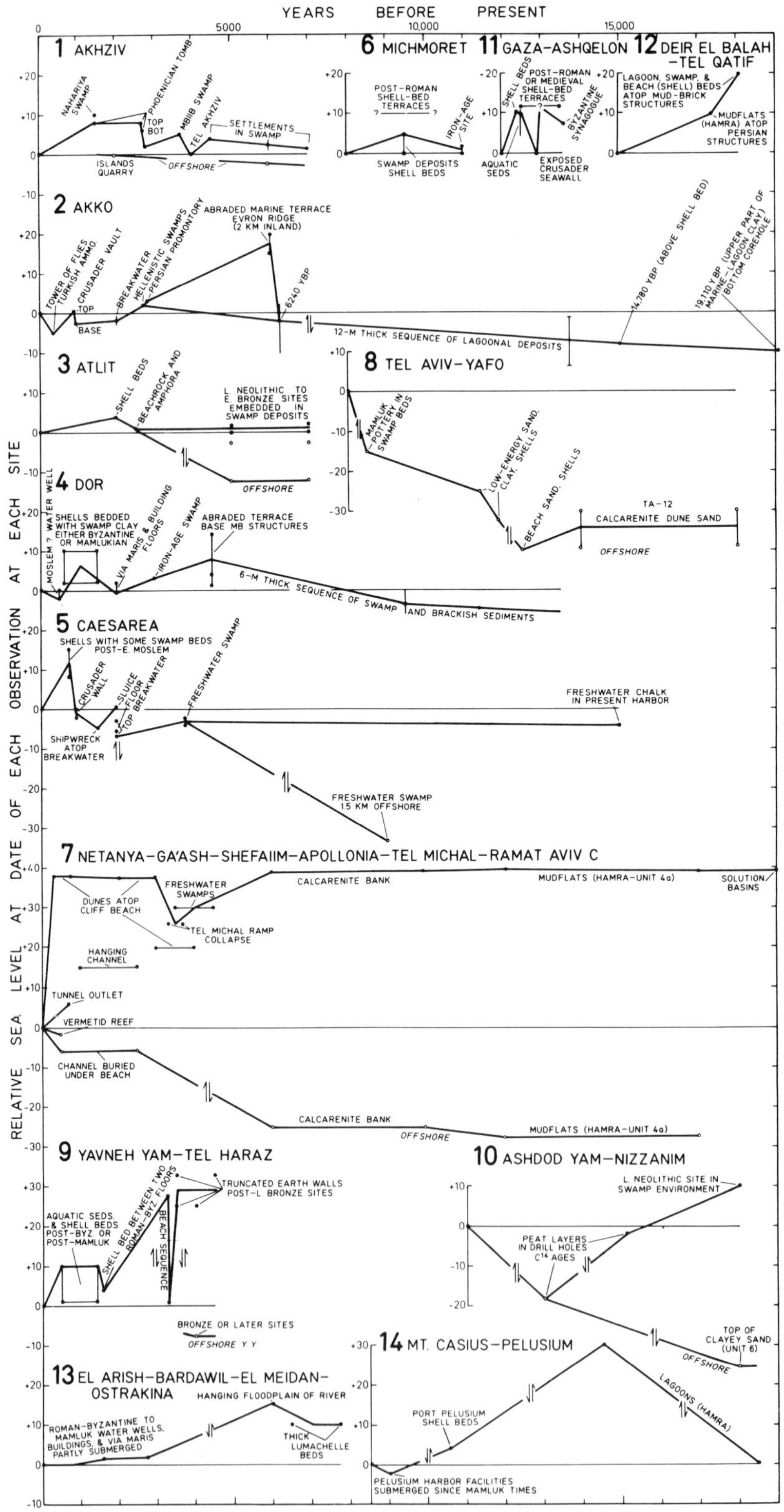
YEARS BEFORE PRESENT
0
5000
10,000
15,000
RELATIVE SEA LEVEL AT DATE OF EACH OBSERVATION AT EACH SITE
1 AKHZIV
NAHARIYA SWAMP
PHOENICIAN TOMB
TOP
BOT.
MBIIB SWAMP
TEL AKHZIV
SETTLEMENTS IN SWAMP
ISLANDS QUARRY
OFFSHORE
6 MICHMORET
POST-ROMAN SHELL-BED TERRACES
IRON-AGE SITE
SWAMP DEPOSITS SHELL BEDS
11 GAZA-ASHQELON
SHELL BEDS
POST-ROMAN OR MEDIEVAL SHELL-BED TERRACES
BYZANTINE SYNAGOGUE
AQUATIC SEDS
EXPOSED CRUSADER SEAWALL
12 DEIR EL BALAH -TEL QATIF
LAGOON, SWAMP, & BEACH (SHELL) BEDS ATOP MUD-BRICK STRUCTURES
MUDFLATS (HAMRA) ATOP PERSIAN STRUCTURES
2 AKKO
TOWER OF FLIES TURKISH AMMO
CRUSADER VAULT
TOP
BASE
BREAKWATER
HELLENISTIC SWAMPS
PERSIAN PROMONTORY
ABRADED MARINE TERRACE EVRON RIDGE (2 KM INLAND)
6240 YBP
12-M THICK SEQUENCE OF LAGOONAL DEPOSITS
14,780 YBP (ABOVE SHELL BED)
19,110 YBP (UPPER PART OF MARINE-LAGOON CLAY) BOTTOM COREHOLE
3 ATLIT
SHELL BEDS
BEACHROCK AND AMPHORA
L. NEOLITHIC TO E. BRONZE SITES EMBEDDED IN SWAMP DEPOSITS
OFFSHORE
8 TEL AVIV-YAFO
MAMLUK POTTERY IN SWAMP BEDS
LOW-ENERGY SAND, CLAY, SHELLS
BEACH SAND, SHELLS
TA-12
CALCARENITE DUNE SAND
OFFSHORE
4 DOR
MOSLEM ? WATER WELL
SHELLS BEDDED WITH SWAMP CLAY EITHER BYZANTINE OR MAMLUKIAN
VIA MARIS & BUILDING FLOORS
IRON-AGE SWAMP
ABRADED TERRACE BASE MB STRUCTURES
6-M THICK SEQUENCE OF SWAMP AND BRACKISH SEDIMENTS
5 CAESAREA
SHELLS WITH SOME SWAMP BEDS POST-E. MOSLEM
CRUSADER WALL
SLUICE FLOOR
TOP BREAKWATER
FRESHWATER SWAMP
SHIPWRECK ATOP BREAKWATER
FRESHWATER CHALK IN PRESENT HARBOR
FRESHWATER SWAMP 1.5 KM OFFSHORE
7 NETANYA-GA'ASH-SHEFAIIM-APOLLONIA-TEL MICHAL-RAMAT AVIV C
DUNES ATOP CLIFF BEACH
FRESHWATER SWAMPS
TEL MICHAL RAMP COLLAPSE
CALCARENITE BANK
MUDFLATS (HAMRA-UNIT 4a)
SOLUTION BASINS
HANGING CHANNEL
TUNNEL OUTLET
VERMETID REEF
CHANNEL BURIED UNDER BEACH
CALCARENITE BANK
OFFSHORE
MUDFLATS (HAMRA-UNIT 4a)
9 YAVNEH YAM-TEL HARAZ
AQUATIC SEDS. & SHELL BEDS POST-BYZ. OR POST-MAMLUK
SHELL BED BETWEEN TWO ROMAN-BYZ. FLOORS
BEACH SEQUENCE
TRUNCATED EARTH WALLS POST-L BRONZE SITES
BRONZE OR LATER SITES
OFFSHORE Y Y
10 ASHDOD YAM-NIZZANIM
L. NEOLITHIC SITE IN SWAMP ENVIRONMENT
PEAT LAYERS IN DRILL HOLES C14 AGES
TOP OF CLAYEY SAND (UNIT 6)
OFFSHORE
13 EL ARISH-BARDAWIL-EL MEIDAN-OSTRAKINA
HANGING FLOODPLAIN OF RIVER
ROMAN-BYZANTINE TO MAMLUK WATER WELLS, BUILDINGS, & VIA MARIS PARTLY SUBMERGED
THICK LUMACHELLE BEDS
14 MT. CASIUS-PELUSIUM
PORT PELUSIUM SHELL BEDS
LAGOONS (HAMRA)
PELUSIUM HARBOR FACILITIES SUBMERGED SINCE MAMLUK TIMES

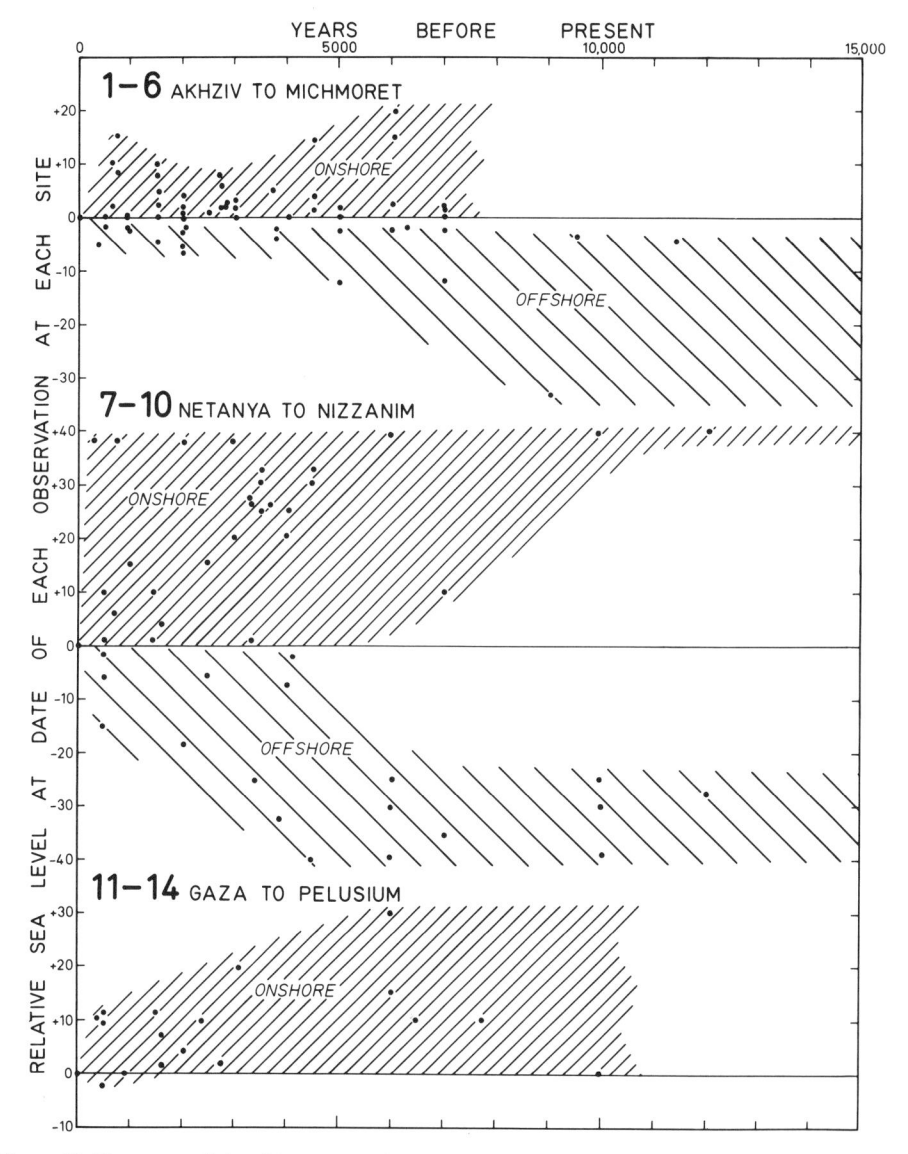

Figure 38. Three generalizing diagrams containing data of Figure 37 plotted together for three segments of the coast: (i) the northern one-fifth of the coast (Akhziv to Michmoret), (ii) the central one-fifth (Netanya to Nizzanim), and (iii) the southwestern three-fifths (Gaza to Pelusium). These diagrams show that the cumulative magnitude of the vertical differential movements across the central segment (80 m) was appreciably greater than across the northern one (30 to 50 m) and apparently also than across the southwestern one (where data for the offshore belt are scarce).

◁

Figure 37. Fourteen diagrams in which present elevations of past sea level indicators are plotted against their ages for the period between 19,000 y BP and the present. Each diagram represents data recovered from an individual site or from a closely associated group of sites, both onshore (solid dots) and offshore (open circles). The lines connecting the data points in all 14 diagrams tell a story of tectonism along the coast in which the offshore belt has predominantly dropped, whereas the onshore one has predominantly risen. They also indicate the repeated occurrence of oscillatory (down and up) movements of the onshore block through the mechanism suggested in Figure 35.

C. Depositional History Relative to Climate, Sea Level, and Coastline

1. Late Pleistocene. (50,000 to 10,000 y BP). The remarkable increase of sand supply from the Arabo-Nubian Massif into nearby basins during the Pleistocene left a significant imprint on physiography. Much of this sand was supplied by the Nile River to the southeastern Mediterranean Sea. The process was influenced by both climatic and tectonic factors. Upon reaching the coast, much of the quartz-sand migrated northeastward along the beaches by longshore wave-induced currents. Excess sand was swept from the beaches and transported landward by the wind to accumulate as dunes. Along the coast of Israel, these dunes became cemented diagenetically to form the friable Kurkar rock unit. Cementation diminished southward (less calcite), so that in northwestern Sinai the sand dunes remained uncemented. The latest important phase of the Pleistocene inland sand supply (II B Unit 1) terminated 50,000 to 40,000 years ago. The overlying generation of sand dunes (Unit 3) has much more limited areal distribution, thereby indicating a diminution of supply. Absence of a coastal cliff during that phase explains the large distances to which these dunes encroached inland, reaching as far east as the foothills geosuture (Fig. 3).

The break in sand supply that followed was rather long, persisting until about 10,000 y BP. During that long break, the lowlands of the present inner shelf and coastal plain were covered mostly by freshwater and brackish lakes. This lake environment gradually changed upward in the sequence into a mudflat one, where hamra and swamp sediments dominated. Both environments indicate low relief near sea level. During the time span of this break (40,000 to 10,000 y BP), the level of the ocean appreciably changed eustatically (by a range of more than a hundred meters). Consequently, the coastline probably shifted relatively great distances back and forth in an east-west direction. Its configuration approached a linear shape but did not reach the present alignment. The climate warmed toward and during the Pleistocene—Holocene transition in correspondence with the sea level rise. However, in the Rub al Khali (southern Saudi Arabia) "Aridity of the present day intensity appears to have begun about 17,000 years BP, " as indicated by the prevalence of desiccation (gypsum deposits) and by the abundance of dune sands (McClure 1978, 253–8). Most of this hyperarid period, which lasted in the Arabian Peninsula until about 9000 y BP, coincided with the latest glaciation phase at high latitudes and with the corresponding pluvial phase in the Dead Sea—Jordan Valley (Neev and Hall 1977). These phenomena of late Pleistocene and Holocene ice-age aridity and interglacial pluviality occurred in Arabia and in the subtropical Sahara, as discussed and explained by Whitney (1983, 28–33) on the basis of regional and global climatic models. In fact, most of the dry and humid climatic peaks noted by Hötzl and Zötl (1978, table 50) to have occured in central and eastern Arabia since latest Pleistocene are out of phase with their contemporary ones in the Dead Sea—Jordan Valley (Neev and Hall 1977). The most significant differences are represented by the extremely dry period in Arabia between 25,000 and 14,000 y BP and the more humid (pluvial) one between 7000 and 4500 y BP.

The time-stratigraphic equivalent for most of the latest Pleistocene (25,000 to 14,000 y BP) hyperarid sediments of Arabia along the coastline of Israel is Unit 4a (the Netanya Hamra, or red loam). Absence of sand dunes in this unit can be attributed to a phase of tectonic quiescence in the Nile Delta region and aridity within the catchment area of the Nile River (mostly the Ethiopian highlands and eastern Sahara).

2. Early to Middle Holocene. (10,000 to 4000 y BP). About 10,000 years ago, a new but feeble phase of quartz-sand supply into the Mediterranean Sea began. Quantities of the quartz fraction diminished away from the source, along the northeastward route of sand migration within the littoral zone. Consequently, environments suitable for production of biogenic sands at the sea bottom increased in northern provinces as compared with southern ones, and the Calcarenitic Bank (Unit 5a) was deposited. The Calcarenitic Bank wedges out landward across the central segment of the coastline, and within a rather short distance eastward, the sand was dissipated within a belt of swamps. Swamp deposits accumulated there, perhaps uninterruptedly, after the beginning of Holocene until about the end of Early Bronze time (about 4000 y BP). The same sequence of swamp deposits dominated both in the present offshore and onshore belts of the Hof Hacarmel and the northern segments of the coastal belt, as well as along the landward side of the southern segment (between Yafo and Rafiah).

It is possible that during the peak of the early Holocene transgression the configuration of the coastline differed from the present one in two respects: (i) Whereas along the central segment it corresponded with about the same area and shape as at present, in the northern two segments (north of Caesarea) it was at least a few kilometers farther west. Unfortunately, no data are available to check this possibility for the southern two segments—south of Yafo. (ii) No coastal cliff existed then at the position of the present coastline (at least for the segments between Rosh Haniqra and Yafo).

The swamp or mudflat sediments that accumulated during this time span (10,000 to 4000 y BP) along the southern segments (south of Wadi Gaza) differ from their more northern equivalents by their relatively lighter color, tan in the south versus dark brown in the north. The transition is a gradual one, and it occurs at the present climatic boundary between the Negev and more northern territories. The opposing attitude of climatic fluctuations in Arabia and in Israel (Dead Sea—Jordan graben) since latest Pleistocene has already been mentioned (Synopsis B 1). Relevant major differences during the Holocene are: (i) relative aridity during the climatic optimum in Israel (7000 to 4500 y BP) versus wet climate in Arabia (9000 to 6000 y BP according to McClure 1978, fig. 84, or 7000 to 4500 y BP according to Hötzl and Zötl 1978, table 50) and in Predynastic Egypt along the Nile Valley (Butzer, 1976, 105), and (ii) the pluvial period in Israel between 4000 and 2500 y BP (Neev and Hall 1977, fig. 5) versus hyperaridity in Arabia between 6000 y BP and the present (McClure 1978, fig. 84).

3. Late Holocene. (4000 y BP to Present). The transition from the Early to the Middle Bronze periods about 4000 years ago is most remarkably expressed by three physical changes across the coastal belt: (i) The present coastline and the adjoining seacliff were initiated by rejuvenation of differential vertical movements. (ii) The sea transgressed eastward across the present littoral belt perhaps more because of subsidence of the sea floor and tilt to the west than to additional eustatic rise of sea level. Consequently, sandy marine sediments accumulated along the outer littoral belt, at first within a high-energy environment and later in a lower energy one (deposited in deeper water). (iii) The continental block east of the coastline was uplifted, thereby rejuvenating erosional processes that entrenched the late Pleistocene drainage pattern into the Uppermost Erosional Surface (II B Unit 2).

The three or four oscillatory vertical movements that occurred during the past 4000 years across the coastline (see above) temporarily established conditions suitable for swamps as well as for landward encroachment of sand dunes from the beaches. These conditions were created and extinguished several times. A sequence of three generations of loose quartz-sand dunes topped the onshore part of the coastal belt during the late Holocene. The first generation was deposited during Middle to Late Bronze ages (4000 to 3000 y BP). These sands are separated from the overlying two younger sands by a dark-brown sandy soil layer, thereby suggesting a relatively long intermission in sand supply that lasted possibly until Late Roman time. The fact that the lower sand layer is appreciably thinner than the upper two ones deserves an explanation, especially because its period of deposition was relatively long. A possible explanation is that thickness of the sand layers was more closely related to the rate of sand supply from the Nile River than to other factors. Such a conclusion is corroborated by other relevant observations made in the region (such as III E 7 and others that are discussed below). This increase in sand supply to Israel could have been generated by a climatic factor, larger waves, a tectonic change, or all of them.

A climatic change could cause increased aridity and sand storms in the Sahara Desert and the Ethiopian Mountains, thereby increasing the airborne sand supply into the Nile catchment area. A tectonic factor could influence the rate of sand supply through the Nile River by a slight northward or northeastward tilt of the Nile Delta. Physiographic changes across the delta suggest such a tilt sometime between the Early Moslem Period (seventh to tenth century AD) and the present. The seven-branched pattern that this delta attained since at least the fifth century BC (as described by Herodotus; Carter 1958, 99) was maintained at least until the fourth century AD (Said 1981, fig. 52c) or even until the ninth century (the Early Moslem Period; Toussoun 1925). Since then, the number of branches has diminished to two: the Damietta and the Rosetta ones. Such a change could be explained by an increase in seaward gradient (a northward tilt) of the delta sometime after the Early Moslem Period. The Post-Mamlukian tectonic subsidence of the city-harbor of Pelusium (III E 7) and of the industrial city-harbor of Tenis (about 10 km south of Port Said), together with an uplift to about ± 50 m msl of the southwestern province of the delta (adjacent and parallel to Wadi Natrun—as observed by the first author), suggests a northward or northeastward tectonic tilt of the entire delta with the pivotal line somewhere in its midst. Butzer (1976, 106) attributed the Post-Roman abandonment of the northernmost delta to autocompaction and storms but did not explain why similar lagoons were not formed along the western fringes of the delta.

D. Cultural History

Cultural history of the region is beyond the real scope of this work; the impact that the natural physical processes have on the cultural history of the region is such a fascinating and important subject that it deserves a separate treatment. Such a study should include botanical and zoological aspects in addition to the geological ones. Nevertheless, we prefer to introduce the following three subheadings that cover material quite closely related to our main subject.

1. Coastline Positions and Their Relation to Settlements. One of the most important physical factors that controlled the development of cultural history in the region was the position of the coastline. This factor must have been effective here until the end of the Early Bronze Period, as inferred from the following two points: (i) After Early Bronze (4000 y BP), the rate of eustatic change of sea level was appreciably reduced. (ii) A coastal cliff was formed by both marine erosion and renewed activity along the coastal fault. It created a physical barrier along which the coastline stabilized. Subsequent east-west landward shift of the Israeli coastline probably was less than the shoreline shift across other continental shelves in the world where similar tectonic movements did not occur. Consequently, the impact of a migrating coastline on human societies that resided along the late Pleistocene coastal plain of Israel since the Middle Bronze Age (the need to change habitat or to move long distances in order to stay in the same habitat) also was reduced.

The results of insistence on the rebuilding of a settlement several times just at the same site along a tectonically active coastline (such as noted at Akhziv, Dor, Caesarea, Apollonia, Tel Michal, and Yavneh Yam) could be measured in terms of cost and benefit, as such a behavior always demanded its tollage. There had to be a good reason (an economical and or a strategic one) to justify rebuilding a site after its destruction by an earthquake. There were other examples, such as at Ashdod and Gaza (the settlements of the Bronze through Iron ages) as well as at Khan Yunes (a settlement established during Mamlukian time—see Figs. 1, 30 for its position), where the sites were established a few kilometers inland. Apparently, such an approach was intended to avoid the most severe effects of earthquakes and tsunamis associated with rejuvenation of the coastal fault.

2. Effects of Coastal Dunes. The crossing of an active sand sea is a cumbersome task for a civilian caravan and even more so for a military convoy that involves transportation of heavy supplies. In addition, there are problems of water supply for the caravans as well as the difficulties associated with extreme climatic conditions. For these reasons, crossing of the northwestern Sinai desert involved tremendous transportation problems. Such difficulties were much increased during and following the phases of intensive sand movement when the dunes encroached inland and blanketed the routes. On the other hand, problems were much relieved during periods when the dunes became stabilized. A rough estimate of the dates of dune stabilization (when it was relatively easy for armies to cross the Sinai desert) is as follows (based on data at III E 7): (i) during Early Bronze times

(5500 to 4500 y BP); (ii) during Late Bronze to Early Roman times (3500 to 2000 y BP); and (iii) during Early Moslem to Mamlukian times (1400 to 500 y BP).

Actual tracks of specific routes between Egypt and Israel (Canaan) are much influenced by the distribution pattern of active sand dunes. Such a suggestion is based on the following considerations: (i) Most parts of the critical segment of the coastal overland route between Egypt and Canaan (Oren 1973), that extends between Qantara (on the Suez Canal) and El Arish, are along the southern inland fringes of Bardawil Lagoon and its adjacent sabkhas. This part of the route is relatively more protected from landward-encroaching coastal dunes. (ii) The Via Maris (Neev and Friedman 1978; III E 7, above) became an active route as soon as the western half of the Bardawil Lagoon arcuate bar was uplifted and emerged to create a stable though very narrow land bridge. Apparently, this long continuous and uniform strip of wet sandy beach served as a comfortable route, especially for pedestrians and camels. (iii) The route between Ismailya (on the central segment of the Suez Canal) and the Central Negev probably was free of dunes until about 500 years ago (Jarvis, 1943; III E 7 above).

3. Tectonic Instability (Earthquakes) and Climatic Changes. The period from Neolithic to the end of Early Bronze times (about 9000 to 4000 y BP) appears to have had rather mild and more uniform climatic conditions as well as a relatively stable tectonic regimen in comparison with the subsequent period. Although the so-called climatic optimum occurred during the Chalcolithic Period (about 6000 y BP), the related cultural and demographic processes reached their peaks somewhat later, near the end of Early Bronze or perhaps even during the Middle Bronze time. This is true for Anatolia and Crete—Santorini as well as for Egypt and the Fertile Crescent (Mesopotamia, Syria, Lebanon, and Israel). It is doubtful whether the same human societies living in the same regions could have reached such high standards of vitality and cultural achievements, if climatic conditions at their time had been the same as at present.

A radical change occurred in the regional cultural and demographic pattern probably after the Early Bronze Period. Differences were caused by both tectonic and climatic

Table 6
Tectonism, Climate, and Culture

Culture	Tectonic Phases	Wet Climatic Phases	Human Migrations
Early to Middle Bronze	+	+	First settlement at Dor, Break at Beit Yerah (Sea of Galilee), Zoar
Middle to Late Bronze	+	+	Santorini, Tel Michal, Yavneh Yam, Tel Haraz
Iron	+	?	Tel Gaza
Persian	+	?	Deir el Balah, Pelusium Harbor
Byzantine	+	+	Yavneh Yam, Gaza Harbor, Akhziv
Mamluk	+	+	Via Maris, Pelusium Harbor, Apollonia, Caesarea

factors. Judging from coastline data, there were perhaps six tectonic phases during that time span: (i) Early Bronze to Middle Bronze; (ii) Middle Bronze to Late Bronze (perhaps associated with the pre-Santorini and Santorini volcanic eruptions); (iii) Middle Iron; (iv) Late Iron to Persian; (v) Byzantine; and (vi) Late Mamlukian. Four more humid climatic phases also occurred: (i) Early Bronze to Middle Bronze; (ii) Middle to Late Bronze; (iii) Byzantine; and (iv) Post-Mamlukian. A correlation may exist between the following breaks in the history of the different dynasties and rules of Egypt and the six climatic and tectonic phases (Table 6). These breaks are the transitions from the Early to the Middle and from the Middle to Late Kingdoms, as well as the conquests of Egypt by the Persians, Early Moslems, and Turks. Mistakes in this correlation probably are relatively minor and can be due to lag effects and inaccuracies in methods of dating or both.

Another aspect of the cultural-climatic problem may be the gradual shift from south to north of the cultural vitality of human societies during the past four thousand years (from Egypt and Mesopotamia through Greece and Rome to central and northern Europe). Such a shift could be influenced by an overall trend of global climatic warming, on which several secondary fluctuations of colder-wetter weather are superimposed.

References

Adler, E., 1985, Submerged kurkar ridges off the northern Carmel coast, Israel: Israel Oceanographic and Limnological Research Institute with Univ. Haifa, Dept. Maritime Civilizations, unpubl. master's thesis, 106 p. (Hebrew with English abstract).

Allen, J. R. L., 1984, Experiments on the terminal fall of the valves of bivalve molluscs loaded with sand trapped from a dispersion: Sedimentary Geology, v. 39, p. 197–209.

Almagor, G., 1979, Relict sediments of Pleistocene age on the continental shelf of northern Sinai and southern Israel: Israel Jour. Earth-Sciences, v. 27, p. 128–132.

_____, and J. K. Hall, 1980, Morphology of the continental margin off northern Israel and southern Lebanon: Israel Jour. Earth-Sciences, v. 29, p. 245–252.

Ambraseys, N. N., 1962; Data for the investigation of the seismic sea-waves in the Eastern Mediterranean: Seismol. Soc. America, Bull., v. 52, p. 895–913.

Anati, E., 1959, Excavations at the cemetery of Tell Abu Hawam (1952): Atiqot, v. 2, p. 89–102.

_____, 1975, Tell Abu Hawam: *in* M. Avi-Yonah and E. Stern, eds., Encyclopedia of Archaeological Excavations in the Holy Land: Jerusalem, Massada Press, v. I, p. 9–12.

Arad, A., and D. Wachs, 1976, Field study of elevated shell deposits along the coast of Israel: Geol. Survey Israel, Internal Rept., 4 p.

_____, A. Ecker, and A. Olshina, 1978, The young (post-Lower Pliocene) geological history of the Caesarea structure (Neev, *et al.*, 1978): Discussion: Israel Jour. Earth-Sciences, v. 27, p. 142–146.

Aubrey, D. G., and K. O. Emery, 1983, Eigenanalysis of recent United States sea levels: Continental Shelf Research, v. 2, p. 21–33.

_____, and _____, 1986, Relative sea levels of Japan from tide-gauge records: Geol. Soc. American Bull., v. 97, p. 194–205.

Avi-Yonah, M., and E. Stern, 1975–1978, Encyclopedia of Archaeological Excavations in the Holy Land: Jerusalem, Massada Press, v. I, II, III, IV.

Avnimelech, M., 1943, Contribution to the geological history of the Palestinian coastal plain; the surroundings of Nahariya: Bull. Jewish Exploration Soc., v. 10, no. 2–3, p. 39–46 (in Hebrew).

_____, 1952, Late Quaternary sediments of the coastal plain of Israel: Research Council Israel Bull., v. 2, no. 1, p. 51–57.

Ayalon, D., 1964, The Mameluks and the naval strength: Israel National Academy of Science Proc., v. 1, no. 8, p. 1–10 (in Hebrew).

Ayalon, E., 1981, Yavneh-Yam: Museum Ha'Aretz, unpubl. archeological rept., 2 p. (in Hebrew).

Bakler, N., 1976, Calcareous sandstone and sands of the Israel Mediterranean offshore aggregate reserves: Geol. Survey Israel, Summary Rept., M. G. 5/76 and UN/UNDP-GSI Offshore Dredging Project 71/522, 49 p.

_____, S. Denekamp, and V. Rohrlich, 1972, Sandy units in the coastal plain of Israel; environmental interpretation using statistical analysis of grain size data: Israel Jour. Earth-Sciences, v. 21, p. 155–178.

———, D. Neev, and M. Magaritz, 1985, Late Holocene ectonic movements at Tel Haraz, southern coast of Israel: Earth and Planetary Science Letters, v. 75, p. 223–230.

Bartov, Y., and Y. Arkin, 1975, Geological photomap of Israel, 1: 500,000: Geol. Survey Israel.

———, Y. Mimran, and I. Karcz, 1977, Lineaments in the coastal plain of Israel: Israel Jour. Earth-Sciences, v. 26, p. 1–14.

Bein, A., and G. Gvirtzman, 1977, A Mesozoic fossil edge of the Arabian Plate along the Levant coastline and its bearing on the evolution of the eastern Mediterranean: Intl. Symposium Structural History Mediterranean Basins, 25–29 Oct. 1976, Split, Technip, Paris, p. 95–110.

Ben-Menahem, A., 1979, Earthquake Catalogue for the Middle East (92 B. C. —1980 A. D.): Boll. Geofisica Teorica et Applicata, v. 21, no. 84, p. 245–313.

Bloom, A. L., 1963, Late-Pleistocene fluctuations of sea-level and postglacial crustal rebound in coastal Maine: Amer. Jour. Science, v. 261, p. 862–879.

———, 1971, Glacial-eustatic and isostatic controls of sea level since the last glaciation: *in* K. K. Turekian, ed., Late Cenozoic Glacial Ages, New Haven, CT, Yale Univ. Press, p. 355–379.

Buchbinder, L. G., and G. M. Friedman, 1980, Vadose, phreatic, and marine diagenesis of Pleistocene-Holocene carbonates in a borehole, Mediterranean coast of Israel: Jour. Sedimentary Petrology, v. 50, p. 395–408.

Butzer, K. W., 1976, Early Hydraulic Civilization in Egypt: Univ. Chicago Press, 134 p.

Carter, H., 1958, The Histories of Herodotus of Halicarnassus: New York, Heritage Press, 615 p.

Chappell, J., E. G. Rhodes, B. G. Thom, and E. Wallensky, 1982, Hydro-isostasy and the sea-level isobase of 5500 B. C. in north Queensland, Australia: Marine Geology, v. 49, p. 81–90.

Curray, J. R., 1965, Late Quaternary history, continental shelves of the United States: *in* H. E. Wright, Jr., and D. G. Frey, eds., The Quaternary of the United States: Princeton, NJ, Princeton Univ. Press, p. 723–735.

———, and D. G. Moore, 1964, Pleistocene deltaic progradation of continental terrace, Costa de Nayarit, Mexico: *in* Tj. H. van Andel and G. G. Shor, Jr., eds., Marine Geology of the Gulf of California: Amer. Assoc. Petroleum Geologists, Mem. 3, p. 193–215.

Dan, J., 1977, Nahal Nizzana, an ancient river in the western Negev: Nofim, 9–10 (Machon Avshalom, Univ. Tel Aviv, Studies in Geography), p. 25–29 (in Hebrew).

———, D. H. Yaalon, and H. Koyumdjisky, 1968–69, Catenary soil relationships in Israel, 1. The Netanya catena on coastal dunes of the Sharon: Geoderma, v. 2, p. 95–120.

Einsele, G., D. Herm, and H. U. Schwartz, 1974, Holocene eustatic(?) sea level fluctuation at the coast of Mauritania: Meteor Forschungsergebnisse, ser. c., v. 18, p. 43–62.

Emery, K. O., 1950, Ironstone concretions and beach ridges of San Diego County, California: California Division Mines, v. 46, 213–221.

———, 1968, Positions of empty pelecypod valves on the continental shelf: Jour. Sedimentary Petrology, v. 38, p. 1264–1269.

———, 1980, Relative sea levels from tide-gauge records: National Academy of Sciences Proc., v. 77, p. 6968–6972.

———, and D. G. Aubrey, 1985, Glacial rebound and relative sea levels in Europe from tide-gauge records: Tectonophysics, v. 120, p. 239–255.

———, and Y. K. Bentor, 1960, The continental shelf of Israel: Geol. Surv. Israel, Bull. 26, p. 25–41.

———, and G. G. Kuhn, 1982, Sea cliffs—their processes, profiles and classification: Geol. Soc. America Bull., v. 93, p. 644–654.

———, and D. Neev, 1960, Mediterranean beaches of Israel: Geol. Survey Israel, Bull. 26, p. 1–24.

Fairbridge, R. W., 1961, Eustatic changes in sea level: Physics and Chemistry of the Earth, v. 4, p. 99–185.

Fink, M., 1969, A preliminary report on the underground water survey at the coastal zone of North Sinai: Tahal (Water Planning Israel), Tel Aviv, PM/727, 18 p. (in Hebrew).

Fitch, T. J., and C. H. Scholz, 1971, Mechanism of underthrusting in southwest Japan: A model of convergent plate interaction: Jour. Geophysical Research, v. 76, p. 7260–7292.

Flemming, N. C., 1968, Archaeological evidence of eustatic changes of sea level and earth movements in the western Mediterranean: Geol. Soc. America, Spec. Paper 109, 125 p.

_____ , A. Raban, and C. Goetschel, 1978, Tectonic and eustatic changes on the Mediterranean coast of Israel in the last 9000 years: Progress in Underwater Science, v. 3, p. 33–98.

Galili, E., 1985, Clay exposures and archaeological finds on the sea bottom between Haifa and Athlit: Univ. Haifa, Dept. Maritime Civilizations, submitted master's thesis, 160 p. (in Hebrew).

_____ , and M. Evron, 1985, Prehistory and paleo-environments of submerged sites along the Carmel coast of Israel: Paleorient, v. 11, p. 37–52.

_____ , and M. Inbar, 1986, Submarine outcrops of clay along the Israeli coast and submerged settlements at the Hof Hacarmel: Fifth Conf. on the Israeli Coastal Studies, 18 March, at Coastal and Marine Engineering Inst., Technion City, Haifa, Abstracts, p. 39–48. (in Hebrew).

Garfunkel, Z., and G. Almagor, 1985, Geology and structure of the continental margin of northern Israel and the adjacent part of the Levantine Basin: Marine Geology, v. 62, p. 105–131.

_____ , and B. Derin, 1984, Permian-early Mesozoic tectonism and continental margin formation in Israel and its implications for the history of the Eastern Mediterranean: in J. E. Dixon and A. H. F. Robertson eds., The Geological Evolution of the Eastern Mediterranean: London, Blackwell Scientific Publications, p. 187–201.

_____ , A. Arad, and D. Wachs, 1977, Shell deposits in the Tel Haraz area: Geol. Survey Israel, Hydro/3/77, 12 p.

Gavish, E., and N. Bakler, in press, The Hof Hasharon coastal zone—geomorphological and sedimentological factors: in A. Shmueli and D. Grosman, eds., The Sharon Volume, Reshafim (in Hebrew).

_____ , and G. M. Friedman, 1969, Progressive diagenesis in Quaternary to Late Tertiary carbonate sediments, sequence and time scale: Jour. Sedimentary Petrology, v. 39, p. 980–1006.

Gifford, J. A., and G. Rapp, Jr., in press, Paleogeography of the central Sharon Coast: in Z. Herzog, G. Rapp, Jr., and O. Negbi, eds., Excavations at Tel Michal, Israel, University of Minnesota Press.

_____ , _____ , and C. L. Hill, in press, Site geology: in Z . Herzog, G. Rapp, Jr. , and O. Negbi, eds., Excavations at Tel Michal, Israel, University of Minnesota Press.

Ginzburg, A., 1971, Offshore Israel. Interpretation of seismic reflection survey: Inst. Petroleum Research and Geophysics, Rept. RS/916-G/71, 17 p.

_____ , and U. Amitai, 1968, North Sinai—El Arish and Romani area. Seismic reflection survey: Inst. Petroleum Research and Geophysics, Rept. S/550/67, 19 p.

_____ , and Z . Ben-Avraham, 1986, The continental margin of the Levant: Israel Geological Society, Ann. Meeting, Ma'alot, Israel, program, p. 46.

Goldsmith, V., and S. Sofer, 1983, Wave climatology of the southeastern Mediterranean: Israel Jour. Earth-Sciences, v. 32, p. 1–51.

Golik, A., 1978, Bathymetry and wave climate model off Haifa, Israel—an oceanographic analysis for anchorage site selection: Israel Oceanographic and Limnological Research, Geol. Dept. Rept. 78/2, 18 p.; Bathymetric map of the vicinity of Cape Carmel, scale 1: 10,000, 1-m contour interval.

Gophna, R., 1977, Archaeological survey of the central coastal plain, 1977: Tel Aviv, v. 5, no. 3–4, p. 136–147.

_____ , and E. Ayalon, 1980, Survey of the central coastal plain 1978–1979; settlement pattern of the Middle Bronze Age—IIA: Tel Aviv, v. 7, p. 147–151.

Gould, H. R., and E. McFarlan, Jr., 1959, Geologic history of the chenier plain, southwestern Louisiana: Gulf Coast Assoc. Geol. Soc. Trans., v. 9, p. 261–270.

Greenfield, L. L., 1984, Reconnaisance seismic (interpretation of the coastal and offshore area from Kfar Darom to Palmahim): Oil Exploration (Investments) Ltd., Rept. , 32 p.

─────, and Z. Bino, 1974, A seismic interpretation of the southern coastal plain of Israel: Inst. Petroleum Research and Geophysics, Preliminary Study, June, 1974, 55 p.

─────, and D. Neev, 1983, Nearshore Ashqelon—Ashdod Area, seismic interpretation: Oil Exploration (Investments) Ltd., Rept. 84/4, 20 p.

Gvirtzman, G., 1969, The Saqiye Group (Late Eocene to early Pleistocene) in the coastal plain and Hashephela regions, Israel: Geol. Survey Israel Bull. 51 (IPRG Report No. 1022, v. 2), maps.

─────, 1981, The findings of the Ga'ash 2 well and their implication on oil exploration in NW Israel: in Oil Exploration Symposium, Jerusalem, P. 29–32.

─────, in press, Geology and geomorphology of the Sharon and its Mediterranean Shelf: in A. Shmueli and D. Grosman, eds., The Sharon Volume, Reshafim (in Hebrew).

─────, and A. Klang, 1981, Caesarea 3, recommendation for drilling: Oil Exploration (Investments) Ltd., Rept. 81/28, 78 p.

Hall, J. K., 1976, Seismic studies, Haifa Bay—Summary Report: Geol. Survey Israel, Geol. Div. and UN/UNDP-GSI Offshore Dredging Project, Field Report 1/76, 106 p.

─────, and N. Bakler, 1975, Detailed bathymetric and hallow marine surveys at five locations along the Mediterranean coast of Israel: Geol. Survey Israel, UNDP Offshore Dredging Project, Field Rept. 1, 21 p.

Hamilton, H. C., and W. Falconer, 1854, The Geography of Strabo: London, H. G. Bohn, 3 vols.

Hamilton, R. W., 1934, Tell Abu Hawam: Dept. Antiquities in Palestine, Quarterly, v. 3, p. 74–80.

Herzog, Z., 1981, Tel Michal—Trading post at the coastline: Qadmoniot, v. 14, no. 3–4, p. 96–103 (in Hebrew).

─────, and A. Horowitz, 1986, Archaeological evidence for the possible tectonic rotation and partial destruction of Tel Michal: Israel Geogr. Soc., Ann. Meeting, December, Abstract (in Hebrew).

─────, O. Negbi, and S. Moshkovitz, 1978, Excavations at Tel Michal, 1977: Tel Aviv, v. 5, no. 3–4, p. 99–130.

Horowitz, A., 1979, The Quaternary of Israel: New York, Academic Press, 394 p.

Hötzl, H., and J. G. Zötl, 1978, Climatic changes during the Quaternary period: in S. S. Al-Sayari and J. G. Zötl, eds., Quaternary period in Saudi Arabia: Vienna, Springer-Verlag, pt. 1, p. 301–311.

Imamura, A., 1929, On the chronic and acute earth-tilting in the Kii Peninsula, Japan: Jour. Astronomical Geophysics, v. 7, p. 31–45.

Inbar, M, and D. Sivan, 1984, Paleo-urban development and Late Quaternary environmental change in the Akko area: Paleorient, v. 9, no. 2, p. 85–91.

Issar, A., 1968, Geology of the central coastal plain of Israel: Israel Jour. Earth-Sciences, v. 17, p. 16–29.

─────, and U. Kafri, 1972, Neogene and Pleistocene geology of the western Galilee coastal plain: Geol. Survey Israel, Bull. 53, 14 p.

Jarvis, C. S., 1943, Yesterday and Today in Sinai: Edinburgh, William Blackwood & Sons Ltd., 231 p.

Johnson, D. W., 1938, Shore Processes and Shoreline Development: New York, John Wiley, 584 p.

Kafri, U., 1972, Nahariyya Geological Map, I–IV, 1: 50,000: Geol. Survey Israel.

———, and A. Ecker, 1964, Neogene amd Quaternary subsurface geology and hydrogeology of the Zevulun Plain: Geol. Survey Israel, Bull. 37, 15 p.

———, and I. Karcz, 1975, On the stability of the Mediterranean coast of Israel since Roman times. A further contribution to the discussion: Israel Jour. Earth-Sciences, v. 24, p. 114–116.

Kallner-Amiran, D. H., 1951–52, A revised earthquake catalogue of Palestine: Israel Exploration Jour., v. 1, no. 4, p. 223–246; v. 2, no. 1, p. 48–62.

Kaplan, J., 1978, Yavneh-Yam: *in* M. Avi-Yonah and E. Stern, eds., Encyclopedia of Archaeological Excavations in the Holy Land: Jerusalem, Massada Press v. 4, p. 1216–1218.

Karcz, I., 1959, The structure of the northern Carmel: Research Council Israel Bull. 8G, no. 2–3, p. 119–130.

Kashai, E., 1966, The geology of the eastern and southwestern Carmel; Hebrew Univ. Jerusalem, unpubl. doctoral dissertation, 115 p. (in Hebrew).

Kenyon, K. M., 1979, Archaeology in the Holy Land: London, E. Benn, 360 p.

Klang, A., and G. Gvirtzman, 1983, Preliminary structural analysis of the Sharon area and its continental shelf: Oil Exploration (Investments) Ltd., Rept. 83/30, 47 p.

Lamb, H., 1930, The Flame of Islam: Garden City, N. Y., Doubleday & Co., Inc., 490 p.

Lapidoth, Israel Oil Prospectors Corp., Ltd., 1972, Total gravity map of north Sinai, scale 1: 250,000: 17 Brodetzki Street, Tel Aviv, Israel.

Levy, J., 1972, The sub-bottom geology and young sediments of Haifa Bay: Hebrew Univ. Jerusalem, Dept. Geology, unpubl. master's thesis, 30 p. (in Hebrew).

———, D. Neev, and Y. Folkman, 1968, Continuous seismic profiling at the site of A. P. C. terminal off Asheqelon: Geol. Survey Israel, Marine Geol. Div., Rept. Q/68/3, 5 p. (in Hebrew).

Levy, Y., 1972, Interactions between brines and sediments in the Bardawil area, northern Sinai. Hebrew Univ. Jerusalem, Dept. Geology, unpubl. doctoral dissertation, 108 p.

———, 1977, Origin and evolution of brines in coastal sabkhas, northern Sinai: Jour. Sedimentary Petrology, v. 47, p. 451–462.

Lewy, Z., D. Neev, and M. Prausnitz, 1986, Late Holocene tectonic movements at Akhziv, Mediterranean coastline of northern Israel: Quaternary Research, v. 25, p. 177–188.

Mazor, E., 1960, Fossil solution basins in kurkar near Nathanya: Research Council Israel Bull., v. 9G, p. 153–158.

———, 1974, "On the stability of the Mediterranean coast of Israel since Roman Times." A discussion. Israel Jour. Earth-Sciences, v. 23, p. 149–150.

McClure, H. A., 1978, Ar Rub Al Khali: *in* S. S. Al-Sayari and J. G. Zötl, eds., 1978, Quaternary Period in Saudi Arabia: Vienna, Springer-Verlag, p. 252–263.

Meshref, W. M., 1982, Regional structural setting of northern Egypt; fig. 2 is aeromagnetic map of northern Egypt, 50 gamma contours: Egyptian General Petroleum Company, 6th Exploration Seminar, Cairo, March 1982, 11p.

Michelson, H., 1970, Geology of the coast of Carmel: Tahal (Water Planning Israel), Ref. HG/70/025, 61 p. (in Hebrew).

———, 1971, Pleistocene tectonic movements in the coastal plain of Israel, emphasizing the Mt. Carmel. Discussion of a paper by Kafri (1970): Israel Jour. Earth-Sciences, v. 20, p. 129–132.

Milliman, J. D., and K. O. Emery, 1968, Sea levels during the past 35,000 years. Science, v. 162, p. 1121–1123.

Moon, F. W., and H. Sadek, 1921, Topography and geology of northern Sinai: Part I—Session 1919–1920, Ministry of Finance, Egypt: Petroleum Research Bull., v. 10, 154 p.

Moore, J. G., and G. W. Moore, 1984, Deposit from a giant wave on the island of Lanai, Hawaii: Science, v. 226, p. 1312–1315.

Neev, D., 1960, A pre-Neogene erosion channel in the southern coastal plain of Israel: Geol. Survey Israel, Bull. 25, GSI Oil Division Paper 7, 20 p.

———, 1967, Geological observations in the coastal plain of north Sinai—a preliminary report: Geol. Survey Israel, Marine Geol. Div., Rept. Q/1/67, 15 p. (in Hebrew).

_____, 1974, Reply to discussion of Mazor, 1974, Israel Jour. Earth-Sciences, v. 23, p. 150–151.

_____, 1975, Tectonic evolution of the Middle Eastern and Levantine Basin (easternmost Mediterranean): Geology, v. 3, p. 683–686.

_____, 1977, The Pelusium Line—a major transcontinental shear: Tectonophysics, v. 38, p. T1–T8.

_____, 1978, The geology of the Sea of Galilee (Lake Kinneret): *in* The Kinneret Booklet: Kinneret Drainage Authority, Zemach, p. 15–26, (in Hebrew).

_____, and N. Bakler, 1977, An outcrop of beach-rocks near Tel Haraz—an indication for a subrecent tectonic movement along the Mediterranean coastline of Israel (abst.): *in* The Annual Meeting of the Israel Geol. Society, Zikhron-Yaakov, March.

_____, and _____, 1978, Young tectonic activities along the coastline of Israel: *in* Hof VeYam (Hakibbutz Hameuhad Publishing House), p. 9–30 (in Hebrew).

_____, and Z. Ben-Avraham, 1977, The Levantine countries—The Israeli coastal region: *in* E. M. Nairn, W. H. Kanes, and F. G. Stehli, eds., The Ocean Basins and Margins, New York, Plenum Press, v. 4A, p. 355–377.

_____, and K. O. Emery, 1967, The Dead Sea, depositional processes and environments of deposition: Geol. Survey Israel, Bull. 41, 147 p.

_____, and G. M. Friedman, 1978, Late Holocene tectonic activity along the margins of the Sinai subplate: Science, v. 202, p. 427–429.

_____, and L. L. Greenfield, 1981, Oil possibilities of the continental margin off Israel, based on seismic interpretation: Oil Exploration (Investments) Ltd., Rept. 81/54, 23 p.

_____, and _____, 1984, Geology of the Mediterranean "Litoral Zone" off Israel: Oil Exploration (Investments) Ltd., Rept. 84/3, Doc. 1687a, 26 p.

_____, and J. K. Hall, 1977, Climatic fluctuations during the Holocene as reflected by the Dead Sea levels: *in* D. C. Greer, ed., Desertic Terminal Lakes: Intl. Conf. on Terminal Lakes, Water Resource Laboratory, Logan, Utah, Proc. p. 53–60.

_____, and _____, 1982, A global system of spiraling geosutures, Jour. Geophysical Research, v. 87, p. 10689–10708.

_____, L. L. Greenfield, and J. K. Hall, 1985, Slice-tectonics in the eastern Mediterranean Basin: *in* D. J. Stanley and F. C. Wezel, eds., Geological Evolution of the Mediterranean Basin, NATO Advanced Research Inst., Erice, Sicily, November 1982, Proc. volume: New York, Springer-Verlag.

_____, J. K. Hall, and J. M. Saul, 1982, The Pelusium Megashear System across Africa and associated lineament swarms: Jour. Geophysical Research, v. 87, p. 1015–1030.

_____, Y. Nir, and Y. Folkman, 1968, Continuous seismic profiles off the Khirbet Ashdod—Yam area: Geol. Survey Israel, Marine Geol. Div. Rep Q/68/4, 3 p.

_____, H. E. Edgerton, G. Almagor, and N. Bakler, 1966, Preliminary results of some continuous seismic profiles in the Mediterranean shelf of Israel: Israel Jour. Earth-Sciences, v. 15, p. 170–178.

_____, G. Almagor, A. Arad, A. Ginzburg, and J. K. Hall, 1976, The geology of the southeastern Mediterranean: Geol. Survey Israel, Bull. 68, 51 p.

_____, E. Shachnai, J. K. Hall, N. Bakler, and Z. Ben-Avraham, 1978a, The young (post-Lower Pliocene) geological history of the Caesarea Structure: Israel Jour. Earth-Sciences, v. 27, p. 43–64.

_____, _____, _____, _____, _____, 1978b, Reply to Arad et al. (1978), Israel Jour. Earth-Sciences, v. 27, p. 146–149.

_____, N. Bakler, S. Moshkovitz, A. Kaufman, M. Magaritz, and R. Gophna, 1973, Recent faulting along the Mediterranean coast of Israel: Nature, v. 245, p. 254–256.

Nektariov of Crete, ca. 1660, Holy World History printed for King of Boi'Bonda: reprinted in Venice during 1729 (copy in St. Catherine Monastary in Sinai).

Newman, W. S., L. F. Marcus, R. R. Pardi, J. A. Paccione, and S. M. Tomacek, 1980, Eustasy and deformation of the geoid, 1000–6000 radiocarbon years B. P. : *in* N. A. Mörner, ed. Earth Rheology and Late Cenozoic isostatic movements: New York, John Wiley and Sons, p. 555–567.

Nir, Y., 1973, Geological history of the Recent and Subrecent sediments of the Israel Mediterranean shelf and slope: Geol. Survey Israel, Marine Geol. Div., unpubl. rept., 179 p.

_____ , 1985, The destruction of the Roman high-level aquaduct and the Herodian harbor at Caesarea: *in* A. Raban, ed., Harbor Archaeology: Univ. Haifa, Center for Maritime Studies, First Intl. Workshop on Ancient Mediterranean Harbors, Caesarea, Proc., Publ. 1, Intl. Series 257, p. 185–193.

_____ , and I. Eldar, 1986a, Ground water levels in Post-Persian (ca. 2500 y BP) water wells as indicators of tectonic activity and sea level changes along the Israel Mediterranean coast: *in* R. W. Carter and R. J. N. Devoy, eds., The Hydrodynamic and Sedimentary Consequences of Sea-Level Change, A Conference on 20–22 March 1986 at University College, Cork, Ireland: International Geological Correlation Programme—Project 200, Program.

_____ , and _____ , 1986b, Subsurface water levels as an indicator for tectonic movements of the coastal zone: *in* Fifth Conference on the Israeli Coastal Studies, 18 March 1986 at Coastal and Marine Engineering Inst., Technion City, Haifa, Abstracts p. 36–38 (in Hebrew).

_____ , and _____ , 1986c, Subsurface water level in ancient wells as an indicator for ancient sea levels and for neo-tectonic changes in the Mediterranean coastal zone of Israel: Geol. Survey Israel, Rept. GSI/34/86, 28 p. (in Hebrew).

_____ , and _____ , 1987, Ancient wells and their geoarchaeological significance in detecting tectonics of the Israel Mediterranean coastline region: Geology, v. 15, p. 3–6.

Olami, Y., and Y. Peleg, 1977, The water supply system to Caesarea Maritima: Israel Exploration Jour., v. 27, p. 127–137.

Oren, E. D., 1973, The overland route between Egypt and Canaan in the Early Bronze Age (Preliminary Report): Israel Exploration Jour., v. 23, no. 4, p. 198–205.

_____ , 1977, Archaeology and trackers—following ancient sites in northern Sinai Peninsula: BaMachane, no. 3 (21st Sept.), p. 16, 18, 19, 27 (in Hebrew).

_____ , 1982, Excavations at Qasrawet in northwestern Sinai (Preliminary Report): Israel Exploration Jour., v. 32, no. 4, p. 203–211.

Ovadiah, A., 1976, Gaza: *in* M. Avi-Yonah and E. Stern, eds., Encyclopedia of Archaeological Explorations in the Holy Land: Jerusalem, Massada Press, v. II, p. 408–417.

Parchamovsky, S., 1981, Stratigraphy and sedimentology of the Kurkar Group (Pleistocene) in the Nizzanim area: Geol. Survey Israel, Rept. S. D. 402/81, 75 p.

Phythian-Adams, W. J., 1923, Palestine Exploration Foundation, p. 11–36 (*in* Ovadiah, 1976).

Picard, L., 1943, Structure and evolution of Palestine with comparative notes on neighbouring countries: Hebrew Univ. Jerusalem, Geol. Dept. Bull., v. 4, 134 p.

_____ , 1955, The geological map of Israel, 1:100,000. Sheet 2—Haifa: Geol. Survey Israel.

Pitman, W. C., III, 1978, Relationship between eustacy and stratigraphic sequences of passive margins: Geol. Soc. America Bull., v. 89, p. 1389–1403.

Prausnitz, M., 1977, The pottery at Newe Yam: *in* Eretz Israel, M. Stekelis Memorial: Israel Exploration Society, v. 13, p. 272–276.

Raban, A., 1981, Recent maritime archaeological research in Israel: Intl. Jour. Nautical Archaeology and Underwater Exploration, v. 10, p. 287–308.

_____ , 1983a, Recent maritime archaeological research in Israel: Intl. Jour. Nautical Archaeology and Underwater Exploration, v. 12, p. 229–251.

———, 1983b, Submerged prehistoric sites off the Mediterranean coast of Israel: *in* P. M. Masters and N. C. Flemming, eds., Quaternary Coastlines and Marine Archaeology: New York, Academic Press, p. 215–232.

———, 1985, The ancient harbours of Israel in Biblical times: *in* A. Raban, ed., Harbour Archaeology: London, Academic Press, p. 10–44.

———, 1986, Archaeological evidence for ancient sealevels at the Mediterranean coast of Israel: Israel Geological Society, Ann. Meeting, Ma'alot, Israel, program, p. 102–105.

———, and Y. Tur-Caspa, 1979, Tel Michal—a submarine survey: Univ. Haifa, Center for Maritime Studies, A letter to Dr. Z. Herzog, Univ. Tel Aviv, Dept. Archaeology, 4 p. (in Hebrew).

———, ———, E. Adler, E. Sivan, and G. Kaplan, 1976, Marine archeological study in Caesarea: Univ. Haifa, Center for Maritime Studies, Final Rept. 2/76 to NP-1 Project, 65 p. (in Hebrew).

Reifenberg, A., 1951, Caesarea—a study in the decline of a town: Israel Exploration Jour., v. 1, p. 20–32.

Riad, S., H. A. El Etr, and A. Mahkles, 1983, Basement tectonics of northern Egypt as interpreted from gravity data: *in* R. H. Gabrielsen, I. V. Ramberger, D. Roberts, and O. A. Steinlein, eds., International Basement Tectonics Association, Publ. 4, 382 p., (p. 209–220 and after figs. 2, 4, 8, 12).

Rim, M., 1950, Dune sand movement and the formation of red sandy soils in Palestine: Hebrew Univ. Jerusalem, unpubl. doctoral dissertation, 54 p.

———, 1951, Sand and soil in the coastal plain of Israel: Israel Exploration Jour., v. 1, p. 33–48.

Ritter-Kaplan, H., 1979, Note: Israel Exploration Jour., v. 29, no. 3–4, p. 239–241.

Ronen, A., 1977, Mousterian sites in Red Loam in the coastal plain of Mt. Carmel, Eretz Israel; M. Stekelis Memorial: Israel Exploration Society, v. 13, p. 183–190.

———, 1980, The origin of the raised pelecypod beds along the Mediterranean coast of Israel (1): Paleorient, v. 6, p. 163–170.

———, and A. Zemer, 1981, Shell accumulation near Ashqelon: Qadmoniot., v. 14, p. 47–51 (in Hebrew).

Rotstein, Y., S. Goldberg, and D. Neev, 1978, Magnetotelluric survey in the northwestern Sinai Peninsula: Inst. Petroleum Research and Geophysics, Rept. MT/194/75, 11 p.

Safriel, U. N., 1975, The role of vermetid gastropods in the formation of Mediterranean and Atlantic reefs: Oecologia, v. 20, p. 85–101.

Said, R., 1981, The Geological Evolution of the River Nile: New York, Springer-Verlag, 151 p.

Shachnai, E., 1974, Transversal geological cross sections in the coastal plain: Geol. Survey Israel, report prepared for the P. S. A. R. Nuclear Power Plant, Nizanim Site.

Shalem, N., 1956, Seismic tidal waves (tsunamis) in the eastern Mediterranean: Geol. Society Israel Bull., v. 3, p. 79–91 (in Hebrew).

Shata, A., 1959, Structural development of the Sinai Peninsula (Egypt): 20th Intl. Geol. Congress, Mexico, p. 225–249.

———, 1960, Ground water and geomorphology of the northern section of Wadi El Arish Basin: Soc. Géographie d' Egypte, vol. 33, p. 217–245.

Shomrony, A., 1983, Geological analysis of geophysical and dip meter logs: Oil Exploration (Investments) Ltd., Rept. 83/74, Doc. 1565a, 20 p.

Shukri, N. M., G. Philip, and R. Said, 1956, The geology of the Mediterranean coast between Rosetta and Bardia; pt. 2. Pleistocene sediments—geomorphology and microfacies: Bull. Inst. d'Egypte, v. 37, no. 2, p. 395–444.

Sieberg, A., 1932, Untersuchungen über Erdbeben und Bruchschollenbau im Oestlichen Mittelmeergebiet: Denkschr. Mediz. Naturw. Ges. Jena, v. 1B, p. 161–273.

Sivan, D., 1981, Paleogeography of Akko area during the Holocene: Univ. Haifa (Humanities—Maritime Civilizations), unpubl. master's thesis, 103 p. (in Hebrew).

———, 1982, Paleogeography of the Akko area in the Holocene Period: *in* The 3rd Symposium on coastal morphology, Univ. Haifa, p. 51–63 (in Hebrew).

Sneh, A., and T. Weissbrod, 1973, Nile Delta, the defunct Pelusiac branch identified: Science, v. 180, p. 59–61.

———, ———, A. Ehrlich, A. Horowitz, S. Moskovitz, and A. Rosenfeld, 1986, Holocene evolution of the northeastern corner of the Nile Delta: Quaternary Res., v. 26, p. 194–206.

Sneh, Y., and M. Klein, 1982, Sea-level changes during the Holocene at the Dor coastline: *in* The 3rd Symposium on coastal morphology, Univ. Haifa, p. 64–77; also 1984, Holocene sea level changes at the coast of Dor, southeast Mediterranean: Science, v. 226, p. 831–832.

Striem, H. L., and T. Miloh, 1975, Tsunamis induced by submarine slumpings off the coast of Israel: Licensing Division, Israel Atomic Energy Commission, IA-LD-1-102, 23 p.

Thatcher, W., 1985, The earthquake deformation cycle at the Nankai Trough, southwest Japan: Jour. Geophysical Research, v. 89, p. 3087–3101.

Toussoun, O., 1925, Memoire sur l'histoire du Nil: Congres Intl. de Geographie Publie au auspices de S. M. Fouad Ier, Roi d'Egypte, Inst. Francais d' Archeologie Orientale, v. 1, 264 p.

Tzur, Y., and U. N. Safriel, 1978, Vermetid platforms as indicators of coastal movements: Israel Jour. Earth-Sciences, v. 27, p. 124–127.

Vitto, F., 1984, The harbor of Jamnae: Qadmoniot, v. 17, p. 76–78 (in Hebrew).

Vroman, A. J., 1958, The geological map of Israel, 1: 50,000, Series 1—Galilee: Geol. Survey Israel.

Wiens, H. J., 1962, Atoll Environment and Ecology: New Haven, Yale Univ. Press, 532 p.

Whitney, J. W., 1983, Erosional history and surficial geology of western Saudi Arabia: U. S. Geol. Survey, technical record TR-04-1, 90 p.

Wreschner, E. E., 1977, Newe Yam—a submerged late Neolithic settlement near Mt. Carmel: *in* Eretz Israel, M. Stekelis Memorial: Israel Exploration Society, v. 13, p. 260–271.

Yaalon, D. H., and J. Dan, 1967, Factors controlling soil formation and distribution in the Mediterranean coastal plain of Israel during the Quaternary: Quaternary Soils, INQUA Congress, Proc. v. 9, p. 322–338.

Yeivin, E., and Y. Olami, 1979, Nizzanim—a Neolithic site in Nahal Evtah, excavations of 1968–1970: Tel Aviv, v. 6, p. 99–135.

Zelinger, A., and Y. Bar Yosef, 1971, Underground water resources in the coastal plain between Rafiah and Sheikh Zuweid: Tahal (Water Planning Israel), HR/71/078, 8 p. (in Hebrew).

———, N. Kolombos, and Y. Bar Yosef, 1971, Underground water resources at Pithat Rafiah, Sheikh Zuweid and Kharuba: Tahal. (Water Planning Israel), HR/71/041, 18 p. (in Hebrew).

Index

Aegean, 56
African Plate, 99
Akhziv, 21, 22
   Harbor, 32, 39
   Tel, 41
   Fault (Transverse), 41, 44
   Canyon, 44, 103
Ahihud Fault, 42
Akko, 11, 39, 41, 89
   Promontory, 14, 42
   Tel (also Mt. Napoleon and Tel Al Fukhar), 42
   Ledge, 43
Alexander the Great, 90
Alexandria, 87, 103
Amphorae, 47, 75
Anatolia, 56, 114
Angular truncation (Wedgeout), 17
Apollonia (Tel Arsuf or Arshaf), 23, 55
Apron (of sediments), 27
Aqueduct, 53
Arab, Arabia(n), 1, 13, 76
   Nubian Massif, 110
   Saudi—, 110
   Peninsula, 110
Archaeology (see specific sites), 5
Articulated bivalves, 15, 32, 43
Ashdod, 69, 92
   Coastline, 22
   Harbor, 26, 72
   Yam, 72
   1 well, 69
   Hof—well, 70
Ashqelon, 69, 73
Assyrian, 76
Atlit Bay, 45, 46
Atlit Fault (Transverse), 47
   Promontory, 47
Ayalon River, 61
   Fault, 61

Babylonian, 76, 97
Bardawil, 83, 84
   Lagoon, 19, 35

Railway Station, 19, 84, 92
   arcuate bar, 19, 89
   inland sabkhas, 37
Beach sand, 26
Beachrock (lumachelle) Terraces, 11, 19, 43, 47, 82
Beibars, 73
Beit Yerah (Sea of Galilee), 114
Bir Abd, 11, 84
   Peninsula, 83, 88
Bir Jamil, 11, 84
Bir Jaradi, 79
Bir Lahfan, 82
Bitter Lake, 11
Bronze, 7, 37
   Early—, 47, 91, 114
   Middle—, 37, 48, 56, 67, 91, 114
   Late—, 37, 56, 67, 75, 91, 44
Burrowers, 16, 55
   Mytilus, 17
   molds, 26
   —ing position, 32
Byzantine, 10, 32, 41, 48, 52, 55, 65, 75, 76, 77, 87, 114

Caesarea, 45, 49, 52, 62, 102, 106
   Aqueduct, 53
   Harbor (Herodian), 13, 23, 38
   Hippodrome, 53
   Coastline, 22
   Roman obelisk, 38
   Crusaders wall (fortress), 38
Cairo, 105
   Suez (district), 105
Calcarenite Bank (Tel Aviv or Beit Yanai Kurkar), 16, 18, 49, 54, 62, 91
California, 3
Canaan, 84, 91, 114
Caravan station, 38
Carmel (Haifa) Nose, 44, 45
Cerastoderma (Cardium) edule (glaucum), 14, 32, 43
Chalcolith, 7, 91
Channel (river), 12

Index

Climatic optimum, 16
Constantinopole, 87
Continental crust, 93
Convolute (load structures), 17
Cretaceous, 43, 44, 52, 69
   Early, 69, 90
   Middle, 69
   Late, 69
Crete, 26, 99
Crusaders, 10, 38, 42, 47, 55, 87, 106
Cyprus, 87, 99
Cyrenaica, 87, 105

Damietta, 112
Dates (archaeological), 10
Dead Sea—Jordan Rift, 23, 110
Deir el Balah, 76
   beach, 35
   evaporites, 94
   brines, 37
"Delta" offshore well, 69
Dor, 14, 21, 32, 45, 47, 102

Earthen ramps, 38, 56, 67
   walls, 35
Earthquake, 56, 87
Egypt, 38, 87, 90, 91, 114
   Predynastic, 111
El Alamein, 103
El Arish, 11, 74, 91
   wadi, 15, 79
Elat, 73
El Kharubeh, 11, 15
El Meidan Railway Station, 19, 82, 87
El Quseima, 93
En Hod, 47
Epipaleolith(ic), 7, 73, 77, 91
Erg, 12, 91
Estuarine, 32, 39, 82
Ethiopia, 111, 112
Et Tineh (bay), 90
   Burge, 89
Europe (northern), 115
Eustatic, 16, 54, 93, 100, 106
Evron Ridge, 14, 42, 43

Fadda (Tel el—) No. 1 well, 21, 93
Fertile Crescent, 114
Flandrian transgression, 17
Flasser, 13
Floodplain (Hamra and swamps), 13
   terraces, 16
Foothills geosuture, 43, 103
Foxhound Reef, 43
Fault coastal, 52, 95
   transverse, 44, 63
   strike slip (wrench), 95

Ga'ash, 23, 49, 55
Gafgafa, 11
Gaza, 10, 21, 45, 52, 62, 75
   Wadi, 75, 111
   Maritima, 76
Geosuture, 43, 90
Giva't Olga, 12
Glacial (stages), 39
Glycymeris, 26, 29, 35, 48, 53, 55, 61, 77
Graded bedding, 13, 32
Gravity (Bouguer), 90
Greek, 56

Hadera Electric Power Plant, 22
   Dune Sands, 23
Hadrian, 53
Haifa Bay, 22, 46, 48
   (Carmel) Nose, 44, 45
Hamada, 12
Hamra, 7, 11, 12, 22, 54, 77, 103
Hassana, 92
Hawaii, 29
Helix (Helicidae), 10, 17, 20, 23, 29
Hellenistic, 10, 76, 91
Hermopolis, 87
Herod(ian), 53
Herodotus, 112
Hillazon Graben, 42
Hippodrome, 53
Hittite, 56
Hod el Kufri, 12, 84
Hof Hacarmel, 51, 130
Hof Hasharon, 45, 55, 57, 77
Holocene, 1, 105, 111
Hydraulic equilibrium, 35, 47
Hygroscopic, 35
Hyksos, 76

Initial dips, 27
Interstitial water, 36
Ionic Ratio, 35
   exchange, 36
Iron Age, 10, 67, 77, 115
Isfiya Fault, 47
Ismailya, 114
Isostatic, 95, 100
Israel, 38

Japan, 99
Jerusalem, 64
Jet (sampling), 61
Jordan Valley, 13
Judean Upwarp (Mountains), 93, 97
Jurassic, 1, 69
   Top—(Base Level), 69
   Peneplane, 69

Index

Khan Yunes, 113
Kefar Darom, 79
Kurdaneh Calcarenite, 43
Kurkar, 7, 12, 56, 77
   Ridge, 3, 44, 47
   Group, 7, 54

Lagoon(al), 39, 47
   evaporitic, 35
LANDSAT, 4, 61, 103
Lebanon, 114
Levant, 1
Load casts (convolute structures), 17, 26, 32
Louisiana, 3

"M" reflector (Horizon), 7, 54, 70
Maa'gan Michael, 22, 45, 102
Magnetotelluric, 90
Mameluk(ian), 10, 42, 48, 52, 56, 62, 67, 75, 87, 92, 115
Marginopora, 19
Mavkiim (Messinian), Formation, 71
Mawassie, 16
Medieval, 67, 74
Mediterranean (eastern) (sea), 12, 99, 111
   Circum—, 13
   sea level, 15
Megaripple, 27
Mesopotamia, 114
Mesozoic, 1
Mexico, 3
Michmoret, 32, 53, 101, 106
Minoan, 26
Moghara-Lagama-Risan Aneiza Mountains, 84
Moslem, 10, 56, 87, 92, 115
Mount Carmel, 1, 21, 43, 45
Mount Casius, 19, 84, 88, 92
   promontory, 21
   peninsula, 88
Mount Qeren, 82
Mud (ball), 12, 16
   (earth) brick (wall), 35, 77
   flat (plain), 79, 82, 103, 110
Musaida, 11, 15

Nabatean, 91
Nahal Besor (Wadi Gaza), 75, 77, 79
Nahal Evtah, 73
Nahal Lavan, 82
Nahal Nizzana, 82
Nahal Oren, 47
Nahal Poleg, 77
Nahariya (plain, trough), 14, 32, 39
Negev, 79, 82
Neolithic, 7, 73, 91
   Early—(Pre-Ceramic), 47
   Late—(Ceramic), 73

Netanya, 12, 54, 57, 106
Netherland, 3
Nile (river, delta), 3, 23, 90, 92, 110, 111
Nilotic fauna, 11
Nizzanim, 21, 70

Ocean, 94
Oceanic crust, 93
Oligocene, 2
Or Aqiva, 45, 49
Oregon, 99
Oscillatory (movement), 3, 48, 54, 55, 57, 66, 67, 74, 75, 77, 89, 99, 100
Ostracodes, 59
Ostrakina (El Felusiat), 38, 84
   Tabba Felusiat, 88

Paleolithic, 7, 82, 93
Paleowatertable (body), 39, 54, 100
Palmahim (disturbance), 7, 45, 69
Patria Ridge, 44
Pelusium (Tel Farameh), 89
   Line, 45, 52, 69, 89
   —iac Branch, 89
Persian, 10, 32, 42, 47, 53, 75, 79, 88, 91, 115
Peru, 99
Philistines ("Sea People"), 76, 77
Phoenician, 41, 105
Photolineament, 84, 89, 103
Pleistocene, 1, 70, 80, 110
Pliocene, 2, 70, 80
Poleg River, 15
Port Said (Tenis), 90, 92
Pottery Sherds, 16, 29, 61, 74
Pumice, 26, 87
Puranella, 43

Qadesh Barnea (evaporites), 93, 94
Qantara, 89, 92
Qasrawet, 91
Qattara Depression, 103
   trend, 105
   Eratosthenes, 104
Qishon River, 43
Quaternary, 7
Qudeirat (Ein), (Wadi), 93

Rafiah, 11, 79
Ramat Aviv C, 22, 59
Ramleh, 64
Rebound, 48, 67, 75
Roman, 10, 32, 41, 48, 53, 65, 88, 91, 106, 115
Romani, 91
Rosetta, 112
Rosh Haniqra, 39, 42, 111
Rub al Khali, 110

Sabkha (Hawash, Hayareah), 35
Sahara, 13, 111
Salah ad Din al Ayoubi, 73
Samson, 76
Santorini (Thera), 26, 56, 67, 115
   Volcanic eruption, 26, 76
Saqiye Group, 7, 54
Sea Level-Relative Changes (eustatic), 39
Seismic (reflection), 7, 54
Sharon Plain, 1, 23
Shefaiim, 17, 23
Sheikh Zuweid (Sabkhat e Sheikh), 11, 79
Shell Beds (lenses, terraces, carpet), 29, 67, 74, 77
   Orientation (concavity), 17, 29, 35, 67
   Structure (packing, imbrication, nestling), 29, 31
Shiqmona, 31
Sicily, 87
Sidon, 74
Sinai (central, northwestern, coastline), 1, 7, 11, 35, 69, 79, 87, 91, 105, 113
Sirbonis (Lac), 87
Solution Basins, 12
Sneh No. 1, 90
St. Catherine (Monastery), 87
Storm Wave (deposits), 27, 29
Suez Canal, 11, 89, 91
Swamp, 7, 32, 39, 53, 59, 77, 110
Synagogue, 76
Syria, 38, 114

Tectonism, Tectonic, 1, 39, 79, 93, 100, 102, 106, 114
Tel Abu Hawam, 43
Tel Ajjul, 75
Tel Aviv-Yafo, 1, 12, 27, 61, 63
Tel Baruch, 59, 77
Tel es Summeiriya, 42
Tel Haraz (Calcarenite, Beachrock Terraces, Beds, Sequence, Fragmented shell sands), 26, 67, 76
Tel Michal, 17, 37, 56, 67, 76, 102
Tel Mor, 101
Tel Qassila, 101

Tel Qatif, 21, 77
Tenis, 92
Terra Rossa, 13
Tertiary, 16
Tide Gauge, 99, 106
Til No. 1 (offshore), 69
Triassic, 69
Tsunami, 27, 42, 89, 105
Tunis, 87
Turkish (Turks), 10, 42, 92, 115
Tyre, 89
Tyrrhenian, 19, 70

Um el Fahm, 43
Unio, 32
United States, 3
U.E.S. ("Uppermost Erosional Surface"), 10, 12, 21, 62, 72

Vermetus (vermetid), 56, 67
Via Maris, 38, 48, 77, 87
Vibrocore, 61

Wadi Azarik, 82
Wadi Hareidin, 82
Wadi Kharubeh, 82
Wadi Natrun, 105, 112
Wadi Silka, 79
Washington (state), 99
Washover Fan, 89
Würm, 105

Yafo (Jaffa), 1, 49, 61, 63, 65, 106
   Formation, 7
   Promontory, 63
Yafo-Lod fault, 95
Yarkon (River, Fault), 22, 23, 49, 56, 59, 61, 63
Yavneh Yam (floor, promontory), 1, 16, 26, 31, 37, 57, 65, 76, 101

Zaranik, 87
Zikim, 73
Zoar (Dead Sea), 114